FIRE FROM THE SKY

Battle Of Harvest Moon And True Story Of Space Shuttles

Tesla: The Electric Magician

The Abduction Controllers

> If you are the legitimate copyright holder of any material inadvertently used in this book, please send a notice to this effect and the "offending" material will be immediately removed from all future printings. The material utilized herein is reproduced for educational purposes and every effort has been made to verify that the material has been properly credited and is available in the public domain.

FIRE FROM THE SKY
The Battle Of Harvest Moon and True Story of the Space Shuttles
Compiled by The Committee Of Twelve To Save The Earth
This edition Copyright 2008 by Global Communications/Conspiracy Journal

All rights reserved. No part of these manuscripts may be copied or reproduced by any mechanical or digital methods and no exerpts or quotes may be used in any other book or manuscript without permission in writing by the Publisher, Global Communications/Conspiracy Journal, except by a reviewer who may quote brief passages in a review.

Revised Edition

ISBN 1-60611-024-1
978-1-60611-024-9

Published by Global Communications/Conspiracy Journal
Box 753 · New Brunswick, NJ 08903

Staff Members
Timothy G. Beckley, Publisher
Carol Ann Rodriguez, Assistant to the Publisher
Sean Casteel, General Associate Editor
Tim R. Swartz, Graphics and Editorial Consultant
William Kern, Editorial and Art Consultant

Sign Up On The Web For Our Free Weekly Newsletter
and Mail Order Version of Conspiracy Journal
and Bizarre Bazaar
www.ConspiracyJournal.com

Order Hot Line: 1-732-602-3407
PayPal: MrUFO8@hotmail,com

AMERICA WAS FULL OF NAZIS!
Soon after cessation of hostilities closed World War Two, hundreds of former Nazi scientists and SS members were secretly smuggled into America to work on military and space programs for the United States government (Operation Paperclip). They were employed by nearly every one of the military-industrial complex companies, developing bombs, missiles, rockets, aircraft and advanced ground vehicles for use in future wars.

Many former Nazis went to work for the Central Intelligence Agency and, indeed, they actually formed the foundation of that agency after the war because they kept accurate records of their enemies (Russia) during the war, and the agents brought their knowledge and contacts information with them.

But the Russians had captured their own cadres of German scientists after the war and put them to work developing the same types of machines for the same purposes. Russia's German scientists actually helped the Soviets beat America into space. Russia launched the first satellite, put the first man into orbit around the planet, and Russian cosmonauts conducted the first space walk. Russia also placed the first automated research vehicle on the moon, an achievement America would not match for decades.

Both countries, and others, made adequate use of Tesla technologies to create weapons and communications devices previously undreamed of, including—if the records are true—aerial disc platforms, or "flying saucers."

Intelligence records show that German scientists had built and test-flown several different types of flying discs. The complete plans for one type were captured at the BMW auto factory in Prague at the close of the war.

From the development of the atomic bomb to the refinement of the space shuttles to the planned future missions to Mars, German scientists were up to their elbows in America's business—military, commercial and industrial—and they still are!

Fire From The Sky is the story of how it all happened and the consequences with which we all must live today. The cold war did not end; it simply went underground.

You might be surprised to learn who is planning your childrens' future.

TABLE OF CONTENTS

PART ONE
FIRE FROM THE SKY: Battle of Harvest Moon and True Story of Space Shuttles

In The Begining..7
USS Thresher and the U-2...8
Total Russian Defense...8
Project Paperclip..9
Operation Sunrise...10
Project Overcast..11
Michael Paine..12
More Assassinations Connections..13
People Of Earth/Shan..14
Nixon, Bush and Donovan..15
Gehlen and the German General Staff...16
William Clark..16
German Scientists and Aliens..18
NICAP..18
Then Came 1947...20
Antarctica..20
Admiral Byrd and Operation Highjump..21
Hitler Escaped!...22
Polar Defenses..26
UFOs: Nazi or Alien?..26
Russian Space Program...26
Scalar Weapons Activated..27
Coalition Insider...28
Northern Book House...28
Kammler..29
Rudolph Hess and Secret Space Base..30
Werner Heisenberg...31
Who Created The Atomic Bomb?...32
German Submarines in the South Atlantic.....................................34
Rand Corporation...35

Leslie Groves	35
Boris Pash	35
German Flying Saucers	38
Falklands Islands War	38
German Economic Miracle	39
Albert Einstein	43
Paul Rosbaud	44
Samual Abraham Goudsmit	46
The Kennedy/Nazi Connection	48
Nazi Imbeciles?	49
Cover and Concealment	49

PART TWO

Nikola Tesla: The Forgotten Genius	52
One: The Man Behind The Mind	53
Two: Tesla's Battle To Give The World The AC Engine	56
Three: Years Of Continuos Rapture	59
Four: Tesla's Military Inventions—The Death Ray	62
Five: Tesla's Wildest Dreams	64
Six: The Forgotten Genius	66

PART THREE

Nikola Tesla—The Greatest Hacker Of All Time	69
The Scene: Colorado Springs, Colorado	69
The Man: Nikola Tesla	70
The Hack: The Tesla Coil	71
The SDI And The Tesla Coil	72
The Soviets Use The Coil	72
Computers And Grounding	73
Star Wars And The Tesla Coil	74
The Tesla Coil Works	74

PART FOUR

Nikola Tesla's Autobiography	75
Introduction	75
Chapter One—My Early Life	76
Chapter Two—Extraordinary Experiences	83
Chapter Three—How Tesla Conceived The Rotary Magnetic Field	89
Chapter Four—The Discovery of the Tesla Coil and Transformer	95
Chapter Five	100
Chapter Six	107

PART FIVE
A New Hypothosis For Alien Abduction
    I. Introduction..118
    II. The Technology...122
    III. Applications...137
    IV. Abductions...152

FIRE FROM THE SKY

FIRE FROM THE SKY: Battle of Harvest Moon & True Story of Space Shuttles by "One Who Knows"
IN THE BEGINNING...

In the March 1919 issue of Electrical Experimenter magazine, details of the Roger's underground communication system were released. This system was later classified SECRET and used to communicate with submarines during World War I. It involved using frequencies through the ground and water. The signals were 5,000 times stronger than signals through the air.

The patents are confusing to most engineers, but to someone who understands, it is obvious that the transmitters were using scalar waves. If you wonder if it could be possible for scientists to devise the type of technology written about in the early Fire From The Sky articles, you need to be aware that this technology has been around for a long time. Actually, for a very long time.

For instance, in 1977, Louis Kervran won the Nobel Prize for showing that plants and animals (his main experiments were with chickens) use "scalar wave" type technology to transmute elements, for instance, turning potassium into calcium. This is impossible according to the "laws" of physics currently taught in schools. The ruling Elite does not want you "common folk" to have this type of knowledge, as it will undermine their control over you. So the "laws" they teach are WRONG.

While the oil barons sabotaged Nikola Tesla's efforts to provide cheap or free energy to the world, the Russians took an interest in his material and developed it.

Nikita Kruschev asked his physicists, specifically Pyorte (Peter) Kapitsa, to develop a system for total defense against missiles and aircraft. By studying Tesla and others they were successful and, in 1960, Kruschev announced the development of a "fantastic" Soviet weapon, one that could destroy all life on the world. ("Kruschev Says Soviets Will Cut Forces a Third; Sees 'Fantastic Weapon'," by Max Frankel, New York Times, Jan. 15, 1960, p. 1.) However, it was not quite ready and in 1962 Kruschev was forced to back

FIRE FROM THE SKY

down during the Cuban Missile Crisis. This caused him to lose much face with his government and people.

U.S.S. THRESHER AND THE U-2

As things were not going well with Kruschev, he decided to use the weapons system before it was fully operational and on April 10, 1963, he successfully detected and destroyed the nuclear submarine U.S.S. Thresher, using an underwater scalar howitzer. The next day, they celebrated by firing a pulse blast creating a tremendous underwater explosion about 100 miles north of Puerto Rico, south of where they had sunk the Thresher.

Col. Tom Bearden described the event: "It left a signature: the sub's surface companion, the U.S.S. Skylark, was in the splatter zone of the underwater scalar interference. That is, spurious EM noise was being generated in all the Skylark's electrical systems, some of which were actually disabled. So intense was the "electronic jamming" that it required over an hour and a half for the Skylark to transmit an emergency message back to its headquarters that the Thresher was in serious trouble and contact with it had been lost.

Some of the Skylark's communication systems actually failed, but later resumed operation inexplicably, once the jamming was gone. That type of "jamming" of multiple bands and multiple electronic equipment, of course, together with the anomalous failure of electronic equipment and its later mysterious recovery, were direct signatures of the use of the exothermic scalar interferometer against the undersea target area in the vicinity of the Skylark.

"The very next day, April 11, 1963, the same Soviet scalar EM howitzer system was tested in the "destroy submarine" pulse mode. A huge underwater EM blast occurred off the coast of Puerto Rico, about 100 miles north of the island. The underwater explosion caused a huge boiling up of a giant mushroom of water about a third of a mile high. The mushroom of water then fell back into the ocean, completing the signature.

"Fortunately the entire incident was seen by the startled crew of a passing U.S. jetliner which was just passing its checkpoint in that area." (See Robert J. Durant, "An Underwater Explosion - or What?" Pursuit, 5(2), April 1972, p. 30-31.) For more information on the Thresher disaster and Skylark problems, see John Bentley, The Thresher Disaster, Doubleday, Garden City, N.Y., 1975, particularly p. 164.

"These two incidents were full-up operational tests of Kruschev's newly-deployed superweapons. He probably staged this dramatic one-two punch in a desperate effort to recover face with the Communist Party after his disastrous facedown by Kennedy in the Cuban Missile Crisis a few short months previously. Apparently the attempt was successful, since he remained in power another year before being deposed."

There is also evidence that the U-2 flight of Francis Gary Powers was shot down by this technology. Bearden says: "In fact, Gary Powers' high-flying aircraft was probably shot down in 1960 by a 'jury-rigged' scalar EM howitzer using modified radars and timed scalar pulses to provide an aerial explosion and EMP." (Fer-De-Lance, by Tom Bearden, p. 65.)

TOTAL RUSSIAN DEFENSE

In 1968, the Soviets made a statement in Military Strategy that the USSR has achieved a 100% defense, and the West has not (Sokolovsky, 3rd Edition). Were they telling the truth, and if so, to what were they referring? It is only a matter of life and death, you

FIRE FROM THE SKY

know.

Dr. Edward Teller said in 1987: "Today, the Soviets have a monopoly on defense and they intend to keep it. We have done practically nothing about civil defense." He also said, "The Soviets have worked for the past 10 years perfecting laser weapons and now have a laser capable of shooting 1,000 miles without its beam spreading more than 5 feet" (Jan.-Feb. 1987 Fusion).

PROJECT PAPERCLIP

Before we continue in time sequence of what happened, I want to go back and point out some connections you need to know. The earlier Fire From The Sky material says that Russia succeeded in developing anti-gravity levitating platforms, which are the same things as commonly called flying saucers. In fact the Soviets used former Nazi scientists to achieve their advances.

The Nazis actually originated the "flying saucers," and they got their ideas and information concerning them from extraterrestrials. This is what all the records indicate. I will give you some leads and if you are serious, you can do your own research and prove it to yourself. You don't have to believe me or anyone else - check it out for yourself!

For information about the Nazi scientists, I suggest you study material about Project Paperclip. (Project Paperclip by Clarence Lasby; The Torbitt Document by William Torbitt; The Nazi Connection to the John F. Kennedy Assassination by Mae Brussell; etc.) A former member of that operation is a good friend of mine. Among the Germans (Austrians) involved in Paperclip was a Communist spy named Henry Kissinger - you've heard of him, perhaps?

Another German was Werner von Braun, who was brought to this country and became head of the U.S. space program. Von Braun worked for a German general named Walter Dornberger, and had been an SS Sturmbannfuhrer since 1937. Dornberger was in charge of Peenemunde. At the end of the war, von Braun and 115 other German scientists surrendered to the Americans and were brought to Fort Bliss, Texas (just across the state line from White Sands Missile Range, New Mexico).

In 1950 they were transferred to the Redstone Arsenal at Huntsville, Alabama. Col. Tom Bearden was a nuclear physicist at Redstone Arsenal. Von Braun's original security report said: "He was an SS officer but no information is available to indicate that he was ardent Nazi. Subject is regarded as a potential security threat by the Military Governor."

Von Braun played down his SS membership and said that it was only honorary, and that "his real reason for working in the Nazi missile program, he said, had been the potential usefulness of his machines in 'space travel'" (Blowback, p. 39).

Dornberger was convicted as a war criminal, then later was secretly brought to the U.S. at the request of von Braun to High Commissioner John J. McCloy. He went to work for Bell Aircraft (Bell Textron) where he worked on the space program as director of R&D (James "Bo" Gritz, Called to Serve, p. 511). He was also a special CIA consultant (The Nazi Hunters, p. 217).

Eventually he served on the board of several aerospace companies. He helped develop a nuclear powered trans-atmospheric vehicle (TAV). These vehicles began operating out of Area 51 in Nevada, and other places. Dornberger became a boss of Bell Aerospace Corporation and had about 30 former Nazi scientists working for him. A man named Stanton Friedman is going around the country saying he has worked on these

FIRE FROM THE SKY

type of nuclear propulsion systems. He sells videos with photos.

McCloy was Assistant Secretary of War and blocked the executions of many Nazi war "criminals." He is the one who was overseer of the internment of Japanese-Americans in concentration camps in California. In 1949 he became High Commissioner in Germany and pardoned convicted war criminals such as Alfred Krupp and Dr. Hjalmar Schact (who went to work for Aristotle Onassis).

He became legal counsel to the "Seven Sisters" oil companies, one of which was managed by the father of CIA agent George de Mohrenschildt who was a Nazi spy in WW II. "George's cousin, the movie producer Baron Constantine Maydell, was one of the top German Abwehr agents in North America, and was recruited by Gehlen..." (Gritz, p. 538).

OPERATION SUNRISE

According to Col. Bo Gritz, former head of U.S. Army Special Forces for Latin America, "General Reinhard Gehlen, Hitler's chief intelligence officer against the Soviet Union, had struck a deal with the Americans (Called OPERATION SUNRISE) that was not, for obvious reasons, released to establishment media. The principal negotiators were Allen Dulles and William Casey of the OSS, Sir William Stephenson for the British, and SS General Karl Wolff, head of the Gestapo in Italy and former chief of Heinrich Himmler's personal staff" (p. 562).

Operation SUNRISE developed into Operation OVERCAST with General Walter Dornberger and Werner von Braun, and then became Project PAPERCLIP, BLOODSTONE AND BELARUS, etc. (ibid.).

John McCloy, by the way, would later serve the Warren Commission and helped cover up the assassination of JFK. He became head of the World Bank, head of the Chase Manhattan Bank, head of the Ford Foundation, chairman of the Council on Foreign Relations, and co-author of Freedom From War, The United States Program For General And Complete Disarmament In A Peaceful World (Department of State Publication 7277).

Von Braun had an assistant named Fred Wolff: "...that matter had been amply met through Dr. von Braun's suggestions (which Wolff sketched out quickly to receive von Braun's check)." War For The Moon by Martin Caidin, E.P. Dutton, 1959, chapter "Project Moon," p. 61 (this book was illustrated by Fred Wolff). Note above that the head of the Gestapo in Italy, Karl Wolff, was working with von Braun. Was Fred's name originally Karl, or was he a son? We are not talking Smith or Jones here, how many men named Wolff (spelled with two f's) that were close friends of von Braun were there in this very small organization?

Gehlen, von Braun and Dornberger continued to have considerable influence on American politics, as evidenced from this quote from Blowback, p. 64: "Gehlen also played a role in the creation of the famous missile gap of the 1950s. 'Gehlen provided us [the CIA] with specific reports on the Soviet ICBM program,' Victor Marchetti says. 'He said, "We have two reliable reports confirming this," and they [the Soviets] have just installed three missiles at that site,' et cetera, claiming that they had contacts among the German scientists captured by the Russians at the end of the war." The intelligence reports were transmitted to the Pentagon through interagency channels, and word about the alarming new development eventually leaked from there into the press.

"Walter Dornberger added fuel to this fire in 1955 by publishing alarming specula-

FIRE FROM THE SKY

tions that the Soviets might attack from the sea, using shorter-range missiles deployed in floating canisters off the coast of the United States. He was deeply involved in the United States' own ICBM program at this point, and his opinions were given considerable weight in public discussions."

PROJECT OVERCAST

On July 19, 1945, the Joint Chiefs of Staff approved a program called Operation Overcast. Under this program, 350 German scientists and technicians would be brought into the United States for a period of six months. The program was labeled Top Secret to keep it from the American public. (Ashman, Charles & Wagman, Robert J., The Nazi Hunters, Warner Books, p. 212.)

When the Nazi scientists were brought into the U.S., they were first put up at Camp Overcast. Camp Overcast was at Wright Field, which later became famous among UFO researchers as Wright-Patterson Air Force Base, home of the infamous Hangar 18. Even Senator Barry Goldwater was not allowed access to this facility.

Rabbi Stephen Wise, head of the American Jewish Congress, discovered that the wife of one of the Wright Field rocket team was a former Nazi Party official and in May 1946 said: "This operation [Paperclip, formerly called Overcast] is all the more deplorable at a time when officials of our government find every possible reason for failing to fulfill the declared policy of President Truman to rescue as many victims of the Nazi terror as our immigration laws permit... As long as we reward the former servants of Hitler while leaving his victims in DP camps, we cannot even pretend that we are making any real effort to achieve the aims we fought for."

Rabbi Stephen Wise is also famous for the quote: "Some call it Communism; I call it Judaism!"

When the Germans were first brought into New York, "At Port Washing, they lived in comfortable conditions at a castle that had been build by the multimillionaire Jay Gould. They soaked in marble bathtubs and ate in an imposing dining room" (p. 203, American Swastika by Charles Higham).

"In August 1945, General Walter Bedell Smith's private plane was used to fly Gehlen and five of his general staff to the American capital. They traveled in plain clothes, one of their members using a violin case for a suitcase. It is interesting to note that Bedell Smith was Eisenhower's chief of staff" (p. 260, American Swastika).

On March 4, 1946, the operation was changed to Operation Paperclip, with no limits on the time or to the number of Germans.

Another German brought in, who was not a scientist, was Otto von Bolschwing. He was educated at the University of London and the University of Breslau. He joined the Nazi Party on April 1, 1932 and developed an import/export business, owned a coal mine, and was involved with several drug companies.

When the war broke out, he joined the SS and became an intelligence officer, working with the German branches of General Electric and Standard Oil. He was in charge of important funds that came through Nazi connections with Allen Dulles in the Schroeder Bank of New York. In 1945 he was contacted by the Army CIC and in 1947 was a member of the Gehlen organization. He came to the United States and got a job with Alfred Driscoll, former governor of New Jersey and president of Warner-Lambert drug company.

Later he joined the Transinternational Computer Investment Corporation (TCI) in Sili-

FIRE FROM THE SKY

con Valley, California and became vice-president of the company. Reinhard Gehlen worked for TCI during the time he was helping Richard Nixon run for President.

MICHAEL PAINE

Those who studied the assassination of President Kennedy perhaps will recall that Lee Harvey Oswald's wife Marina was staying with Ruth Paine. On April 30, 1961, Oswald married Marina Pruskova in the Soviet Union. He wrote to U.S. Senator John Tower for help in returning to the United States, and it was granted. Remember, Oswald had denounced and left the United States, then he asked a U.S. Senator for help in returning, and got it! Why did he pick Tower to ask, and why did Tower help him? Tower took Lyndon Johnson's place in the Senate and later became head of the Armed Services Committee.

A special non-quota immigrant permit was issued for Oswald's wife. Oswald and Marina arrived in the U.S. on June 13, 1962 and went to Dallas. "He returned to Dallas on October 2, 1963, and was met by fellow CIA agents George de Mohrenschildt and Ruth and Michael Paine. Michael Paine worked for Nazi war criminal Gen. Walter Dornberger at Bell-Textron in Dallas" (Gritz, p. 529). Next page - "Most of Oswald's contacts in Dallas, in fact, were with persons hired by Dornberger."

The majority of people who testified about Oswald before the Warren Commission were carefully selected Dornberger associates. Gritz says of these very people: "Eastern European and Russian emigre groups supplied by Gehlen were the personnel initially trained for these missions at a special camp set up at Oberammergau in 1946, under the command of General Sikes and SS General Burckhardt, and with the assistance of Henry Kissinger and Lucius Clay. The camp held 5,000 anti-communist elements who were prepared there and called themselves "Special Forces" (p. 564).

This was the origin of the U.S. Army Special Forces and on the next page Gritz says: "Many of the remainder underwent special guerrilla training as Special Forces recruits at Fort Bragg, North Carolina and helped form the nucleus of the present-day Green Berets. They would later be quite at home at their first assignment - the SS Bad Tolz Flint Kaserne in the heart of the Bavarian Alps."

And on page 566 Gritz says: "Gehlen's immediate staff of about 350 agents, in fact, were brought en masse to the U.S. Army's Historical Division. Almost all resistance to using Nazi war criminals to accomplish the CIA's missions seemed to have been overcome by the time Allen Dulles became Director in 1953." The Nazi SS Death's Head insignia was adopted as the symbol of the U.S. Army Special Forces (p. 567).

CIA agent George de Mohrenschildt's boss in the CIA was George Bush. De Mohrenschildt had a close friend, John W. Mecom, who was one of the incorporators of the San Jacinto Fund which was used to launder Bush's drug money. ("Surreptitious Entry: The CIA's Operations in the United States," by Thomas B. Ross of the Chicago Sun Times in The CIA File, edited by Robert L. Borosage and John Marks (Viking, 1976), and quoted in The Mafia, CIA & George Bush by Pete Brewton, p. 317.)

De Mohrenschildt had another friend, Jean de Menil, president of Schlumberger Corporation. Jim Garrison tells of Schlumberger being the source of weapons involved in anti-Castro operations and in Algeria. In 1977, hours after arranging to meet an investigator for the House Select Committee on Assassinations, de Mohrenschildt joined the long line of people involved in the Kennedy assassination who "committed suicide."

FIRE FROM THE SKY

If you have the stomach to check into it, you will find that Presidents Johnson, Nixon, Reagan and Bush shot their way into the Presidency. And people keeping a list have identified over 30 people close to President Clinton who have been murdered or at least died under mysterious circumstances. If you count the wars, our Presidents have been responsible for the deaths of thousands of people. Tell me, friend, are you a Republican or a Democrat?

Oswald told a public stenographer that an "engineer" (Michael Paine) offered to publish a book about the Soviet Union for Oswald if he would write it. The Paines began to subsidize the Oswalds and later Mrs. Oswald moved in with the Paines, where she and Ruth chatted every day in Russian.

Lee Harvey Oswald then went to New Orleans and became involved with the "Fair Play For Cuba Committee." The head of that committed was a Jew named V.T. Lee, real name Tappin. Researchers of Lee Harvey Oswald must take into account the fact that there were several people claiming to be Oswald.

While living with the Paines, Oswald practiced shooting with a rifle he kept in their garage. Some say he took a pot-shot at General Walker at this time. In September, it was announced that President Kennedy would visit Dallas, and three weeks later Mrs. Paine called Mr. Truly, the manager of the Texas School Book Depository and got Oswald at job working there, under the name of "O.H. Lee." (New York Post, Dec. 10, 1963, p. 22.)

MORE ASSASSINATION CONNECTIONS

Immediately after Kennedy was assassinated there were three main investigations launched - by the Texas Attorney General, the FBI, and the U.S. Congress. On Dec. 9, 1963, seventeen days after the assassination, the Communist Worker Newspaper demanded that the three investigations be stopped and that only Earl Warren do the investigation. Three days later, President Johnson ordered the three groups to stop and put Earl Warren in charge, exactly as the Communists had ordered.

Warren immediately began destroying evidence. While the other groups were finding information of multiple people involved, Arlen Specter came up with the "magic bullet" theory to explain what happened. No one else supported that theory except Gerald Ford, but that became the conclusion of the Warren Commission. Gerald Ford, whose real name was Leslie Lynch King (American Heritage Dictionary, 1979), in his book Portrait of the Assassin, page 51, tells about Lee Harvey Oswald being on the payroll of the American Red Cross while in Russia. The current head of the Red Cross is Elizabeth Dole, the wife of Senator Bob Dole. Specter has become prominent recently in the Waco and Ruby Ridge investigations, and is campaigning for President. Does it sound like maybe the Communists were behind the assassination of Kennedy?

If only it were that simple! We need to pay attention to who and what these people are, as their names come up in all kinds of strange places.

Ruth Paine's husband Michael worked as an engineer at Bell Aerospace for the German ex-General Dornberger, head of research for Bell. Paine was part of the Gehlen operation.

Werner von Braun became a close personal friend of J. Edgar Hoover and soon after he came to the U.S. he also became a close personal friend of Lyndon B. Johnson. Von Braun worked with Hoover in security projects at the Tennessee Valley Authority, the Redstone Arsenal and later in the National Space Agency. In 1958 Lyndon Johnson, ma-

7

FIRE FROM THE SKY

jority leader of the Senate, helped push through the National Space Act, which gave funding to von Braun.

The Navy and Air Force were in charge of the U.S. missile programs when Russia launched its Sputnik satellite in October of 1957. Two weeks later, they launched the much larger Sputnik II which carried a dog into space. The Russians had put a six-ton package into orbit, while two months later the Navy tried to launch a three-and-half-pound grapefruit-size satellite on their Vanguard missile. It rose a grand height of four feet and blew up, on national television. Eisenhower was reminded about the little-known bunch of Nazis at Huntsville, so he gave them the go-ahead. Less than two months later, the (ex) Nazis put America's first satellite, Explorer I, into orbit on January 31, 1958.

"Sputnik forced two space agendas on the United States, one public, the other top secret." (Burrows, William E., Deep Black - Space Espionage And National Security, Random House, 1986, p. 138.)

Reinhard Gehlen was head of the Nazi Abwehr spy organization during WW II, and at the end of the war he approached the OSS and offered to work for them, with his team and records. They accepted and brought many of his team into the U.S. under Projer Paperclip.

Gehlen remained chief of the West German Intelligence service until he retired in 1968. Frank Wisner, who worked for Allen Welsh Dulles, was a Wall Street lawyer who became head of Dulles' Secret Intelligence Branch and was responsible for the Gehlen organization. Working with Wisner were Harvard grad Harry Rositzke who worked in the same room with Arthur Schlesinger, Jr. and Richard Helms, who later became Director of the CIA in 1966.

One of Wisner's team was George Bookbinder, who later became President of the Rand Development Corporation. It was the Gehlen organization that dug the famous Berlin tunnel. They, especially the Rand Corporation, became good at digging tunnels (except they have not quite conquered that annoying "hum"!).

PEOPLE OF EARTH/SHAN

The book Air America says, during the Vietnam conflict, "An HQ was established in Singapore where Frank Wisner, the Deputy Director of Plans for the CIA, went personally to head the operation." (Robbins, Christopher, Air America, New York: Avon Books, 1979, p. 70).

Air America was the secret CIA airline involved in Operation Phoenix in the Vietnam war. One of the pilots was John Lear of UFO fame. The name Phoenix was a translation from the Phung Hoang, a mythical bird the Vietnamese said had magical powers to bring news of peace. The CIA bought drugs from Khun Sa, leader of the "Shan" people.

Bo Gritz, in Called To Serve, tells that Khun Sa tried to STOP the drug trade and was forced to continue by the Americans. On page 300, Gritz tells that President Reagan offered to recognize Shanland as a new and independent nation. I suppose it is "only coincidence" that the command ship ("flying saucer") of the ships involved with UFO legend Billy Meier was called the "Phoenix" and the extraterrestrials involved said that their name for Earth was "Shan."

The man in charge of the CIA Vietnam drug operation was Richard Armitage, who later became Assistant Secretary of Defense. Armitage shipped the drugs to Manuel Noriega in Panama, who shipped them to George Bush, head of the CIA and later Presi-

FIRE FROM THE SKY

dent, at Bush's drug bases in Mena, Arkansas, Homestead Air Force Base in Florida, and through the Zapata and Black Rose and such Bush family operations.

Armitage had a best friend named Erich von Marbod, also a Gehlen Organization person and a friend of Bo Gritz. At the end of the war in Vietnam, "he [Armitage] and Erich secreted tons of munitions in strategic caches around Southeast Asia. Erich's friends read like a global Who's Who. He was a best friend to the Shah of Iran. He is also very close to James Schlesinger, who was appointed Director of the CIA by Richard Nixon in December 1972. Schlesinger later became Secretary of Defense from 1973-1975 and Secretary of the Department of Energy from 1977-1979" (Gritz, p. 300). Erich "...was a protege of Henry Kissinger."

NIXON, BUSH & DONOVAN

On page 572 of his book, Gritz says: "The Indonesian campaign marked the entry of the CIA into large-scale operations, and although it was a failure, the more the Agency failed in the future, the more it grew and prospered. Oddly enough, the man who had helped back Dulles and Frank Wisner [remember, Wisner was over Gehlen's Nazi spy network] on the campaign was Richard Nixon."

In 1969, Richard Nixon was in California campaigning and one of his campaign supporters was Reinhard Gehlen, former Nazi head of the German Secret Service (Abwehr). Gehlen was with a high-tech firm called TCI (Transinternational Computer Investment Corp.) that worked on classified Defense Department projects. His translator for German projects was Helene von Damme, who was also Governor Ronald Reagan's personal appointments secretary and personal secretary to Reagan when he became President. Von Damme later became U.S. Ambassador to Austria. Von Damme was former secretary to the Nazi German High Command.

William Donovan, head of OSS, and Allen Dulles, head of OSS in Europe under Donovan (who later became head of the CIA until President Kennedy fired him - it was said that he told Kennedy, "You can't fire me, you don't even know who I work for!"), and J. Edgar Hoover, head of the FBI, brought Reinhard Gehlen and his Abwehr spy group into the United States. One of the men involved was counter-intelligence officer William P. Clark. Clark married Werner von Braun's niece, Joan von Braun (Brauner). Clark at one time was a member of the Council on Foreign Relations.

Clark moved to San Luis Obispo in California and joined Ronald Reagan. He became President Reagan's National Security Advisor on the National Security Council. A suit was filed in Southern California naming William Clark as being involved in the Kennedy assassination. Researchers Mae Brussell, William Torbitt, District Attorney Garrison, and others say Lyndon Johnson, J. Edgar Hoover, Werner von Braun, and Walter Dornberger were involved in the Kennedy assassination. Also involved were Richard Nixon, George Bush and Allen Dulles.

Col. Bo Gritz, in Called To Serve (p. 534), quotes a memo written by an FBI staff assistant in 1947: "Nixon intervened on behalf of a Chicago gangster who was about to be called as a witness before a congressional committee... It is my sworn statement that one Jack Rubinstein of Chicago, noted as a potential witness for hearings of the House Committee on Un-American Activities, is performing information functions for the staff of Congressman Richard Nixon, Republican of California. It is requested Rubinstein not be called for open testimony in the aforementioned hearings. That same year Rubinstein

FIRE FROM THE SKY

moved to Dallas, Texas, and changed his name to JACK RUBY..."

Sam Giancana bragged that Nixon was controlled by the "Mob," see the book Double Cross written by his brother.

GEHLEN AND THE GERMAN GENERAL STAFF

Dick Russell in The Man Who Knew Too Much is one of the researchers with many details of the involvement of Nixon, Bush, and Dulles and said, "Willoughby was in regular correspondence with Allen Dulles - before JFK fired Dulles - and with ex(?) Nazis who ran the CIA's European-based spy network" (p. 707).

Gehlen was responsible for reviving the Nazi German General Staff after the war by placing his agent Adolph Heusinger in charge of the German General Staff. Der Spiegel said: "It is quite true that General Gehlen had engaged the former Chief of Wehrmacht Opertions for a purpose other than his espionage service. The West German spy boss did not at that time think of confining himself to merely collecting and sifting information. Two years before Adenauer offered soldiers to the Allies, General Gehlen was, with General Heusinger, already engaged in assembling a new general staff high command." (Der Spiegel, Feb. 29, 1956.)

The Heusinger Wehrmacht were involved in the space race (remember, it was the Germans who started rockets, "flying saucers," etc.). The book Heusinger of the Fourth Reich by Charles R. Allen, Jr., said: "The conservative columnist Edgar Ansel Mower on September 28, 1962 reported that the West German newspaper Die Welt of Hamburg devoted a lengthy series to the vigorous efforts being made by the West German Defense Ministry to perfect 'death rays' (LASERS) which, when fired from a space platform, 'WOULD BURN, VAPORIZE, DESTROY ANY KNOWN MATTER AND MATERIAL BY ITS FANTASTIC ENERGY CONCENTRATION OF MILLIONS OF WATTS and, from the DISTANCE OF THE MOON, WOULD TAKE EXACTLY 1.3 SECONDS TO KILL." (Long Island Daily Press, September 28, 1962). Note they were talking, in 1962, of lasers from a Moon base.

WILLIAM CLARK

Paperclip Operation member William Clark was one who pressured to pardon Ollie North. Clark has a ranch in California called the "Eagles Nest." There was (is?) a machine gun in Clark's living room which came from a National Guard Armory robbery in Oxnard, California. The rest of the weapons from the robbery were stored at a hideout at the Branch Davidian compound in Waco, Texas. When "they" wanted "their" guns back, David Koresh did not want to give them back. Oh, friends, why don't you check up on your leaders?! Why waste your time on soap operas, when the real thing is so much more "interesting"?!

As another interesting "coincidence," not that our present Jewish Chairman of the Joint Chiefs of Staff Gen. John Shalikashvili (who succeeded the part-Jewish, part black CFR member Gen. Colin Powell) speaks English with a foreign accent and was born in Soviet Georgia. The media has reported that his father was a major in the Nazi Waffen SS. In spite of this, he is the darling of the Zionists, with strong support from Les Aspin, the Simon Wiesenthal Center, Senator Carl Levin, etc.

When Reagan became Governor of California, he appointed William Clark as Superior Court Judge in San Luis Obispo County. Later Reagan appointed him Deputy Secretary of State. When James Watt resigned as Secretary of the Interior, William Clark replaced him. Reagan appointed Clark's wife Joan Brauner (von Braun) Clark as alternate

FIRE FROM THE SKY

United States representative to the United Nations General Assembly.

Ray Renick says: "The American headquarters of the Gehlen Organization is in San Luis Obispo County. The main office is called "Eagles Nest." Many public officials, judges, supervisors and law enforcement personnel are personal friends and business associates (in drug trafficking, no less) with the Gehlen Organization and "Eagles Nest." Judge William P. Clark and Mrs. Joan Clark (nee von Braun, Brauner) are the executives behind the Gehlen Organization, "Eagles Nest" and the Zapata Cattle Company's drug trafficking interest. [The cattle are brought in from Mexico. Cattle have four stomachs.] Ronald Reagan is a slient partner in the San Luis Obispo cattle/drug business. Remember, Clark was one of the original architects of "Project Paperclip"! The Zapata Cattle Company is affiliated with George Bush's Zapata Oil Company of Houston, Texas (REF: "The SLO Connection," Barrons article "The Mexican Connection") - Sept. 19, 1988.

A major law firm for the Gehlen Organization is Sinsheimer, Schiebelhut, and Baggett.

The Gehlen Organization, copying Hitler's New Order, established a concentration camp system in San Luis Obispo County. It was called the California Specialized Training Institute. It developed plans called the King Alfred Plan, Operation Cable Splitter, Operation Garden Plot, and REX-84 and was later renamed as the Federal Emergency Management Agency (FEMA). You can get more information on these subjects from Militia of Montana, Bo Gritz, Spotlight Newspaper, etc.

Also brought in under Paperclip was Henry Kissinger. The U.S. Army 44th CIC and 970th CIC Detachments negotiated the surrender of the German Army in Northern Italy and Austria in Operation Sunrise from which Paperclip took over. Later the Vatican provided documents and help for many Nazis to escape to South America, including Martin Bormann.

Prince Bernhard of the Netherlands created a group that became known as the Bilderbergers. Many "conservative" researchers have come to recognize the Bilderbergers as an important force for the "New World Order." What they probably don't know, though, is that Bernhard was a former Nazi SS storm trooper.

Some of the Paperclip surrender operation personnel included Theodore Shackley and Heide Kingsbury (daughter of General Galland, designer of the Messerschmidt ME 262). Kingbury became secretary and court transcriber to Judge William Clark. Shackley became head of Operation Phoenix in Vietnam (Laos). Shackley was head of JM Wave, code name of the CIA Miami office during the Bay of Pigs and Kennedy assassination events (Furiati, p. 41). (Furiati, Claudia, ZR Rifle - The Plot To Kill Kennedy And Castro, Ocean Press, Victoria, Australia, 1994. From declassified Cuban records of the Kennedy assassination.)

For more information see Reinhard Gehlen, Master Spy (I can't find my copy at the moment and don't remember the author). In 1968, after the Kennedy assassination, Gehlen retired to his chalet in Bavaria. The chalet was a gift from Allen Dulles. The General Was A Spy by Heinz Hohne and Hermann Zolling,, Project Paperclip by Clarence Lasby, Shootdown by R.W. Johnson (tells about Clark's involvement in the shootdown of Korean Airlines 007), Project Paperclip by Ray Renick, and the Torbitt Document by William Torbitt are all resources for more information. The most accurate source of information for a general overview are the Phoenix Journals and CONTACT newspaper.

GERMAN SCIENTISTS AND ALIENS

FIRE FROM THE SKY

Here is something you should think seriously about. The ONE thing that "everybody" agrees on. Christians, atheists, Republicans, Democrats, Communists, whatever, is that the Nazis were degenerate, sick, nuts, weird, the ultimate evil. I ask you: realistically, how can this be?

Is it possible that this is another "lie?" You ask, am I saying the Nazis were not evil? What is your definition of evil? Does the evidence support what you believe? How can a whole nation of Germans - many of them our brothers and sisters and direct ancestors - all be totally evil? Were they that different from us? Was our government telling us the truth? Has the government ever told us the truth about ANYTHING?

Let's go back to Werner von Braun. IN 1959, (in News Europa, Jan. 1, 1959), von Braun states this about extraterrestrials in an interview: "We find ourselves faced by powers which are far stronger than we had hitherto assumed, and whose base of operations is at present unknown to us" (when asked about the deflection of a U.S. satellite). "More I cannot say at present. We are now engaged in entering into a closer contact with those powers, and in six or nine months' time it may be possible to speak with more precision on the matter."

The great German space pioneer Hermann Oberth said, "We cannot take credit for our record advancement in certain scientific fields alone; we have been helped." When asked who helped, he said: "The people of other worlds." (Robin Collyns, Did Spacemen Colonize the Earth? London: Pelham Books, 1974, p. 236.)

Noted German rocket expert Dr. Walter Riedel said: "I'm convinced that saucers have an out-of-world basis." (April, 1952, LIFE magazine, p. 96.)

The American Weekly of October 24, 1954, quoted Professor Oberth of Germany: "It is my thesis that flying saucers are real and that they are space ships from another solar system."

General Douglas MacArthur, quoted in the The New York Times, Oct. 8, 1955, said "The nations of the world will have to unite - for the next war will be an interplanetary war. The nations of the Earth must someday make a common front against attack by people from other planets."

There is plenty of proof that "flying saucers" are real. The questions now are, what are they, and from where do they come?

NICAP

The National Investigations Committee On Aerial Phenomena (NICAP) was founded in 1956 by Navy physicist Thomas Townsend Brown. Brown is known as the discoverer of the electrogravitic capacitance effect. He was former Vice President of Douglas Aircraft (one of the founding groups of the RAND Corporation). NICAP gained a reputation as being a CIA front operation. For many years it was headed by Marine Major Donald Keyhoe.

In Der Weltraum Rueckt Uns Nagher, Blanvalet Verlag, Chapter III, by; Major Keyhoe, he says that the U.S. infiltrated 600 scientists into Bohemia in tank crew uniforms, in 1945, to check out some of the U.F.O. bases. Vice-Admiral Roscoe Hillenkoetter, a former director of the CIA, was a board member of NICAP for years.

Colonel Joseph Bryan III, chief of the CIA psychological warfare staff and Count Nicolas de Rochefort of the same CIA staff were board members. Karl Pflock was chairman of NICAP's Washington sub-committee. John Acuff "who was alleged to have CIA affilia-

FIRE FROM THE SKY

tions" per the UFO Encyclopedia by John Spencer, took over as head of NICAP. Then Acuff did a curious thing, according to Cosmic Patriot Files, Vol. 2, by the "Committed of 12 to Save the Earth," edited by Commander X, p. 137, Acuff sold classified CIA documents to a Nazi organization in Canada called Samisdat.

Samisdat is the publisher of two books called UFOs, Nazi Secret Weapon? by Mattern-Friedrich and Secret Nazi Polar Expeditions by Christof Friedrich, both of which were available from Samisdat Publishers, 206 Carlton St., Toronto, ONT., M5A 2L1, Canada, or from Liberty Bell Publications, Reedy, WV, 25270.

A video called UFO Secrets of WW II German Flying Saucers and one called UFO Secrets of the Third Reich, both produced by the American Academy of Dissident Scientists, are available and a phone number from the tapes is: 310-473-9717. (American Academy of Dissident Scientists, 10970 Ashton Ave. #310, Los Angeles, CA 90024. One of their Presidents is Vladimir Terziski.

Acuff was kicked out and replaced by CIA agent Alan Hall in 1979. Christof Friedrich campaigned to become Prime Minister of Canada. A Jewish radio announcer interviewed Friedrich to try to discredit him, but the result was the firing, blacklisting, and subsequent persecution of the Jewish moderator.

Cosmic Patriot Files (currently available from ads in UFO publications and most UFO book dealers) says in Vol. 2, p. 131 that in 1945 the Germans began transferring their flying saucer projects to a secret underground base near the South Pole. Also in 1945, General Hans Kammler disappeared from Germany and went to the South Pole on German U-Boat U-977, and German flying saucers began appearing over the United States.

Samisdat was selling a manuscript called "The Lightning & the Sun" by Savitri Devi, a "guru" from India whose book connected roots of Naziism with the pyramid in Egypt and Pharoah Akhn-aton and the "ancient cult of the Sun."

Willard McIntyre, a friend of Stuart Nixon, who was the assistant to NICAP President John (Jack) Acuff, accused Acuff of selling the material to Samisdat and of intending to merge Samisdat and NICAP. One NICAP board member, the Jewish Senator Barry Goldwater, was quite upset upon learning about the involvement with Samisdat, considered a Nazi organization.

Goldwater was busy running for President and no doubt would not appreciate the link to Nazis and UFOs. The head of his Presidential Campaign Committee was someone you have perhaps heard of, named Ronald Reagan. Goldwater was Chairman of the Senate Intelligence Committee and the Senate Armed Services Committee. He tried to obtain entrance to the infamous Hangar 18 at Wright-Patterson and was denied. There was more going on with this situation than we are allowed to know.

Anyway, Acuff had to go and was forced out. A new board was voted in which included two new board members: one was Senator Goldwater's aide, Charles Lombard, and the other was John Fisher. If you recall, in the early Fire From The Sky writings, I said that General George Keegan, head of Air Force Intelligence, inspired the founding of the American Security Council to try to warn the American public of what was happening. The President of the American Security Council was - did you guess it? - John Fisher. A Co-Chairman of the Council was Senator Robert Dole. The members of this council did not understand who was the real enemy, and they were sabotaged.

"NICAP continued to have confidential UFO data leaked to it during Acuff's tenure.

FIRE FROM THE SKY

Late in 1976, for example, an officer in the Pentagon provided Acuff with copies of a number of classified documents, including the now-famous Iranian report and several other 'hot' reports." This had to be stopped, so Acuff was canned and retired CIA agent Alan Hall was brought in to replace him. "Not much is known about Hall's background, except he evidently worked in some technical capacity - perhaps with the Office of Scientific Intelligence..." My-Oh-My. What tangled webs.

THEN CAME 1947

The famous Roswell crash occurred in 1947. That year, Operation Majestic-12 was supposedly established by Truman to control the UFO situation, the National Security Act was passed, Project SIGN was established at Wright-Patterson and the CIA was established. Admiral James Forrestal was soon appointed Secretary of Defense, later to be murdered when he was tossed out of a hospital window by CIA agents, because he wanted to tell about the flying saucers.

The Roswell, New Mexico, crash of a flying saucer in 1947 has been described by the government as nothing but a weather balloon. Yet, an investigation by the Government Accounting Office and others has shown that all records pertaining to this event were illegally destroyed.

Another strange thing about this event is that the government must have released HUNDREDS of these "weather balloons" in 1947 - or - perhaps they were not weather balloons? A file in the MUFON computer bulletin board called 1947.SIT lists the reported sightings of UFOs during 1947, sorted by state. There were 853 events and 3283 witnesses reported. How many more were not reported? Quite a lot of "weather balloons," don't you think?

In 1951, Congress was talking about turning Antarctica into a nuclear test area, but suddenly changed their mind when Washington was buzzed by UFOs and pictures of flying saucers over the White House appeared on the front pages of newspapers.

ANTARCTICA

In early 1980, I received the following letter from Christof Friedrich of Samisdat, written in 1979, the same year John Acuff was kicked out of NICAP for selling classified CIA documents to Samisdat. As it is too long, I will quote only part of it.

"SEARCH FOR HITLER'S ANTARCTIC U.F.O. BASES. Due to an overwhelming number of letters and telephone calls requesting details about our new books, new products, speaking tours, psychic research projects and our intensive experimental UFO-construction programs, we have to use this less personal form of keeping in touch with our many friends and collaborators around the world.

"Your response to our most recent mailout and activities has been most encouraging! We have received orders and enquiries from as far away as Nomea in the South Pacific, Easter Island, Chile, Argentina, Brazil, Venezuela, Panama, Mexico, Soviet Satellite countries, China, South Africa, Persia, the Congo, Australia, Japan, as well as from every country in Western Europe and almost every state in the U.S.A.

Not only is this response extensive, it is massive - a clear indication on the part of knowledgeable UFO researchers and members of the public that they are tired of the 'junk food' being served up by old-line UFO groups and publications who expound the official CIA-KGB alibi that all UFOs are extraterrestrial. What the UFO-watching world wants now is the real meat of the matter - a serious investigation of UFOs whose origins

FIRE FROM THE SKY

are terrestrial. SAMISDAT is the only organization making such an effort, but we are not alone, for we have thousands of supporters like yourself who want to know the truth which the saucer-charlatans have for 30 years tried to cover up with fairy tale fantasies of 'little green men.' It is people like yourself who have made SAMISDAT the most active UFO organization and publisher on Planet Earth!

[I want to insert a question to readers who consider themselves serious UFO researchers. Have you ever heard of Samisdat? That's what I thought. Continuing:]

"Certainly we can be proud of this achievement which is the result, not only of our own Herculean efforts and sacrifices, but of your faithful support during this 5-year-long struggle against the forces of vested interest, deceit and prejudice which have attempted to hide the UFO story under a cloak of childish nonsense and outright lies.

For many years we have determinedly pursued this new course of investigation, firm in the knowledge that man is able to achieve that which he perceives. Our researchers' keen sense of direction and perception has guided them unerringly in their discovery of seemingly insignificant clues and the derivation of meaningful patterns therefore. Only such devoted and painstaking research could succeed in unEarthing the present array of facts which indicate the Earthly origin of most flying saucers. As one vital discovery has led to another, we have reached certain conclusions which are logical and inescapable, however unpopular they may be today.

"Our discoveries have led us into the production of a number of currently suppressed and sometimes vilified books which are now underground best-sellers. UFOS - Nazi SECRET WEAPON? was our first title, now sold out in five complete editions. Our second book, SECRET Nazi POLAR EXPEDITIONS, is coming up fast and has sold out two full editions. Foreign language translations of these books are selling briskly, and it is becoming obvious to everyone that the media-enforced blockage of the truth has now been broken. Three additional books are currently under production and these will round out our Phase I Publishing Program: THE CIA-KGB-UFO COVERUP, THE ANTARCTICA THEORY and THE LAST BATTALION.

"During the course of our research, we have discovered some of the original German flying saucer scientists who are still alive! These space pioneers are, of course, old men now in their 70s and 80s. Our interviews with them will be incorporated into our regular lecture program as well as into our future books.

"We have also been able to establish research teams in Canada, the U.S.A. and in particular, Germany, whose task it is to rediscover basic principles of wingless flight which brought the original Nazi UFOs into being. Already, these teams have designed and constructed small scale models, some using conventional power and others which have propulsion systems unprecedented in today's aerospace technology. With additional research, we hope to make available several different models in kit form for hobby-builders." END OF QUOTE.

ADMIRAL BYRD AND OPERATION HIGHJUMP

Also in 1947, Admiral Richard E. Byrd led 4,000 military troops from the U.S., Britain and Australia in an invasion of Antarctica (Operation Highjump and follow-up), but encountered heavy resistance from Nazi flying saucers and had to call off the invasion. A Rear-Admiral who was in that invasion has retired in Texas, and said he was shocked when he read the Fire From The Sky material. He knew there were a lot of aircraft and

FIRE FROM THE SKY

rocket shoot-downs but did not realize the situation was so bad.

The invasion of ANTARCTICA consisted of three battle groups from Norfolk, VA, on Dec. 2, 1946. They were led by Byrd's command ship, the ice-breaker Northwind, and consisted of the catapult ship Pine Island, the destroyer Brownsen, the aircraft-carrier Phillipines Sea, the U.S. submarine Sennet, two support vessels Yankee and Merrick, and two tankers Canisted and Capacan, the destroyer Henderson and a floatplane ship Currituck. A British-Norwegian force and a Russian force, and I believe some Australian and Canadian forces were also involved.

On March 5, 1947 the El Mercurio newspaper of Santiago, Chile, had a headline article "On Board the Mount Olympus on the High Seas" which quoted Byrd in an interview with Lee van Atta: "Adm. Byrd declared today that it was imperative for the United States to initiate immediate defence measures against hostile regions. The admiral further stated that he didn't want to frighten anyone unduly but that it was a bitter reality that in case of a new war the continental United States would be attacked by flying objects which could fly from pole to pole at incredible speeds. (Earlier he had recommended defence bases at the North Pole.) Admiral Byrd repeated the above points of view, resulting from his personal knowledge gathered both at the north and south poles, before a news conference held for International News Service."

When Byrd returned to the States, he was hospitalized and was not allowed to hold any more press conferences. In March 1955, he was placed in charge of Operation Deepfreeze which was part of the International Geophysical Year (1957-1958) exploration of the Antarctic. He died, some have suggested he was murdered, in 1957. UFO researchers are familiar with a diary purported to be Admiral Byrd's diary which tells of an entrance to a hollow Earth at the poles and a being called THE MASTER. The diary is generally considered to be a hoax, but even if it is a hoax, it is an indication that there was SOMETHING going on upon which to build the hoax.

UFO researchers are also aware of strange sightings of flying saucers with swastikas or iron crosses on them, "aliens" speaking German, etc. An example is the American Reinhold Schmidt, whose father was born in Germany, who tells in his book Incident At Kearney (Nebraska) that he was taken on a flying saucer on several occasions. He said the crew spoke German and acted like German soldiers. He said they took him to the Polar region (if someone were making up a story, why would they claim to be taken, of all places, to the pole?)

After returning he was subjected to persecution by the U.S. Government. His description of the flying saucers matched pictures captured from the Germans. In 1959, three large newspapers in Chile reported front page articles about UFO encounters where the crew members appeared to be German soldiers. IN the 1960s there were reports in New York and New Jersey of flying saucer "aliens" who spoke German, or English with a German accent.

In the Julius and Ethel Rosenberg atomic espionage trials, they spoke of "warships of space." Since they had access to top secret information, about what were they talking?

HITLER ESCAPED!

I remember hearing, in the 1950s, rumors that Hitler had escaped to a secret Nazi base at the South Pole. In 1952, Dwight D. Eisenhower said: "We have been unable to unearth one bit of tangible evidence of Hitler's death. Many people believe that Hitler

FIRE FROM THE SKY

escaped from Berlin."

When President Truman asked Joseph Stalin at the Potsdam conference in 1945 whether or not Hitler was dead, Stalin replied bluntly, "No." Stalin's top army officer, Marshall Gregory Zhukov, whose troops were the ones to occupy Berlin, flatly stated after a long thorough investigation in 1945: "We have found no corpse that could be Hitler's."

The chief of the U.S. trial counsel at Nuremburg, Thomas J. Dodd, said: "No one can say he is dead." Major General Floyd Parks, who was commanding general of the U.S. sector in Berlin, stated for publication that he had been present when Marshall Zhukov described his entrance to Berlin, and Zhukov stated he believed Hitler might have escaped. Lt. Gen. Bedell Smith, Chief of Staff to Gen. Eisenhower in the European invasion and later Director of the CIA, stated publicly on Oct. 12, 1945, "No human being can say conclusively that Hitler is dead."

Col. W.J. Heimlich, former Chief, United States Intelligence, at Berlin, stated for publication that he was in charge of determining what had happened to Hitler and after a thorough investigation his report was: "There was no evidence beyond that of hearsay to support the theory of Hitler's suicide." He also stated, "On the basis of present evidence, no insurance company in America would pay a claim on Adolph Hitler."

Nuremburg judge Michael Mussmanno said in his book Ten Days to Die, "Russia must accept much of the blame (to the extent that it still exists) that Hitler did not die in May 1945." However, Mussmanno stated that he interviewed Hitler's personal waiter, his valet, his chauffeur, his two secretaries, pilots, top generals, etc., and they all agreed perfectly that Hitler committed suicide. He said they could not have gotten together afterward and made up a story that agreed in perfect detail without one flaw anywhere, so they must be telling the truth and he was absolutely convinced that Hitler committed suicide. The story at first sounds convincing, until you realized that they could have memorized a story BEFOREHAND and these were all people who almost WORSHIPPED Hitler. Do witnesses ever agree perfectly in detail in real life?

Former Secretary of State Jimmy Byrnes in his book Frankly Speaking (as quoted in the April 1948 The Cross and The Flag): "While in Potsdam at the Conference of the Big Four, Stalin left his chair, came over and clinked his liquor glass with mine in a very friendly manner. I said to him: 'Marshal Stalin, what is your theory about the death of Hitler?' Stalin replied: "He is not dead. He escaped either to Spain or Argentina."'

I still have the September, 1948, issue of a magazine called The Plain Truth with the headline article: "IS HITLER ALIVE, OR DEAD?," subtitled: "Here is summarized the conclusions of an exhaustive three-year investigation - together with reasons for believing Hitler may be alive and secretly planning the biggest hoax of all history."

Another article in November, 1949, says "The Nazis went underground, May 16, 1943!" and details a meeting at the residence of Krupp von Bohlen-Halbach, the head of I.G. Farben, etc., at which they planned "for World War III."

Another article in August, 1952, entitled "HITLER DID NOT DIE," subtitled "Adolph Hitler's fake suicide in his Berlin Bunker now is exposed as History's greatest hoax! Positive evidence comes to light that Hitler did not die - here's new evidence that Hitler is alive, directing Nazi underground, today!"

The June, 1952, issue of The Plain Truth is headlined: "HITLER May Be Alive!" The article states: "Now, NEW FACTS, or purported facts, leak out. It's reported now that in 1940

FIRE FROM THE SKY

the Nazis started to amass tractors, planes, sledges, gliders, and all sorts of machinery and materials IN THE SOUTH POLAR REGIONS - that for the next 4 years Nazi technicians built, on an almost unknown CONTINENT, Antarctica, the Fuhrer's SHANGRILA - a new Berchtesgaden.

The report says they scooped out an entire mountain, built a new refuge completely camouflaged - a magic mountain hide-a-way. The recently discovered continent is larger than Europe - 5,600 miles from Africa, 1,900 miles from the southern tip of South America, 4,800 miles from Australia.

It is NOT a mere ice-covered surface, but a real continent, with plains, valleys, mountain peaks up to 15,000 feet. The temperature in the interior is around zero (?) in the summer, and never drops below 20 or 30 degrees below in the winter. In other words, it is not as cold as in parts of North Dakota or Canada."

Bonjour magazine, the Police Gazette, and the Paris newspaper Le Monde all had articles about Hitler's South Pole hideaway. Admiral Doenitz, in 1943, stated, "The German submarine fleet has even now established an earthly paradise, an impregnable fortress, for the Fuhrer, in whatever part of the world." Although he did not specify where the exact location was, Bonjour pointed out that in 1940 Nazi engineers had begun construction of buildings that were to withstand temperatures to 60 degrees below zero.

There have been strong rumors, from the end of the War, that Hitler escaped to the South Pole. Yet, most people simply REFUSE to believe the evidence, the idea that Hitler survived the war is just unacceptable! It is too upsetting to too many people!

There is plenty of PROOF that the Americans and Russians LIED about what happened to Hitler, and there are strong rumors that he escaped to Antarctica. There is ample proof that a major group of Nazis escaped to Argentina. What do YOU think? Why did Admiral Byrd lead an invasion to Antarctica, and why the extreme secrecy about the whole situation?

In 1981, Donald McKale wrote Hitler: The Survival Myth to try to lay to rest the questions about what happened to Hitler. The flyleaf says: "In this book a distinguished historian examines the postwar world's most absorbing and persistent mystery, revealing why it has endured and where the mystery leads" (emphasis mine). The back flyleaf says "Absolute certainty about what happened still eludes us today."

Just recently on TV there are STILL programs telling "at last, the final, once and for all, this is the real story" about what happened to Hitler, yet they all do not really answer the question. A recent TV program, called "What Really Happened to Adolph Hitler," after investigating numerous stories, ends by saying that, in spite of Glasnost and the new freedom of access to Russian files, the files on Hitler are still some of the most highly classified items of the Soviets.

The Diario Illustrado of Santiago, Chile, January 18, 1948 issue, said: "On 30th of April, 1945, Berlin was in dissolution but little of that dissolution was evident at Templehof Airfield. At 4:15 p.m. at JU52 landed and S.S. troops directly from Rechlin for the defence of Berlin disembarked, all of them young, not older than 18 years.

The gunner in the particular plane was an engineer by the name of B... whom I had known for a number of years and for whom I had endeavored to get exemption from military service. He sought to tank up and leave Berlin as quickly as possible. During this re-fueling interval Mr. B... was suddenly elbowed in the ribs by his radio operator

FIRE FROM THE SKY

with a nod to look in a certain direction.

At about 100-120 meters he saw a sleek Messerschmitt Jet Model 332 [an editorial comment says this should be an ARADO 234]. Br. B.. and the radio operator saw, and without any doubt whatsoever, standing in front of the jet, their Commander in Chief, Adolf Hitler, dressed in field-grey uniform and gesticulating animatedly with some Party functionaries, who were obviously seeing him off.

For about ten minutes whilst their plane was being refuelled the two men observed this scene and around 4:30 p.m. they took to the air again. They were extremely astonished to hear during the midnight military news bulletin, some seven and a half hours later, that Hitler had committed suicide."

On a Canadian Broadcasting Corporation program called As It Happens, September 17th, 1974 at 7:15 p.m., a Prof. Dr. Ryder Saguenay, oral surgeon from the Dental Faculty of the University of California at Los Angeles, said that Hitler had ordered a special plane to leave from Berlin with all medical and dental records, especially X-rays, of all top Nazis for an unknown destination. He said that the dental records used to identify Hitler's body were drawn from MEMORY by a dental assistant, who disappeared and was never found.

An editorial in Zig Zag, Santiago, Chile, January 16, 1948, states that on April 30th, 1945, Flight Captain Peter Baumgart took Adolf Hitler, his wife Eva Braun, as well as a few loyal friends by plane from Tempelhof Airport to Tondern in Denmark (still German controlled). From Tondern, they took another plane to Kristiansund in Norway (also German controlled). From there they joined a submarine convoy. (U.F.O. Letzte Geheimwaffe des III Reiches, Mattern, pp. 50-51.)

The Jewish writer Michael Bar-Zohar in The Avengers, p. 99, said: "In 1943 Admiral Doenitz had declared: 'The German U-boat fleet is proud to have made an earthly paradise, an impregnable fortress for the Fuhrer, somewhere in the world.' He did not say in what part of the world it existed, but fairly obviously it was in South America."

The German writer Mattern said that Admiral Doenitz told a graduating class of naval cadets in Kiel in 1944: "The German Navy has still a great role to play in the future. The German Navy knows all hiding places for the Navy to take the Fuhrer to, should the need arise. There he can prepare his last measures in complete quiet."

The Germans say they were in contact with extraterrestrials. Now consider what Ronald Reagan, who was involved with the formerly Nazi Gehlen spy organization, said to Soviet leader Mikhail Gorbachev at the November 1985 Geneva summit conference: He told him, "How much easier your task and mine might be in these meetings that we held if suddenly there was a threat to this world from another species from another planet outside in the universe. We'd forget all the little local differences that we have between our countries, and we would find out once and for all that we really are all human beings here on this earth together." (International Herald Tribune and Daily Telegraph, 5 Dec. 1985.)

On September 21, 1987, Reagan spoke before the General Assembly of the United Nations and said: "I occasionally think, how quickly our differences worldwide would vanish if we were facing an alien threat from outside this world. And yet I ask, is not an alien force already among us?"

On May 4, 1988, at Chicago's Palmer House Hotel, Reagan said: "I've often wondered,

FIRE FROM THE SKY

what if all of us in the world discovered that we were threatened by an outer... a power from outer space, from another planet."

You of course have heard about Reagan's Star Wars program. If you study what was reported after the Gulf War about the Patriot missiles, you will find that the Patriot missile program and the Star Wars program were a big lie and the money was spent on something other than what we were told. The Patriot missiles never shot down a Scud, as learned by Congressional inquiry and reported by Israel.

There are so many facets to this story, it is hard to explain one part because it will not make sense unless you understand the other parts.

POLAR DEFENSES

One thing that Admiral Byrd stated in a press conference after his defeat at Antarctica was that the Antarctic continent should be surrounded by a "wall of defence installations since it represented the last line of defence for America." Although the U.S. and Russia had been allies during the war, suddenly the "Iron Curtain" was created and we and the Russians became enemies.

Both the Soviets and the United States ringed the poles with defense and detection bases, and in between was the barren no-man's-land of the poles where absolutely nobody lived, or did they? Could it be that we pretended we were protecting against the Russians and they pretended they were protecting against us, while really we and they were both scared of what was in between us - the Nazi Last Battalion?

UFO researchers should now begin to see the light of why the Navy has always been in the lead of UFO research. And you should now understand why, right from the beginning, they issued shoot-to-kill orders against any UFOs and why the situation was so highly classified! And anti-communist researchers have more clues now as to why we were giving aid to the Soviets at the same time we were calling them our enemies!

UFOs - NAZIS OR ALIENS?

Let me be sure you understand, though, that NOT ALL UFOs ARE NAZIS. Originally they were Nazi with some alien. Later the U.S. developed UFOs, and the Russians, and who knows who else. But all along there really were extraterrestrials, that is from where some of the technology originally came. Read the lives of Walter Russell, Nikola Tesla, the world's most advanced mathematician Ramanujan, etc., and they all say they were in contact with "gods" (The Goddess Namagiri, in the case of Ramanujan) or they had "enlightenment" from a "cosmic messenger" as in the case of Walter Russell. Russell is one who understood true physics, as opposed to the deceptions taught in modern physics.

RUSSIAN SPACE PROGRAM

Let's return to the origin of the Russian space program. The Russians also captured many German rocket and space scientists. Later the chief Russian physicist was Kapitsa, who once headed an atomic research laboratory at Cambridge University. (Assault on the Unknown, The International Geophysical Year by Walter Sullivan, McGraw-Hill Book Co., New York, p. 56. Part of the IGY explorations were covers for secret investigations into the Nazi UFO base at Antarctica, see books referenced elsewhere.) The Russians were successful in their endeavors and in 1972, at a meeting of Communist leaders in Prague, Brezhnev stated that the Soviets would be able to dominate the world by 1985. He specifically stated they would control the oceans, 90% of the land, and the air and space. He said they would control, not invade and conquer.

FIRE FROM THE SKY

In 1974, the construction of the Tara directed-energy facility at Saryshagan was begun.

In 1975, a Soviet article in International Life talks about weather war, changing the nature of lightning, increasing the power of lightning, and using directed energy of tremendous power at specific targets. It tells of using "atmospheric electricity" to suppress mental activity of large groups of people.

On June 13, 1975 - he repeated his call for a ban on doomsday weapons to visiting U.S. Senators. They could not understand what he was talking about.

In August 1975 - Ponomarev made the same proposal to a group of U.S. congressmen visiting the Kremlin, same result.

In November of 1975 - large amounts of hydrogen gas with traces of tritium were detected at Semipalatinsk by U.S. Air Force TRW reconnaissance satellites. General George Keegan had been paying special attention to this facility ever since one of his men warned him of something "fishy" there in 1972. This was evidence confirming his suspicions of Soviet particle beam research.

In October-December of 1975 - the Soviets destroyed at least five U.S. satellites over the Indian Ocean.

In 1976 - the State Department revealed that the U.S. Embassy in Moscow had been continuously under some sort of microwave radiation attack from the Soviets. Two ambassadors were killed, other people got sick. All Embassy employees were given a 20% hazardous duty pay increase.

In 1976 - Soviet nuclear physicist Rudakov visited the U.S., and gave a talk which was immediately classified and the blackboard ripped down and carried away. Material which was open public scientific material in the USSR was considered classified here in the U.S. Who was being kept in the dark?

March 30, 1976 - a huge unexplained boom occurred over the Netherlands. Probable Soviet scalar howitzer test.

July 4, 1976 - Independence Day! Russia joined our celebrations by activating its giant Woodpecker transmitters causing worldwide interference in all frequencies from 3 to 30 MHz. Transmissions have been continuous ever since. Later the U.S. government said these were merely Russian over-the-horizon radar.

September 10, 1976 - European Airways Flight 831, Moscow to London, saw a huge blinding ball of light below them. Pilot contacted Soviets, was told to not ask questions. This was probably a test to measure the British reaction and to determine if the British knew what it was.

In 1976 - Sweden detected evidence of nuclear explosions from Semipalatinsk but without seismic activity.

In 1976 - Legionnaires Disease strikes in downtown Philadelphia. Kills 34, 187 others got sick. Dr. P. David Beter said this was actually caused by Soviets releasing plutonium gas, but Bearden says it was a scalar electromagnetic attack.

SCALAR WEAPONS ACTIVATED

March 24, 1977 - a luminous patch of light appeared off the coast of Spanish Sahara, Africa, and a large globe of dynamic lights appeared over it. Bearden says this was a test of the Tesla shield which shields everything within it from any outside attack.

June 11, 1977 - Soviet scientist gave a report to Los Angeles Times journalist Robert

FIRE FROM THE SKY

Toth (who was in Moscow) which spoke of energy coming from the vacuum of space. KGB quickly arrested both and charged them with possessing Soviet state secrets. Most American scientists at the time thought energy from the vacuum was nonsense.

September 26, 1977 - Russia launched the Intercosmos 17 octagon space vehicle and destroyed the U.S. moon base, as mentioned in earlier Fire From The Sky material. Soviets also destroyed our spy satellites and "took the high ground." Russia has prevented us from controlling space ever since.

December 1977 and later - mysterious unexplained booms began occurring off the U.S. coasts. This was, according to Bearden, Soviet weapon registration and calibration, and according to Beter was warnings to our government.

Also in 1977 - Russia began weather war in earnest. Two huge hot spots in the Pacific were created which caused an El Niño effect and resulted in one of the most severe winters on record. For more information, read Tom Bearden's materials and check his reference material.

January 27, 1978 - all three engines fail on a Boeing 727 off U.S. east coast, restart one by one as plane falls 8,000 feet. Bearden says this was a Soviet test and warning. Four planes crash in 6 days NW of Las Vegas in February, 1978. From this point on the aircraft events and crashes are too numerous to list and are still ongoing. Atmospheric booms were reported over Texas coast, Nova Scotia, South Carolina.

April 2, 1978 - 39 pilots in a race off Florida experience "time loss" on synchronized watches. Unexplained lights and lighted objects seen and tracked on radar over Florida.

For more information on scalar EM bird kills, earthquakes, Tesla shield observations, crashes, and much more as part of Soviet man-caused events, see Tom Bearden's material, Dr. Beter's material, and related material from other authors. There are far too many for me to list.

COALITION INSIDER

In December, 1978, I received Vol. 1, No. 1 of the Coalition Insider, a report of the Coalition for Peace Through Strength. This was published by the American Security Council, started by General George Keegan after he resigned as head of Air Force Intelligence to become a private citizen so he could warn about the Soviet particle beam and other weapons developments. The back page article entitled "Soviets Have Satellite Killers" says: "At a news conference recently, Defense Secretary Harold Brown revealed that the Soviet Union has placed into operation a space interceptor satellite capable of shooting down U.S. military and civilian satellites." How did he know the capabilities of these interceptors? Because they had already knocked out our satellites!

The article further stated: "Last year, the Soviet Union denounced the U.S. for even considering the development of a similar space interceptor satellite, capable of shooting down Soviet interceptor satellites, before they could knock out our reconnaissance satellites. Any such plans, warned Moscow, would be in 'direct violation' of the treaty for peaceful uses of space. But, the Soviets already had a 'killer satellite' of their own!"

The co-chairman of the press conference is pictured; his name was Senator Robert Dole.

NORTHERN BOOK HOUSE

Also in 1978 I received a packet of Communist literature from the Soviet distributor Northern Book House, Box 1000, Gravenhurst, Ontario, Canada. At the time, I consid-

FIRE FROM THE SKY

ered the material as worthless nonsense garbage. Now, as I review it, I am shocked. They talk about humans and animals responding to "electromagnetic waves." They talk about Soviet scientist Dr. N. A. Kozyrev's study of earthquakes on the moon. They talk about getting energy out of the vacuum.

They brag about the "world's first supersonic aircraft," the Soviet TU-104, introduced in 1956 (they ignore the German supersonic bomber code-named Horten XVIII, made in 1945). I'll just quote the article: "Remember back to 1956? World's first jet passenger plane. Changed whole course of flying (vastly increased people carried).

When NN [Northern Neighbors, publication of Northern Book House] said it (15 years ago), hor-hor-hor, such exaggerating! Plane was, of course, famous Soviet TU-104, long far ahead of USA. Now they've [Russia] got the TU-144 supersonic aircraft.

And where is USA? Where NN said it would be. Far behind USSR's. But darn it all, we missed out! We didn't say USA would not have any SST at all, like it hasn't. Sorry, but don't expect to see us exaggerate all the time. These days it's hard to see how far behind USA is falling."

Oh, but now we are far ahead of them, we are told. Our supersonic passenger transport is the, ah, er, it's the - somebody help me out here, please? And our space station is the ah, er, oh - never mind. We have Disney World, so there!

They quote a U.S. News & World Report article "U.S. Superiority Has Ended," April 5, 1971. The centerfold of the magazine is a spread of pictures of the inside of their space station and the four men working there for months at a time. They point out that the U.S. astronauts have to crash land in the ocean on return, while Soviet astronauts land on the ground.

The next page is an article condemning Zionism as racism! One of the articles tells of the Russian educational system. In their system, there is no homework, all study is done at school. Everybody learns another language starting in Grade One. In some of the schools physical training consists of three hours a day! No wonder they win all the Olympic medals. Oh well, they are probably just bragging.

KAMMLER

Anybody familiar with Nazi Germany will be familiar with Himmler, Speer, Bormann and such but few have ever heard of Hans Kammler. Kammler was a General in the SS, rather an accomplishment any way you look at it. Kammler "was regarded by many in the Nazi hierarchy as the most powerful man in Germany outside the Cabinet." (Blunder! How the U.S. Gave Away Nazi Supersecrets to Russia, by Tom Agoston, Dodd, Mead & Co., p. 4.)

Kammler, whose position of authority was directly under Himmler, was in charge of Hitler's most secret projects, specifically projects such as the world's first jet engines and rockets. He had over 14 million people working for him, mostly building underground factories. Agoston said his projects were equivalent to being in charge of building the Great Pyramids of the Coliseum in Rome. Speer said that he believed that Kammler was being considered to take his (Speer's) position.

Working under Kammler in charge of rockets was General Walther Dornberger, who with Dr. Werner von Braun, developed the V-2 rocket. Working with Kammler at the "Reich's most advanced high-technology military research center" at the Skoda armament complex in Pilsen, Czechoslovakia was General Dr. Wilhelm Voss. Some of the

FIRE FROM THE SKY

projects at Skoda remain secret to this day, but it is acknowledged that among the projects was one by Dr. Franz Josef Neugebauer, "a specialist in thermal systems for aircraft nuclear propulsion." (Agoston, p. 12.)

Albert Speer, in his book Spandau, The Secret Diaries, brags that it was he who ordered Werner Heisenberg to stop building an atomic bomb and concentrate on a "uranium motor" for aircraft. Towards the end of the war, Hitler even made Goering and Speer subordinate to Kammler. Eisenhower admits in Crusade In Europe that the Nazis were within 6 months of developing advanced weapons that would have changed the outcome of the war.

RUDOLPH HESS AND SECRET GERMAN SPACE BASE

Rudolph Hess, Hitler's best friend and second in command, went to England to try to stop the war with Britain and was arrested as a "war criminal" on May 10, 1941 and was kept from having any contact with the public until he was recently murdered. He was the only prisoner in Spandau prison. Ones who paid any attention to his situation at all have wondered what was the big secret he knew that made him so dangerous to the Allies? Perhaps the answer is revealed in Friedrich's book Secret Nazi Polar Expeditions on page 34: Hess "was entrusted with the all-important Antarctic file... Hess, himself, kept the Polar File..."

If you look at a map of Antarctica you will see that a portion of Queen Maud Land is called new Schwabenland. This is the part of the continent nearest to South Africa. The Germans made a major expedition to this area in 1938-1939 and began the construction of a major base. For details of this expedition, see the book by Friedrich. This book has pictures of the warmwater ponds and other information that will surprise you. It has maps showing that Admiral Byrd's Operation Highjump (Naval Task Force 68) military invasion landed on the side opposite the German bases. The book tells of a major food item in the area called krill. Ever heard of "Krill?" The maps of Operation Highjump say that they left the German side of the continent unexplored.

A man who was very influential in modern German post-war politics was Hans-Ulrich Rudel, a frequent guest speaker in German military and political circles. Rudel was the man groomed by Hitler to become his successor. It is known that Rudel made frequent trips to Tierra del Fuego at the tip of South America nearest Antarctica. One of Martin Bormann's last messages from the bunker in Berlin to Doenitz mentioned Tierra del Fuego.

The book, UFOs, Nazi Secret Weapon? says (p. 8) "Hitler's appraisal of the Jews can best be summed up as contained in 'THE PROTOCOLS OF THE LEARNED ELDERS OF ZION.' This is a very important aspect of the whole U.F.O. story, because in it, we find the seeds for many far-reaching decisions made 30 years later." Do you have any idea what such a politically "incorrect" subject such as the PROTOCOLS could have to do with UFOs?

A book called America's Aircraft Year Book tells about the U.S. using captured German scientists at Ft. Bliss and Wright Field. "Among those in the German group at Wright Field were Rudolph Hermann, Alexander Lippsisch, Heinz Schmitt, Helmut Heinrich, and Fritz Doblhoff and Ernst Kugel. Hermann was attached to the Peenemunde Research Station for Aerodynamics, where Germany's V-2 rockets were hatched and launched against England. A specialist in supersonics, he was in charge of the supersonic wind tunnel at Kochel in the Bavarian Alps. He also was a member of the group entrusted with Hitler's futuristic plans to establish a space-station rocket-refueling base revolving as a satellite

FIRE FROM THE SKY

about the Earth at a distance of 4,000 miles - a scheme which he and certain high-ranking AAF officers in 1947 still believed to be feasible."

Later evidence shows that most or all of the craft and flying saucer scientists disappeared. The available evidence indicates they went to South America or Antarctica.

The El Mercurio and Der Weg papers told of a large submarine convoy discovered by the British Navy at the end of WW II. All available Allied units engaged the convoy and were totally destroyed except for the Captain of one destroyer, who was reported as saying, "May God help me, may I never again encounter such a force."

On July 10, 1945, more than two months after the end of the War, the German submarine U-530 surrendered to Argentine authorities. The Commander was Otto Wermoutt. The sub had a crew of 54 men (the normal sub crew was 18 men) and the cargo consisted of 540 barrels of cigarettes and unusually large stocks of food. The Commander was 25 years old, the second officer was 22, and the crew was an average of 25 except for one man who was 32 years old. This was an unusually young crew and upon questioning it was learned that they all claimed that they had no relatives.

A map from a Spanish book called Is Hitler Alive? with the route of the Fuhrer convoy shows it passed alongside South Georgia Island, where later a secret underground base was the focus of a secret battle during the Falkland Islands War.

On April 4, 1944 at 4:40 a.m. the German submarine U-859 left on a mysterious mission carrying 67 men and 33 tons of mercury sealed in glass bottles in watertight tin crates. The sub was sunk by a British submarine and most of the crew died. One survivor on his death bed about 30 years later told about the expensive cargo and some divers checked out his story and found the mercury. For what purpose was this mercury to be used? And where were they trying to take it?

There are many other stories of other U-boats and German survivors, mostly in the Southern Hemisphere. The Germans and other European nations required very meticulous registration records of everybody, including their relatives, employment, addresses, children, etc., and at the end of the war the Allies, cross checking these records, taking into account casualties and deaths, determined that there were 250,000 persons unaccounted for.

WERNER HEISENBERG

Hitler signed the order for the atomic bomb to be built on September 26, 1939. The top scientist on this project was Dr. Werner Heisenberg. (Powers, Thomas, Heisenberg's War, Alfred A. Knopf, 1993, p. 16.) Heisenberg won the Nobel Prize for physics in 1932 "for the creation of quantum mechanics." He was professor of theoretical physics at Leipzig and later Director of the Max Planck Institute for Physics. His best friend, until the war, was Niels Bohr. Edward Teller received his doctorate by studying under Heisenberg (Powers, vii).

Thomas Powers wrote the book Heisenberg's War, The Secret of the German Bomb, in which one of the main themes was trying to account for the fact that Germany was far ahead of the rest of the world in developing the bomb and yet the Allies were astonished when they found the primitive experimental reactor at the end of the war that was supposedly the best the Germans were able to accomplish. Excuses such as German inefficiency, etc., do not fit the evidence, and to say that the Germans were more moral than the American Jews that developed the bomb is not politically acceptable.

FIRE FROM THE SKY

It is known that the Germans were also working on the hydrogen bomb, and the Allies frantically bombed the heavy water plants. There are many books and movies about the heroes who stopped the German nuclear efforts, yet somewhere in the hoopla you find that at least one large load of heavy water was never accounted for.

In a speech in June 1949, Vannevar Bush tells that the Allies were extremely concerned that the Germans were ahead of them on the bomb, but finally found out "they had not accomplished five percent of the undertaking which had been brought to success... in this country." He blamed their failure on typical German "regimentation in a totalitarian system." But if you think about it with an open mind, you should realize that "regimentation in a totalitarian system" is usually MORE efficient, especially when it comes to making weapons.

Powers explores Heisenberg's explanation that the Germans "had used their influence as experts to direct the work into the channels which have been mapped in the foregoing report." But the "foregoing report" did not explain what happened. Powers said: "His account is incomplete. Something is withheld" (p. 482). On the last page he sums up by saying, "No one denies what Samuel Goudsmit found in southern Germany in 1945 - a small-scale program of atomic research that posed no threat to the Allies. It is the difficulty of assigning reasons for the failure that have kept the issue tender for nearly fifty years."

When Field Marshall Erhard Milch visited the Gottow laboratories in 1945 where atomic research was being carried out, he asked Heisenberg, "How big would a bomb have to be in order to destroy New York or London?" Heisenberg replied: "About as big as a pineapple, and we will have a basketful for the Fuhrer by Christmas...!" (Mattern-Friedrich, UFOs, Nazi Secret Weapon?, p. 77. Some of the material in the book came from classified documents obtained from the CIA. See elsewhere in this text.) (It takes 33 pounds of highly-enriched uranium or 13 pounds of plutonium to make a small atomic bomb).

In 1943 Niels Bohr escaped from Denmark to London and reported that Germany was making the bomb. They also had proof that the Germans had "cornered the major supplies of uranium and also of thorium."

WHO CREATED THE ATOMIC BOMB?

Boris Pash, head of security for the Manhattan Project, and scientist Samuel Goudsmit followed the lead tanks into Paris and into Germany, looking for the German nuclear laboratory, which they found in Strasbourg. This was called Operation Alsos (Greek for "Groves"). Peter Goodchild in his book J. Robert Oppenheimer, Shatterer of Worlds, p. 110 said: "Very soon a picture of the Germans' progress began to emerge. They revealed that Hitler had been told of the possibilities of a nuclear weapon in 1942 and that there had been a whole series of uranium pile experiments.

But the crucial facts were that even as late as August 1944 the experiments were still at an early stage. The Germans had neither the certain information that an explosive chain reaction was possible, nor did they have the material or the mechanism to make their bomb. It was apparent that the project had moved forward hardly at all since 1942. There were one or two people in Washington who, when they read Goudsmit's final report, suspected that the information had come too easily, but most people believed it."

It is possible that Germany DID develop the bomb, and the Allies kept it secret? In

FIRE FROM THE SKY

Heisenberg's War, p. 481, Vannevar Bush is quoted as saying in June 1949: "The Nazis wanted an atomic bomb; we knew that. They had as good a chance at it as we had. In the tense years up to 1945 we thought that they were close competitors, even that they might be six months ahead of us. Then after Stuttgart fell and the Alsos mission did its work, we found out. The Nazis had not even reached first base." Surprise, surprise. Or was it lie, lie?

My best guess, based on the evidence, is that there is a strong possibility Germany DID develop the atomic bomb! The Americans managed to capture some of them in early 1945, then on August 6, 1945, dropped one on Hiroshima. This would account for J. Robert Oppenheimer's curious statement that the bomb dropped on Hiroshima was made in Germany. Could the Germans have taken some bombs with them when Hitler escaped? Was the submarine convoy protected by nuclear weapons, and were they what stopped Operation Highjump? Perhaps not, that is just conjecture, but I strongly suspect we got the "bomb" from the Germans.

In Blowback, "the first full account of America's recruitment of Nazis, and its disastrous effect on our domestic and foreign policy" by Christopher Simpson, he states: "On July 6 [1945] the Joint Chiefs of Staff (JCS) specifically authorized an effort to 'exploit... chosen, rare minds whose continuing intellectual productivity we wish to use' under the top secret project code-named Overcast... At first this was justified on the grounds that German scientists might be useful in the continuing war against Japan" (p.33).

When the Allies found the German atomic bomb laboratory, they were amazed that it was just a small concrete reactor in a cave, too small to go critical. Yet they went to considerable trouble in a top secret program to grab these scientists because they might be useful in defeating Japan? What were they going to do, throw radioactive concrete at the Japanese? Tom Agoston in Blunder! says (p. 38) that "Unknown to Allied scientists, the Germans had been able to build up a sizeable stockpile of U-235 and had held up to two tons, as well as two tons of heavy water."

William Stevenson, in A Man Called Intrepid, says "The Germans had the man [Heisenberg] whose theoretical work was the basis of the bomb" (p. 456) and "In the military field, the view prevailed in 1939 that the country with the greatest chance of bringing together the pieces was Germany."

Let's see now, the atomic bomb was a German idea, they had the best scientists, they had a proven ability to develop advanced weapons, they had plenty of raw material, and yet their "bomb" consisted of nothing more than some radioactive concrete in a cave in a hill at the base of a church? (Heisenberg's War, p. 421.) The German laboratory was captured on April 21, 1945, then three months later on July 16 a bomb was tested at Alamogordo, New Mexico. Then on August 6, 1945, one was dropped on Hiroshima, and August 9 on Nagasaki. This is not counting the nuclear explosion in the Oakland, California, area, but we are not supposed to know about that.

Pash and Goudsmit in Operation Alsos captured several tons of uranium and "it was shipped to Britain and then the United States, transformed into uranium hexaflouride gas for isotope separation at Oak Ridge, Tennessee, and finally in the form of U-235 used to destroy Hiroshima." (Heisenberg's War, p. 362.)

Most classified files from World War II have been routinely declassified under the provisions of the U.S. Freedom of Information Act. Tom Agoston (Blunder!, p. 124) said of

FIRE FROM THE SKY

the Alsos information, "The files continued to be suppressed and remain under lock and key in Washington, well beyond the thirty-year rule. The motive for this remains a four-decade mystery."

He also said that the testimony of Albert Speer, referring to General Kammler, "The transcript continues to be classified beyond the normal thirty-year rule, and is not expected to be made public before 2020."

Kammler disappeared at the end of the War and it was reported that he committed suicide (four different versions). If he were dead, why the secrecy? Kammler was regarded as "the most important man in Germany outside the Cabinet." The chain of command was Hitler to Himmler to Himmler's Deputy SS General Karl Wolff to SS General Oswald Pohl to Kammler, and later the link was more direct.

Dr. Wilhelm Voss told Agoston what happened to Kammler was a "hot matter" that could not be revealed. Agoston said one of Kammler's close associates was Rudolph Hess, who flew to Britain on a secret mission in May 1941. "The secret British file that might explain why he flew to Britain will remain closed until the year 2020" (p.160).

What clinched the proof for me was when I read in Phoenix Journal #18 (Blood And Ashes), speaking of the Manhattan Project, "Of course, they utilized the German production urn and, actually, the bomb used on Japan was constructed in Germany" (p. 159). The author of those Journals is "One Who Knows."

GERMAN SUBMARINES IN SOUTH ATLANTIC

The newspaper France Soir had the following account: "Almost 1-1/2 years after cessation of hostilities in Europe, the Islandic Whaler, "Juliana" was stopped by a large German U-boat. The Juliana was in the Antarctic region around Malvinas [now Falkland] Islands when a German submarine surfaced and raised the German official naval Flag of Mourning - red with a black edge.

The submarine commander sent out a boarding party, which approached the Juliana in a rubber dinghy, and having boarded the whaler demanded of Capt. Hekla part of his fresh food stocks. The request was made in the definite tone of an order to which resistance would have been unwise. The German officer spoke a correct English and paid for his provisions in U.S. dollars, giving the Captain a bonus of $10 for each member of the Juliana crew. Whilst the food stuffs were being transferred to the submarine, the submarine commander informed Capt. Hekla of the exact location of a large school of whales. Later the Juliana found the school of whales where designated."

The French Agence France Press on 25 September 1946, said: "The continuous rumours about German U-boat activity in the region of Tierra del Fuego (Feuerland, in German), between the southernmost tip of Latin America and the continent of Antarctica are based on true happenings."

There have been stories and books written about Germans counterfeiting U.S. currency and otherwise obtaining American money printing plates, which may account for the German use of American money.

The Guinness Book of World Records says that the "greatest unsolved robbery" was the disappearance of the entire German treasury at the end of the war.

RAND CORPORATION

In January 1946 industrialist Donald Douglas approached the Army Air Force with a

FIRE FROM THE SKY

plan for government and industry to work together on long range strategic planning. This was called Project RAND, a name coined by Arthur Raymond from Research ANd Development. Much of their first government money went to the von Braun team. (McDougall, Walter al. ...the Heavens and the Earth, A Political History of the Space Age, Basic Books, New York, 1985, p. 89.)

LESLIE R. GROVES

Groves is known as the General in charge of the Manhattan Project which built the Atomic Bomb. He was chosen because he is the one who supervised the building of the Pentagon, and by 1942 was in charge of all U.S. military construction everywhere. After the war he went to work for Remington Rand Corporation.

BORIS PASH

"The stakes in the search for the scientific expertise of Germany were high. The single most important American strike force, for example, was the Alsos raiding team, which targeted Axis atomic research, uranium stockpiles, and nuclear scientists, as well as Nazi chemical and biological warfare research. The commander of this assignment was U.S. Army Colonel Boris Pash, who had previously been security chief of the Manhattan Project - the United States' atomic bomb development program - and who later played an important role in highly secret U.S. covert action programs.

Pash succeeded brilliantly in his mission, seizing top German scientists and more than 70,000 tons of Axis uranium ore and radium products. The uranium taken during these raids was eventually shipped to the United States and incorporated in U.S. atomic weapons." (Simpson, Christopher, Blowback, Collier Books, New York, 1988, p. 26.)

"Another notable Bloodstone veteran is Boris Pash, a career intelligence officer identified in the Final Report of the U.S. Senate's 1975-1976 investigation into U.S. intelligence activities as the retired director of the CIA unit responsible for planning assassinations" (Blowback, p. 108).

Blowback, p. 152-153 says: "The records of Operation Bloodstone add an important new piece of information to one of the most explosive public issues of today: the role of the U.S. government - specifically the CIA - in assassinations and attempted assassinations of foreign officials. According to a 1976 Senate investigation, a key official of Operation Bloodstone is the OPC officer who was specifically delegated responsibility for planning the agency's assassinations, kidnappings, and similar 'wet work.'

"Colonel Boris Pash, one of the most extraordinary and least known characters in American intelligence history... his work for U.S. intelligence agencies places him in the critical office given the responsibility for planning postwar assassination operations... Colonel Pash is one of the few remaining originals of U.S. intelligence, and his experience in 'fighting the communists' goes back to the 1917 Russian Revolution.

He was in Moscow and Eastern Europe in those days with his father, a missionary of Russian extraction, and the young Pash spent much of the Soviet civil war working on the side of the White armies, then with Czarist refugees who had fled their country. In the 1920s Pash signed on as a reserve officer with the U.S. military intelligence service... he... played a role in the internment of Japanese civilians in California, and was soon assigned as chief counterintelligence officer on the Manhattan Project, the supersecret U.S. effort to develop the atomic bomb. (More than a decade later it was Colonel Pash's testimony that helped seal the fate of scientist Robert Oppenheimer in the well-known

FIRE FROM THE SKY

1954 security case.)

Before the war was out, it will be recalled, Colonel Pash led the series of celebrated special operations known as the Alsos Mission that were designed to capture the best atomic and chemical warfare experts that the Nazis had to offer.

"After the war Colonel Pash served as the army's representative on Bloodstone in the spring of 1948, when the tasks of that project, including recruiting defectors, smuggling refugees out from behind the Iron Curtain, and assassinations, were established. Bloodstone's 'special operations,' as defined by the Pentagon, could 'include clandestine warfare, subversion, sabotage and... assassination,' according to the 1948 Joint Chiefs of Staff records. In March 1949, Pash was assigned by the army to the OPC division of the CIA... His five-man CIA unit, known as PB/7, was given a written charter that read in part that 'PB/7 will be responsible for assassinations, kidnapping, and such other functions as from time to time may be given it... by higher authority.'"

From Dulles by Leonard Mosley (A Biography of Eleanor, Allen and John Foster. London: Hodder & Stoughton, 1978.), we find, p. 459: "But now he [Allen Dulles] was interested in the more sinister Agency experiments in mind-bending drugs, portable phials of lethal viruses, and esoteric poisons that killed without trace. Allen's sense of humor was touched when he learned that the unit working on these noxious enterprises was called the Health Alteration Committee (directed by Dr. Sidney Gottlieb and Boris Pash)... Richard Bissell... had now succeeded Frank Wisner as deputy director of Plans..."

To learn more about the mind-control and torture experiments of Pash and Gottlieb, read Journey Into Madness: The True Story of Secret CIA Mind Control and Medical Abuse by Gordon Thomas (Bantam Books, New York, 1989).

One of the people they killed was Frank Olson (a CIA germ warfare doctor whose specialty was anthrax), while they were working on Subproject-68, also known as MK-ULTRA. MK-ULTRA started as Project Bluebird, set up on April 20, 1950, by CIA Director Admiral Roscoe Hillenkoetter (who later was a member of NICAP), and on July 20, 1950, they began using sodium amytal, Benzedrine and other drugs to "brainwash" prisoners.

In September 1950, the Miami News published an article under the headline BRAIN WASHING TACTICS which was considered the first formal use of the term. One of Gottlieb's partners was Dr. Harold Wolff, who appears to be a Paperclip doctor. He worked with Parke-Davis and "...remained closely connected with the M-K Ultra brainwashing project" (p. 191). He helped set up an apartment and introduce LSD to the hippies in San Francisco, and worked on Project Mindbender (a Manchurian-Candidate type operation) with William Buckley.

Isn't it interesting that so many of the participants in the most secret of secrets of World War II are still very involved in the Kennedy assassination and other more current affairs. Many books and articles have been written about the CIA being involved in the JFK assassination, and now you know that the man in charge of CIA assassinations was Boris Pash, formerly chief of security for the Manhattan Project. He was also head of the group trying to capture Hitler's advanced technology, including "flying saucers" and other secrets.

The book ZR Rifle - The Plot To Kill Kennedy And Castro by Claudia Furiati, p. 36, says that a man named William Harvey had been in charge of the CIA post in West Berlin until 1960, then was placed in charge of CIA assassinations by Richard Bissell in 1961. The

FIRE FROM THE SKY

plans to assassinate political leaders was code-named ZR-RIFLE, headed by Harvey. Bo Gritz said on p. 525 of his book: "The Kennedy assassination was code-named 'ZR-RIFLE'." It seems apparent to me that Harvey and Pash were wearing the same pair of pants.

In 1941, Ian Fleming, the future creator of the "James Bond" stories, and at that time a high ranking officer of British Intelligence, suggested to William Donovan that he set up a specially trained and selected assassination unit. PB/7 (Pash Boris Seven) was the original of the "Agent 007" concept. If my memory is correct, I believe Nixon stated that William Harvey was the real 007.

I assume Pash was Agent 001, or perhaps he had seven agents working for him (originally five). If you want to understand more of how these various factions such as CIA, KGB, Nazis, Communists, FBI, etc., can be fighting each other and working together at the same time, you need to understand who was above them, controlling them. To understand that, look to British Intelligence! You will find British Intelligence to be an operation of British and European Royalty and "Aristocracy"!

E. Howard Hunt, while in prison in December, 1975, in an interview with the New York Times, said that the head of the CIA assassination unit was Boris Pash. Pash was assigned to Angleton at this time (see Final Judgment, p. 207). Angleton was head of the Israel desk of the CIA and was very pro-Israel. He was also closely involved with Meyer Lansky.

In Cold Warrior, the biography of James Jesus Angleton by Tom Mangold, he says on page 362: "I would like to place on the record, however, that Angleton's closest professional friends overseas, then and subsequently, came from the Mossad (the Israeli intelligence-gathering service) and that he was held in immense esteem by his Israeli colleagues and by the state of Israel, which was to award him profound honors after his death." His place was taken after his death by William Colby. When Kissinger wanted to "get LaRouche," he turned to Angleton for help. Angleton's tombstone is in Hebrew.

On page 97 of Final Judgment, Piper says that "The ZR/Rifle Team, in fact, was one of Angleton's pet in-house CIA projects, which he ran in conjunction with his CIA colleague, William Harvey."

According to Claudia Furiati, Joseph Schreider was in charge of the CIA laboratories and of developing poisons for assassinations, and says that Harvey was in charge of political assassinations, working out of the Miami office run by [Paperclip] Shackley, and was working with Schreider to try to poison Castro. Above we have Boris Pash and Sidney Gottlieb working together in the same manner. We have Pash and Harvey in the same locations, doing the same jobs, in charge of the same projects - talk about featherbedding. I believe that Harvey was actually at headquarters in Langley, over Shackley in Miami.

Blowback, p. 153, says that Pash "...served as the Army's representative on Bloodstone in the spring of 1948, when the tasks of that project, including recruiting defectors, smuggling refugees out from behind the Iron Curtain, and assassinations, were established. In March 1949, Pash was assigned by the Army to the OPC division of the CIA."

Harvey died June 6, 1976, according to Dick Russell, and Pash was in his 80s in 1988 according to Simpson.

GERMAN FLYING SAUCERS

Hitler's advanced technology included intercontinental ballistic missiles, vertical take-off aircraft, jet engines, cruise missiles, sound cannons, and many other advanced items.

FIRE FROM THE SKY

The Allies captured plans for what became the Boeing 747 Jumbo jet. Among the most secret items captured were plans for flying disks, that were at first called "Krautmeteors." Based on the evidence, they were built as early as around 1933 and went into mass production in 1940. Scientists involved in these projects were Bellonzo, Schriever, Miethe and Victor Schauberger.

Schauberger developed the "flying hat" type disc that was later seen over the United States. The final version was the Bellonzo-Schriever-Miethe Diskus, as large as 135 feet and some up to 225 feet in diameter. They traveled over 2,000 km/hr and were planned to go over 4,000 km/hr. In 1945 they could reach a speed of 1,300 mph and an altitude of 40,000 feet in less than three minutes. The Germans developed the Delta wing craft, and were working on stealth technology, etc.

Many pilots saw the strange craft over Germany. However, as soon as a craft was built, Hitler ordered it disassembled and shipped somewhere - probably Antarctica. None of the craft were captured by the Allies, although some of the scientists were captured and then mostly disappeared, but can somewhat be traced to Bell Textron and to places such as Area 51, which, surprise!, is infamous for its UFO sightings.

Here are some examples of news items during WW II concerning Germany's UFOs, from the New York Times:

NEW YORK TIMES, December 14, 1944:

"Floating Mystery Ball Is New German Weapon. SUPREME HEADQUARTERS, Allied Expeditionary Force, Dec. 13 - A new German weapon has made its appearance on the western air front, it was disclosed today.

"Airmen of the American Air Force report that they are encountering silver colored spheres in the air over German territory. The spheres are encountered either singly or in clusters. Sometimes they are semi-translucent."

and,

"SUPREME HEADQUARTERS Dec. 13 (Reuters) - The Germans have produced a "secret" weapon in keeping with the Christmas season.

"The new device, apparently an air defense weapon, resembles the huge glass balls that adorn Christmas trees. There was no information available as to what holds them up like stars in the sky, what is in them or what their purpose is supposed to be."

FALKLAND ISLANDS WAR

The Falkland Islands War had more to do with Nazis than with Argentina. For more details of what happened please refer to the Phoenix Journals.

The Germans, from their Antarctica base, began to infiltrate into Argentina, Chile, etc., and bought large tracts of land and swept up corporations. They also invested in corporations in Germany and elsewhere, with plans to make a comeback. They used the German treasury, captured treasure from other nations, and counterfeit American currency printed on real U.S. currency printing plates given to the Russians and captured by the Germans.

Some plates were stolen by Assistant Secretary of the U.S. Treasury Harry Dexter White (real name Weiss) under Henry Morgenthau and sent to the Soviets for use in occupied Germany. He also arranged for the mass theft of tons of our special money-paper. When J. Edgar Hoover went to President Truman with all the evidence that the Assistant Secretary of the Treasury was a Communist spy and thief, Truman of course removed Weiss

FIRE FROM THE SKY

(White) from his job - and promoted him to head of the International Monetary Fund. I kid you not, look it up. The story has a rather common ending - when a controversy developed in the press concerning this incident, Weiss became a "suicide."

GERMAN ECONOMIC "MIRACLE"

For more information on how the "economic miracle" was accomplished after the war by the Germans, you can read such books as Martin Bormann, Nazi in Exile by Paul Manning ("...Bormann became the guiding force in the 'economic miracle' that led to the rebirth of German industry and finance in the thirty-five years following political and military defeat. In the waning months of World War II, as the Third Reich was tottering and finally crumbling in defeat, Bormann set up 750 corporations scattered among those nations that had remained neutral. Those corporations received the fleeing wealth of Germany and became the power base that enabled Germany to climb back to economic and political strength." From flyleaf). This book expands on the meeting in Strasbourg on August 10, 1944, mentioned in Michael Bar-Zohar's book The Avengers.

In 1986, while researching these subjects, we received 161 pages under a Freedom of Information search concerning what happened to the German treasury at the end of WW II. Many of these documents had been SECRET until declassification to fulfill our request. One document was No. 19,489, November 27, 1944, Subject: Transmitting Intelligence Report No. EW-Pa 198 [?, barely readable] by G-2 Economic Section, the Secretary of State, from Lt. Col. John W. Easton, Economic Warfare Division.

The cover letter stated "I have the honor to enclose Intelligence Report No. EW-Pa 198 by G-2 Economic Section, SHAEF [Supreme Headquarters Allied Expeditionary Forces], dated November 7, 1944, describing the plans of German industrialists for the post-war resurrection of Germany. Among the topics dealt with in this report are: patents, financial reserves, exportation of capital, and the strategic placing of technical personnel." It is obvious that Manning quoted from these documents in his book on Bormann.

In describing the meeting of August 10,1944, in Stasbourg, some sentences in the documents stand out: "German industrialists must, it was said, through their exports increase the strength of Germany. They must also prepare themselves to finance the Nazi Party which would be forced to go underground as Maquis (in Gebirgverteidigungsstellengehen). From now on the government would allocate large sums to industrialists so that each could establish a secure post-war foundation in foreign countries.

Existing financial reserves in foreign countries must be placed at the disposal of the Party so that a strong German Empire can be created after the defeat. It is also immediately required that the large factories in Germany create small technical offices or research bureaus which would be absolutely independent and have no known connection with the factory. These bureaus will receive plans and drawings of new weapons as well as documents which they need to continue their research and which must not be allowed to fall into the hands of the enemy" [author emphasis].

The last sentences in this document are, "After the defeat of Germany the Nazi Party recognizes that certain of its best known leaders will be condemned as war criminals. However, in cooperation with the industrialists it is arranging to place its less conspicuous but most important members in positions with various German factories as technical experts or members of its research and designing offices."

Some of the documents were concerning "Looted Gold (1945-1948). Accession Num-

FIRE FROM THE SKY

ber 56-75-101, Agency Container Number 169, File Number BIS/2/00." These documents concern Germany's "looted" gold being transferred to the Bank for International Settlements in Switzerland. One important paragraph (#9) says: "It is clear both from correspondence and from testimony that the management of the B.I.S. during the war was 'in the hands of the Administration Council, in which the Axis representatives have an authoritative influence,' and that in 1942 the Germans favored the reelection of President McKittrick whose 'personal opinions' they characterized as 'safely known'."

Enclosed in the file is a clipping from the New York Times, date not included but appears to be in 1945, that states: "McKITTRICK SLATED FOR POST AT CHASE. He Will Take Over Duties as Vice President of Bank Here Next Autumn. Thomas H. McKittrick, American banker who has served as president of the Bank for International Settlements [B.I.S.] since the beginning of 1940, will become a vice president of the Chase National Bank of New York next fall, Winthrop W. Aldrich, chairman of the board of Chase, announced yesterday." The article ends by quoting McKittrick: "I realize it is my duty to perform a neutral task in wartime. It is an extremely difficult and trying thing to do, but I do the best I can."

Another formerly Top Secret document declassified was "Subject: Conversation in Switzerland with Mr. McKittrick, President of the Bank for International Settlements" from Orvis A. Schmidt to Secretary of the Treasury Morgenthau, dated March 23, 1945. It describes McKittrick's dealings with the real head of the Nazi banking system, a Vice President named Puhl.

"Puhl was described by McKittrick as a career banker who had been with the Reichsbank for some twenty years, who does not share the Nazi point of view... the Swiss National Bank said that in order to be sure they were not obtaining looted gold they had requested a member of the Reichsbank, whom they regarded to be trustworthy, to certify that each parcel of gold which they purchased had not been looted. The person who had done this certifying was Puhl."

Puhl was Reichsbank Senior Vice President Emil Johann Rudolf Puhl. He was in charge of taking booty into the bank and was in charge of it for the Nazis. His Senior Shipping Clerk Albert Thoms said that they needed up to thirty men to help him sort and repack the valuables, which consisted of "millions in gold marks, pounds sterling, dollars and Swiss francs, 3,500 ounces of platinum, over 550,000 ounces of gold, and 4,638 carats in diamonds and other precious stones, as well as hundreds of pieces of works of art" (p. 226, Aftermath, Ladislas Farago, Avon, 1974).

This material was shipped out of the country in Operation Fireland or Aktion Feuerland in German, which Farago explained in a footnote in his book on Bormann: "The transaction was named 'Land of Fire' after the archipelago of Tierra del Fuego at the southern extremity of Argentina and Chile, the area to which some of the shipments were originally consigned" (p. 228). On the next page Farago said: "Only a relatively small portion of the SS treasure was impounded by Bormann and sent overseas in the course of Aktion Feuerland. Much of it is still missing."

Germany had developed self-sufficiency before the end of the war, and was manufacturing their own oil, produced "butter" from coal, invented powdered milk, developed freeze drying, learned to store flour indefinitely, were growing their food in greenhouses on chemical "soil," etc. These projects were also necessary for survival of the secret UFO

FIRE FROM THE SKY

force, which Hitler called the "Last Battalion," at the Antarctic.

The counterfeiting of British and American money was under Operation Bernhard. The fake British notes have been often discussed in books and articles about Bernhard, but the fake American currency is not as well known. Recently the U.S. announced that it was issuing new money to counteract the counterfeit, which was said to be coming from Saddam Hussein and Lebanon. It would be more correct to say it is coming from South America, but that money is supposed to all be drug money. Life gets complicated.

When CONTACT newspaper first ran the series on Fire From The Sky, it followed with a reprint of the information about the truth about the Falkland Islands War. In that series, it revealed that the Russians, working with Rockefeller forces, defeated the British Bolshevik forces on South Georgia Island.

If you have not read that series, this information may not make sense to you. It is important to know that information, if you intend to try to understand what is happening. Nazi forces were involved in the Falkland Islands War, on the side of the Russians. This is hard to believe if you have no idea of what IS.

The Russians were nationalists, as opposed to the Zionist Bolsheviks who took their country away from them. The Zionist Bolsheviks were trained in the lower East Side of New York City and financed by New York and London bankers. They invaded Russia, killed the Tzar and many Nationalists and took over the government.

Can you begin to see how someone like Boris Pash, with a Russian Nationalist family background, could work with Nazi Gestapo and SS agents? Even the American General George Patton said we should have fought WITH the Nazis against the Bolshevik Communists. Patton said there was an international conspiracy of Zionist bankers who were the world's problem (see Patton's Papers, Vol. 2, p. 735 for example).

In 1982, on April 20, Hitler's birthday, the Russian/Rockefeller/Nazi commando force broke through and inserted a neutron bomb into the underground naval base at South Georgia Island.

For more of the story of what really happened in the Falkland Islands crisis, read the January 17, 1995, issue of CONTACT: The Phoenix Project newspaper or Phoenix Journal #13, Skeletons In The Closet. (Contact, Inc., P.O. Box 27800, Las Vegas, NV 89126 or call 1-800-800-5565. For Phoenix Journals, write Phoenix Source Distributors, Inc., P.O. Box 27353, Las Vegas, NV 89126 or call 1-800-800-5565. The phone numbers are the same, but the mailing addresses are different.)

Alexander Haig was the General representing the Rockefellers. In his book Caveat, the chapter on the Falklands starts: "On March 28, 1982, a Sunday, the British Ambassador, Nicholas ("Niko") Henderson, brought me a letter from Lord Carrington. A party of Argentineans, wrote the foreign secretary, had landed nine days earlier on the island of South Georgia, a British possession lying in the South Atlantic a few degrees above the Antarctic Circle and some 600 miles to the east of the Falkland Islands, a British Crown colony." I'll bet you thought the Falkland Islands War was about the Falkland Islands!

Much ado was made in the media about the conflict between Jeane Kirkpatrick and Alexander Haig. Kirkpatrick is a Zionist and was the U.S. Ambassador to the United Nations. She has a regular feature column in The Jewish Press newspaper, "The Largest Independent Anglo-Jewish Weekly Newspaper." Haig has had a long relationship with Henry Kissinger, to whom Haig became senior military advisor in 1969. Remember that

FIRE FROM THE SKY

Kissinger came out of the Paperclip Operation personnel.

In January 1982, Reagan replaced his national security advisor, Richard Allen, with William P. Clark, another Paperclip person, and who was Haig's deputy. Nixon said, "When you see the lights burning late in Henry's [Kissinger] office, it's usually Al Haig." (War In The Falklands, the Full Story by the Sunday Times of London Insight Team, Harper & Row, New York, 1982, p. 123.)

If you doubt the fact that the Nazis never gave up and that they planned to continue the war after their defeat in Germany, and planned to make a comeback to finally achieve their goal, then perhaps you should read the following books:

Connell, Brian, A Watcher On The Rhine, William Morrow & Co., New York, 1957. "Old wine in new bottles," how the Nazis have come back into power.

Horne, Alistair, Return To Power, Fredrick A. Praeger, Inc., New York, 1956. "The struggle for unification, rather than any revival of Nazism, may one day force Germany out of the Western camp."

Tetens, T.H., The New Germany And The Old Nazis, Random House, New York, 1961. "A frank and often shocking account which details how 'Hitler's own' have managed to return to power in almost every walk of German life..."

Winkler, Paul, The Thousand-Year Conspiracy, Charles Scribner's Sons, 1943. "Secret Germany behind the mask."

White, Theodore H., Fire In The Ashes, William Sloane Associates, New York, 1953. The fire of Nazism in the ashes of Europe.

Sayers, Michael and Kahn, Albert E., The Plot Against The Peace, Book Find Club, New York, 1945. "...uncovers Nazi Germany's secret plans for a Third World War."

Schultz, Sigrid, Germany Will Try It Again, Reynal & Hitchcock, New York, 1944. Does the title give you a clue?

Dornberg, John, Schizophrenic Germany, MacMillan Company, New York, 1961. "Is the new West Germany of the postwar years as democratic as we have been led to believe, or does Nazism still smolder?"

Lord Russell, Brigadier, of Liverpool, C.B.E., M.C., Return of the Swastika?" David McKay Co., New York, 1969. Russell was part of the Nuremberg prosecution team.

There are more, these just happen to be the ones in my personal library. I read them, mostly about 20 or 30 years ago. I do not mean to give the impression that Germany is the source of the world's problems; Germany has simply been a part of a much bigger picture. Other valuable books that will give you insight are:

Bacque, James, Other Losses, Stoddart Publishing Co., Canada, 1989. The truth about how Eisenhower murdered thousands of German prisoners of war AFTER the surrender. Many of those starving soldiers and piles of dead bodies you have seen in atrocity photos were NOT Jews, they were Germans. Don't argue with me, read the book. General George Patton wrote in 1945 that Eisenhower was using "practically Gestapo methods" in torturing and killing German POWs. You can obtain the book probably from Spotlight Newspaper if you can't find it otherwise.

Sutton, Anthony C., Wall Street And The Rise Of Hitler, '76 Press, Seal Beach, Calif., 1976.

ALBERT EINSTEIN

Albert Einstein is a good example of another deception and hoax involved with the

FIRE FROM THE SKY

atomic bomb program. When many people think of the atomic bomb they think of Einstein. He was presented as the world's greatest scientist, and a hero of the atomic bomb program. Upon closer inspection, you will find that his major contributions were his use of his influence to obtain President Roosevelt's support for the bomb and he was the one personally responsible for bringing the major Communist atomic spy Klaus Fuchs into the Program. The Russians know nothing about the atomic bomb until Fuchs brought it to their attention in 1942. (Heisenberg's War, p. 524).

Thanks to Fuchs, (and to a massive amount of Secret material illegally shipped through Lend-Lease) they were able to explode their own bomb in 1949. Einstein was a communist cell member with Fuchs. Fuchs was the top scientist on the Manhattan Project and he gave the atomic secrets to the Soviets. (Jordan, George Recey, From Major Jordan's Diaries, Harcourt, Brace and Co., New York, 1952.)

We are taught that Einstein is the author of the Theory of Relativity, yet evidence has come for the proving that the real author was Mileva Maric, Einstein's first wife.

Einstein had a reputation at the Swiss Polytechnic Institute in Zurich of being a man with poor work habits and was often reprimanded for laziness during all his school years, including the University. He developed a romance with classmate Mileva who helped him with his math. His autobiography says "In my work participated a Serbian student Mileva Maric who I married later." She had an illegitimate daughter in 1902, which they gave up for adoption. They got married in 1903, separated in 1912 and divorced in 1919. This is when Einstein married his cousin Elsa. The original manuscript of the The Theory of Relativity submitted for publication had Maric's name on it as co-author.

For more proof, see the article "Theory of Relativity - Who is its Real Author?" by Dr. Rastko Maglic and J. W. McGinnis, President, International Tesla Society, in the Jul/Aug 1994 issue of Extraordinary Science magazine, which contains references for further documentation.

Einstein was a hoax and fraud saddled on the scientific community to prevent them from learning too much and to promote Jews as being superior, sort of Nazism in reverse.

Einstein's famous equation "E=MC squared" is WRONG, or at best only partially correct. His definition of energy is WRONG, his definition of mass is WRONG, C is defined as the top speed possible for anything, then it is squared, which would be even faster and thus contradicts the definition. Light is described as a constant, which is WRONG as defined. In a higher understanding, light does not move, our perception of the speed of light is WRONG.

Those who REALLY understand, and who can prove it by creating matter out of "nothing" for instance, say that the original WHITE LIGHT is invisible and still. Read books by Walter Russell for more information.

Einstein was a Zionist with membership in at least 16 Communist front organizations such as Friends of the Soviet. Einstein was head of the Jewish Black Book Committee, which was listed as a Communist front in the 1947 House Un-American Activities Committee Report.

The correct science being discovered and revealed by such as Nikola Tesla, Walter Russell, Tom Bearden, Andrija Puharich, etc., was suppressed to prevent humanity from achieving energy independence (and thus political and military independence) from the Rockefeller/Rothschild oil/nuclear energy barons. This same technology leads to understanding of good health, and thus independence from the drug/medical crowd, who happen to be the same oil crowd crooks.

PAUL ROSBAUD

Rosbaud was one of Britain's top spies in Nazi Germany. He worked as scientific adviser for the publishing firm of Springer Verlag. He came to know Albert Einstein, Peter Kapitsa, Niels Bohr, Ernest Rutherford, Leo Szilard, Otto Hahn, and others of importance in the quest for the Bomb. Kapitsa was the one later credited by Tom Bearden with creating Russia's advanced Tesla technology weapons. Kapitsa won the Nobel Prize in 1978 for his work on the physics of low temperatures and very strong magnetic fields, areas that were pursued in developing anti-gravity platforms.

Rosbaud was code named The Griffin. History books say that the Allies found out from The Griffin that Germany did not have the atomic bomb, and thus the military could advance with more confidence. A book entitled The Griffin by Arnold Karmish (Houghton Mifflin, Boston, 1986, on page 199, chapter titled "Double-Cross" tells of this):

"On Sunday, December 26, 1943, the day the Scharnhorst was sunk, the major headline in the London Sunday Express was THE SECRET WEAPON MAY NOT COME OFF. Beneath it was a long and accurate feature article by Kai Siegbahn, the son of Lise Meitner's reluctant host, Manne Siegbahn. He explained the fundamentals of nuclear energy and described the prewar research. As for the bomb, Siegbahn concluded: 'Despite all the secretiveness about researching in the uranium problem, I venture to say that the uranium bomb is still non-existent, except as a research objective It is rather difficult to say if it is possible at all to construct such a bomb, but for the present it seems as if an essential link is missing for making the uranium bomb a reality.'

Even more remarkable, the Sunday Express went beyond Siegbahn's opinion to assure its readers that 'it may therefore be a source of consolation to know that able Swedish atoms-scientists believe that the Germans have not succeeded in creating atom explosives.' The Express explained its sources for the information by saying, 'Swedish scientists had close contacts with German scientists until the Germans recently arrested Norwegian professors and students.' Among those recently arrested was, of course, Odd Hassel.

"Press security on the atomic bomb was extremely tight in the United States and even tighter in Britain, so the article's appearance seemed at first a puzzle. The Express was owned by William Maxwell Aitken, Lord Beaverbrook, formerly minister of war production and now lord privy seal. Lord Beaverbrook was intimately familiar with the history of the atomic bomb project and its present course, and he was in constant touch with his editors about what they should print. It was quite clear, then, that Kai Siegbahn's article was no accident - but what was its purpose?

"It was not hard to discern the reassuring purpose of the message to the British public. Rumors about Hitler's secret weapons had been rife, and the actions against Rjukan had focused attention on the bomb. But the Gestapo and the Abwehr also read the British papers.

"From the exploit of Jacques Allier to the attacks on the Norwegian installations, the Germans had kept reading the lesson that heavy water was essential for atomic research and that the Allies would do anything to halt production. Now, an article by a distinguished neutral scientist - apparently published with official approval - carried the strong implication that the British were still in a research stage and without much hope of 'making the uranium bomb a reality.'

"The article was, of course, a deliberate SIS plant, conceived in the Double-Cross Committee (The XX Committee), chaired by John Masterman of MI-5."

Lies were and are standard operating procedure for both sides. The article continues: "The top SIS expert on the Abwehr was Frank Foley [who worked with Masterman] of Section V, so he was recruited to the XX Committee as a senior advisor. In the early months, his work was interrupted by a special assignment, conducting the lengthy interrogation of Rudolf Hess. When he returned four months later, Foley took up the deception business once more."

So you see that the ones involved with lying about the bomb were the same ones very interested in what was said by Rudolf Hess. Hess' information remained highly classified long after the war, until he was recently murdered so that they could close Spandau Prison and keep him from talking. In the book Journey Into Madness, The True Story of Secret CIA Mind Control And Medical Abuse by Gordon Thomas, p. 152, tells of one of the heads of the CIA mind-control programs, Dr. Grant Cameron, going to Nuremberg to "establish the state of mind of Rudolf Hess." I wonder if that is "establish" as in "to determine," or as in "to create."

Rosbaud was a close friend with Goudsmit who ran Operation Alsos with Boris Pash. Goudsmit "formed a close friendship with Rosbaud that endured until Paul died" (p. 241).

After the war, Rosbaud formed Pergamon Press with Robert Maxwell. Maxwell went on to become a British "press baron" (p. 250, The Griffin) and was working with the Israeli Mossad selling Israeli briefcase nuclear bombs like the ones used in the New York Trade Center bombing. (Interview with Galen Winsor by Tom Valentine, Radio Free America, March 23, 1993. These bombs were used by Special Forces as early as 1960 per Sgt. Joe Garner, "Army vet tested nuclear 'suitcase bombs' in 60s," Houston Chronicle, January 23, 1995. Also see "Backpack Nukes for 'Nam, Inside SF's Super-Secret A-Bomb Project" in Soldier Of Fortune, May 1995.)

The information that spy Rosbaud, who was Jewish, provided is mentioned in a U.S. Department of Justice memorandum dated April 26, 1955, which reads: "[Rosbaud] returned to Germany determined to assist England and its allies at all costs. This he accomplished. The records in this matter contain official corroboration that Dr. Rosbaud remained in Berlin during World War II for the purpose of obtaining certain technical intelligence for the United States and the United Kingdom. This information was extremely useful and invaluable for the allied cause and involved great risk on the part of Dr. Rosbaud. His activities on behalf of the allied cause were successful and of such importance that even today they cannot be disclosed and are still highly classified."

When you read the book, you see that the most important information that Rosbaud provided was the non-existent status of the German bomb. Yet, the exact details are still "highly classified." So what's the big deal, why is the information still above top secret (top secret items have been declassified)? Makes one wonder, doesn't it?

Another curious "coincidence" is that, after Samisdat published the Nazi UFO information, two journalists from Springer Publishers flew to Toronto to interview Ernst Zundel (head of Samisdat) in person. Samisdat used to sell an audiotape of the interview.

FIRE FROM THE SKY

SAMUEL ABRAHAM GOUDSMIT

Another curiosity is Goudsmit. He turns up in interesting places. He supported Oppenheimer during Oppenheimer's espionage trials. The APRO (Aerial Phenomena Research Organization, founded in 1952) Bulletin, August 1975, contained information obtained from declassified (and well sanitized) CIA records concerning the Robertson Panel which was convened in 1953 to study UFOs. Dr. H.P. Robertson was an expert in cosmology at California Institute of Technology, director of the Weapons System Evaluation Group in the Office of the Secretary of Defense and a CIA classified employee.

The panel was convened by the Office of Scientific Intelligence of the CIA and included Dr. Samuel Abraham Goudsmit, theoretical physicist and Chairman of the Physics Department, Brookhaven National Laboratories. Goudsmit was rather a heavy dude to be "wasting" time on UFOs that the government maintained did not exist. Other OSI panel members were Panel Chairman Dr. Howard Percy Robertson, on leave from his job as professor of Mathematical Physics at California Institute of Technology to be full time to OSI; physicist Dr. Luis Walter Alvarez, University of California, Berkeley, a specialist in magnetism and microwaves (it was speculated that the Roswell UFO was shot down by microwaves) and according to UFO researchers a member of Majestic-12 and the Jason Group; geophysicist Lloyd Viel Berkner, President of Associated Universities, Inc., which operated the particle accelerators of the Brookhaven National Laboratories (according to David Jacobs, The UFO Controversy in America, Berkner "accompanied Admiral Byrd" on Antarctic expeditions. Berkner is generally listed as a member of Majestic-12 and the Jason Group); astronomer Dr. Thornton Leigh Page, Deputy Director, Office of Operations Research, Johns Hopkins University and formerly a physicist with Naval ordnance.

Others included Frederick Clark Durant, a rocket engineer; astronomer Dr. Joseph Allen Hynek, Ohio (home of Wright-Patterson) State University who was also a consultant to the U.S. Air Force Air Technical Intelligence Center (which did the UFO Blue Book Project). The Panel interviewed a long list of Generals and Chiefs and other Big Boys and Heavy Dudes.

Fred Durant met regularly with Stuart Nixon, assistant to John Acuff, head of NICAP. (Timothy Good, Above Top Secret, William Morrow & Co., New York, 1988, p. 349.) Durant worked with von Braun, Krafft Ehricke, Harvard astronomer Fred Whipple, Maryland physicist Fred Singer, Navy Commander George Hoover and others on Ehricke's Moonbase and Marsbase projects.

Army General John Medaris was in charge of the Army Ballistic Missile Agency over von Braun and on March 20, 1959, received a directive for a study of a manned lunar base. "General Medaris organized a crash effort to carry out the study, which became Project Horizon. Less than three months later, on June 8, the study was completed.

On the first page of the study (four or five volumes of which have been declassified), the conclusions are stated: Military, political and scientific considerations indicate that it is imperative for the United States to establish a lunar outpost at the earliest practicable date... Project Horizon represents the earliest feasible capability for the U.S. to establish a lunar outpost" [Project Horizon 1959, vol. 1, p. 1]. (Marsha Freeman, How We Got To The Moon, The Story of the German Space Pioneers, 21st Century Science Associates, Washington, D.C., 1993, p. 210.)

FIRE FROM THE SKY

Ehricke worked with Dornberger at Bell until 1954 when he went with Convair Astronautics in California which was in charge of building space stations and the lunar base. The Washington Star, December 29, 1958, described the Convair station as "the brainchild of Krafft Ehricke." Durant, Whipple and George Hoover were part of the Office of Naval Research. Whipple's assistant, J. Allen Hynek, was part of the Robertson Panel, as was Durant.

In UFO researcher William Steinman's correspondence with Grant Cameron, he states: "I contacted Dr. Alvarez in private, when he admitted that he did take part in the recovery of a saucer in Mexico. He would not go into detail concerning the events and who else was involved." Steinman wrote the book UFO Crash At Aztec which is an excellent source for more information on these men. Unfortunately it is a large, heavily documented book but with no index.

Dr. Lloyd Berkner is also listed in Assault On The Unknown, The International Geophysical Year as the head of the American part of the International Geophysical Year study. He was radio man on the first Byrd Expedition to the Antarctic and developed the sounder that charts the radio-reflecting layers of the atmosphere. Berkner was Chairman of the Space Science Board of the National Academy of Sciences. Operation Highjump is not mentioned, but Berkner was part of Operation Deepfreeze at the Antarctic in 1957-1958, headed by Byrd until his death, as were Werner von Braun and Frederick C. Durant. Berkner became a Navy Rear Admiral.

Another Antarctic scientist was Dr. Carl Augustus Heiland, who worked with Vannevar Bush and who was part of the on-site recovery team of the Aztec UFO crash (p. 85, UFO Crash At Aztec). He appears to be a Paperclip scientist, as he received his Doctorate from the University of Hamburg. Another very important scientist was Dr. Eric Henry Wang. I will not go into his story at this time, except to quote Steinman: "The subject of Dr. Eric Henry Wang remains one of the most touchy and sensitive areas in all ufology" (p. 282). Dr. Eric Wang was head of the Office of Special Studies of the Air Materials Command at Wright-Patterson AFB. He was an Austrian-born graduate of the Vienna Technical Institute and "a close associate of Victor Schauberger." (Hamilton, William F., Cosmic Top Secret, Inner Light, 1991, p. 23.) Steinman's book has a whole chapter on Nazi German "flying disk" projects, many of which used Schauberger's designs.

Goudsmit concluded that UFO sightings were "due to a formation of ducks or other birds." The official conclusion of the panel was that interest in UFOs was dangerous and that the situation should be downplayed and covered up. Jacobs said that Robertson showed the final report of the panel to General Charles Cabell, director of Air Force intelligence and later Deputy Director of the CIA in charge of clandestine operations, "who expressed satisfaction with it."

Cabell's brother Earl was the Mayor of Dallas during the Kennedy assassination, and apparently was the one who ordered the motorcade to change routes into the ambush area. Earl later went to work for Howard Hughes. General Cabell was the person who briefed President Kennedy prior to the Bay of Pigs invasion. Robert Groden in High Treason quotes Victor Marchetti as saying that Clay Shaw, David Ferrie, E. Howard Hunt, Frank Sturgis, Bernard Barker, Charles Cabell, and Richard Nixon "were all working together in the CIA's Bay of Pigs planning operation."

Kennedy later fired Cabell. Cabell and Richard Bissell were in charge of the U-2 pro-

FIRE FROM THE SKY

gram. Lee Harvey Oswald was given a job within one week of his arrival in Dallas working on maps for the U-2 flights (Jim Garrison, On The Trail of The Assassins). In 1957, Oswald was a radar operator at the U-2 base in Atsugi, Japan.

General Cabell ordered the re-activation of Project Grudge on October 27, 1951, and on December 11, 1951, Major General John A. Stamford, "having replaced Major General Cabell as director of intelligence, was given a full briefing of the service's UFO program by Captain Edward J. Ruppelt and Colonel Frank Dunn, chief of the Air Technical Intelligence Center." (Flammonde, Paris, UFOs Exist! Ballantine Books, New York, 1976, p. 392-393.)

According to Leonard Moseley, Dulles, p. 366, Bissell "was a friend of Frank Wisner, and had first met Foster [John Foster Dulles] when Eleanor threw a party at McLean for her brothers, Vice-President Nixon, Bob Bowie, and other members of the administration." I don't have the proof, but I'll bet that Cabell and Bissell and Boris Pash were very cozy, especially when Cabell was second in command under Allen Dulles. Recall that Wisner was the CIA head of the Gehlen Nazi spy group.

THE KENNEDY-Nazi CONNECTION

JFK's father, Joseph Kennedy, had a reputation of being pro-Nazi or at least pro-Hitler. Joe was a bootlegger and a member of the Mafia, although he hated the Jewish Mafia (Mishpucka) boss Meyer Lansky (real name Maier Suchowljansky). He was U.S. Ambassador to Britain but was recalled because of his pro-Hitler viewpoint. His code clerk was Tyler Kent, which is a story in itself.

In the book Final Judgment by Michael Collins Piper, you will find a story about DeWest Hooker. Hooker was a good friend of both Joseph Kennedy and George Lincoln Rockwell, Commander of the American Nazi Party. Piper tells of the arrangement made with Hooker and Rockwell to help JFK get elected. Hooker said, "Frankly, as far as I'm concerned, it was my work that got Johnny Kennedy in the White House." I suggest you read the book, it is available from Spotlight Newspaper or Liberty Lobby. If I quote small portions from it you probably would find it too hard to believe! I assure you the story is true, for I know well the man who was the bodyguard and stenographer/scribe to Commander Rockwell.

When Senator Joe McCarthy was conducting the hearings on Communists in the government, his assistant, seated at the same desk beside him, was Robert Kennedy. The Senator at the desk beside McCarthy was Senator John F. Kennedy. JFK was an insider who KNEW the source of the problems. When he became President, he fired the CIA heads, installed his brother as Attorney General, and said he was going to put the United States back on the silver standard, stop the Vietnam War, eliminate government involvement with the Mafia, and eliminate the Federal Reserve problem. It has also been reported that he was going to tell the truth about UFOs. Ten days after he gave a speech at Columbia University making these statements, he was murdered.

Nazi IMBECILES?

When Dornberger went to work for Bell, Bell recruited another former German army scientist, Krafft Ehricke, "who had been an adviser on the German wartime atom bomb project" according to Jack Manno, Arming The Heavens (Dodd, Mead & Co., 1948). We read a book that says Germany had no atomic bomb project, we read another that says they did. Manno said that Wolfgang Noggerath was brought in and put in charge of what became the Polaris missile. Willy Fiedler was brought in and made chief of planning of

FIRE FROM THE SKY

the underwater launch systems for submarines.

Let me summarize for you the story as presented. We Americans were far ahead of the stupid Nazi Germans, although we had not yet made any atomic bombs. As the war was ending, we sent in teams and frantically searched for the German atomic scientists. We captured some of those dumb, incompetent scientists, quickly brought them to the United States in top secret programs that are still highly classified, we put those stupid losers in CHARGE of our projects, and we suddenly started making Atomic Bombs. And missiles - and satellites - and whatever else.

I just want to be sure you got the story straight.

COVER AND CONCEALMENT

Speaking of lies and deception, it would be reasonable to think that if our spy satellites were destroyed in 1977, as stated in Fire From The Sky, then there would have been all kinds of repercussions and a lot of people who depend on those satellites would know about it. How was the truth kept secret?

One part of the answer is revealed in a book called The Falcon And The Snowman by Robert Lindsey (Pocket Books, New York, 1979). This book tells the story of Christopher John Boyce. Boyce went to work for TRW on July 29, 1974. TRW is the company that made the Viking probe that went to Mars and the satellites which provided General George Keegan with information on the Russian activities at Semipalatinsk and such.

Boyce worked in the top-secret "black box" section, he was the man with the keys and codes to access the vault. He had access to Projects Rhyolite, Argus, Pyramider and "Project 20,030" files, projects which involved spy satellite data coming to the American base at Pine Gap (code named Moreno), Australia, near Alice Springs. He learned things that upset him, such as the CIA interference in Australian elections, the U.S. was lying to other governments, etc. Read the book for more of the story. He began stealing and selling secret documents to the Russian Embassy in Mexico and in January, 1977, he was arrested and charged with espionage.

"It came out during the Boyce-Lee trial that data from these satellites goes to a readout station in Australia - but not the one that monitors the early warning satellites. Instead, the data goes to a CIA-run complex in a valley called Pine Gap. After the Pine Gap computers have processed the data, it goes to the TRW Defense and Space Systems headquarters in Redondo Beach, California" (p.111, The New High Ground by Thomas Karas).

It was claimed that as a result of his selling secrets to the Soviets, the Soviets changed and encoded their transmissions, camouflaged their facilities, etc., so that the spy satellites suddenly no longer worked. Stansfield Turner, director of the CIA, said the results of Boyce's spying were "distressing, perhaps appalling."

As a result of his spying, we are told, the CIA no longer had satellite coverage of Iran, for instance, leading to the Iranian hostage crisis. Do you remember when the CIA was criticized for being surprised at the fall of the Shah and for not foreseeing the Iranian Hostage Crisis? In truth the U.S. DID know beforehand, as they orchestrated those events, but it is too much to try to cover here. Oh, what a tangled web... NOTHING is as it is presented to the public by our media and leaders.

"Our intelligence community is in disarray. A major satellite intelligence system, developed and deployed at a cost of billions of dollars over the past decade, without Soviet knowledge, has been compromised by intelligence procedures as porous as Swiss

FIRE FROM THE SKY

cheese." This was a statement made on December 8, 1878, by William Clements who was Deputy Secretary of Defense at the time Boyce worked in the Vault and who later became governor of Texas.

Would you be surprised to learn that Boyce may have been manipulated/set-up? Even the author of the book noticed mysteries: "Why TRW would place a $140-a-week, twenty-one-year-old college dropout in such a sensitive national-security position in the first place is, at least in retrospect, a puzzle. Circumstantially, TRW's decision to leave the Pyramider papers unlocked in the vault where Chris could read them shortly before his departure suggests they could have been left as bait. And there was the mystery of Daulton's [Boyce's assistant in crime] fingerprints on the circuit boards.

An FBI fingerprint expert testified that he had found Daulton's prints on a circuit board from one of the encrypting machines in the vault. Yet both the two spies, when denials meant nothing regarding whether they might be convicted or not, insisted that Daulton had never entered the vault nor had he ever touched the circuit boards. And certainly, the presence of a U.S. Embassy official at the Soviet Embassy on the morning of Daulton's arrest added another curiosity to the case" (p. 422).

Boyce's partner Daulton claimed that all along he was working undercover for the CIA. "The affair of the snowman and the spy who called himself the Falcon was an episode that demonstrated amazing ineptitude on the part of the Central Intelligence Agency" (p. 423).

Boyce's defense attorney George Chelius later developed a lucrative law practice in Orange County, California, catering to businessmen and land developers (p. 427).

A similar event was when William Kampiles sold the Russians a complete manual on the KH-11 (sometimes called the Big Bird, but technically not the same) satellite in March 1978. Kampiles was an operations clerk at CIA headquarters and resigned in October 1977, just after the Russian destruction of our satellites. In February 1978 he went to Athens, Greece. On February 23, he went to the Soviet Embassy and started making arrangements to sell them the documents. He was arrested and went to trial in November 1978 and was sentenced to 40 years.

The facility at Pine Gap, Australia, is something that needs a closer look. Stan Deyo, in The Cosmic Conspiracy, tells of a multi-national consortium at Pine Gap that have "radical atmospheric vehicles." In other words, UFOs have been seen going in and out of Pine Gap. Deyo mentions that Dr. Vannevar Bush (claimed to be a member of MJ-12) made repeated visits to the area. Deyo says they are conducting research on crashed UFO residue at Pine Gap.

I will close this section with something to ponder: Astronomer Dr. James Greenacre and four colleagues at a conference on "Moon Problems" in New York in 1964 said that on 29 October 1963 they observed several colorful spots on the moon that moved in formation. One month later Greenacre observed the same phenomena.

The May 1966 issue of UFO Nachrichten. Vol. 117, said: "Prof. Dr. Greenacre saw on or close to the moon at least 31 space craft of gigantic size. Some were from 300 meters to 4.8 kilometers long. They were in motion while being observed through the telescopes. Also, clearly discernible were numerous smaller craft approximately 150 meters in diameter, which moved past or alongside the huge craft, the 'mother craft' occasionally changing color, as in the often-reported, pulsating style."

FIRE FROM THE SKY

Keep looking up.
DISCLAIMER: "I know one thing for certain; that I know no thing (nothing) for certain." - Me.
"It's what you learn after you know it all that counts." - Earl Weaver.

NICOLA TESLA: The Electric Magician
by D. Trull

Who is the single most brilliant person of the past century? Several candidates spring immediately to mind: Albert Einstein, Thomas Edison, Stephen Hawking... but few people's lists would include the name of the man who may be the greatest genius of all time: Nikola Tesla.

Tesla pioneered the alternating current engine, the foundation of virtually every elec-

FIRE FROM THE SKY

The Forgotten Genius

trical invention used today. He invented the bladeless turbine. He created the fluorescent light and the arc lamp. He invented radio. He developed the logic circuits used in modern computers. With over 700 patents in his name, Tesla shaped our current technological landscape more than any other individual.

How, then, did this great man end up dying destitute and in obscurity? Why are his staggering achievements unknown to most people, and excluded from recognition in history books and the Smithsonian Institute? The most common explanation is that Tesla ruined his notoriety with the increasingly outlandish efforts of his later years, which included wireless transmission of power, free energy systems, thought recorders, Martian communicators and earth-shattering death rays.

Did Tesla's extraordinary mind decline into insanity... or was he simply far, far ahead of his time? Was there a conspiracy to keep the incredible truth of his discoveries from becoming widely known?

In this series, Editor D. Trull examines the life, accomplishments and bizarre eccentricities of the century's greatest inventor.

ONE
THE MAN BEHIND THE MIND

In the small village of Smiljan, Croatia (then Austria-Hungary), Nikola Tesla was born exactly at the stroke of midnight between July 9 and 10, 1856 — an incidental schism that befits the beginnings of a man who always seemed out of time with the world around him.

From early childhood, it was apparent that Nikola possessed an extraordinary mind.

FIRE FROM THE SKY

His father, Milutin Tesla, was a minister who trained Nikola to strengthen his memory and reasoning skills through a variety of regular mental exercises. But Tesla gave the highest credit for his talents to his mother's side of the family, whom he referred to as a long line of inventors. Despite Djouka Tesla's lack of formal education, she created numerous original tools for sewing and other tasks around her household.

Tesla had an older brother, Dane, whom he considered his superior in every way. When Nikola was five and Dane was twelve, Nikola was jealous of Dane's white stallion, which their father said Nikola was too young to ride. One day Nikola used a blow gun to shoot a pea at the horse, causing it to throw Dane from its back. Dane later died from his injuries. Feelings of guilt over this tragedy haunted Tesla throughout his life. No matter how great his achievements, he always believed that Dane could have outdone him.

During his early life, Tesla was stricken with illness time and time again. He suffered a peculiar affliction in which blinding flashes of light would appear before his eyes, often accompanied by hallucinations. Much of the time the visions were linked to a word or idea he might come across; just by hearing the name of an item, he would involuntarily envision it in realistic detail. The flashes and images caused Tesla great discomfort, and by the time he reached his teens he had taught himself to repress them from occurring except in certain times of stress. When they did happen, they sometimes had a nature that might be described as psychic.

In one case, the young Tesla recklessly attempted to swim beneath a large floating structure that extended further than he realized. Finding himself trapped in the dark water with no sign of the surface, a flash appeared, and with it a vision of a small opening to air. Tesla's vision turned out to be correct, and the strange curse apparently saved him from drowning. Upon the deaths of his father and mother, Tesla claimed to have detailed premonitions just before each passing. In his later years, Tesla boasted of successfully transmitting an image from his mind into that of a person in another room.

Shortly after his graduation from high school, Tesla suffered a devastating bout with cholera and nearly died. He was bedridden for nine months, and doctors announced that he would not live much longer. Tesla was occupying his still-active mind by reading as much as his body would permit, when he encountered a strange new kind of literature: *"Innocents Abroad,"* by Mark Twain. Tesla was captivated by the humor and humanity of this up-and-coming American author, whose work so raised his spirits that he made a miraculously abrupt recovery to health. Years later in the United States, Tesla met Samuel Clemens and was able to thank him for having saved his life. Clemens went on to be-

FIRE FROM THE SKY

come one of Tesla's few close friends.

Tesla underwent another debilitating trauma a few years after recovering from cholera. This time, the nature of the illness and its causes were a complete mystery. Tesla's physical senses, which had always been remarkably acute, seemed to go inexplicably into overdrive, paralyzing him with an overabundance of sensation. The ticking of a pocket watch had become painfully deafening to him, even from several rooms away. He needed rubber cushion inserted beneath the feet of his bed to lessen the vibrations from outside passersby, which felt to him like an earthquake. Exposure to light was excruciating not only for his eyes, but to the surface of his skin, as well. After a time, the crippling condition eased, and Tesla returned to normal sensory perception with a mental breakthrough that led him to the invention of the alternating current motor.

The physical and emotional travails of Tesla's early life undoubtedly helped shape him into the singular man he was: a man of immense brilliance, and a nearly equal level of eccentricity. Tesla shunned physical contact with other people, with a special aversion to touching hair. To avoid shaking hands with people he met, he lied that he had injured his hands in a laboratory accident. He apparently never took part in a romantic relationship of any kind. A female acquaintance who grew enamored of Tesla reportedly once took the initiative to kiss him, causing the startled inventor to flee in agony. Still, Tesla exhibited some appreciation for feminine beauty by demanding that his secretaries conform to an exacting standard of dress and physique. His female employees were forbidden to wear pearls, which Tesla for some reason found hideously repulsive.

Other behaviors of Tesla's seemed to drift into the realm of compulsive-obsessive disorder. He required any repeated actions in his daily life (such as the footsteps he took in a walk) to be divisible by three, and would keep repeating them until he arrived at a suitable total. Quantities of twenty-seven were the most prized of all, since that number was three cubed. Tesla also felt compelled to calculate the exact volume of his food before he ate it. This involved measuring his meal portions with a ruler and dipping pieces in water to determine how many cubic centimeters they displaced. He was especially fond of saltine crackers because of their uniformity of volume. Many times, such as during the heat of a major project, Tesla would forget to eat altogether, and work for days without sleep. At one point his all-consuming devotion to the laboratory brought on an exhaustion so severe that for several days he lost all memory of who he was.

Tesla asserted that it was not until he reached adulthood that he discovered he was an inventor. He discounted his early years (perhaps unreasonably) as a time of undisciplined impulses, entirely lacking focus. But he did invent a wide array of creations and schemes as a child. The first was a simple hook-and-line device for catching frogs. All his young friends imitated it, and the mechanisms performed so well that the local frog population was nearly eradicated. He also built a miniature water wheel which was unique in that it propelled itself without blades. This memory would later inspire his innovation of the bladeless turbine.

The young Tesla created a remarkable machine powered by another natural energy source: June bugs (or, as Europeans call them, May bugs). He glued sixteen of the live insects to the blades of a small windmill-like structure, and they set the rotor spinning vigorously in their vain attempt to fly away. Some accounts have jokingly cited this effort as one of Tesla's rare failures, although the inventor himself remained rather proud of

FIRE FROM THE SKY

the June bug motor. In his autobiography, Tesla explained why he discontinued his research into insect energy:

"These creatures were remarkably efficient, for once they were started, they had no sense to stop and continued whirling for hours and hours and the hotter it was, the harder they worked. All went well until a strange boy came to the place. He was the son of a retired officer in the Austrian army. That urchin ate May-bugs alive and enjoyed them as though they were the finest blue-point oysters."

Adding one more entry to his long list of idiosyncrasies, after beholding that spectacle Tesla refused ever to touch another insect again.

TWO
TESLA'S BATTLE TO GIVE THE WORLD THE INNOVATION OF THE AC ENGINE.

Tesla began his college education at Graz Polytechnic Institute, pursuing studies of the topic that fascinated him above all others: electricity. He had done fairly well in grade school, but his lack of facility at freehand drawing kept him from excelling in technical courses. But in college, Tesla was delighted to find, he was permitted to focus exclusively on what he was best at.

FIRE FROM THE SKY

He studied feverishly almost around the clock, in a routine that began at 3 a.m. and ended at 11 p.m., every day. He aimed to impress his parents with his scholarly achievements, in part because his father had been reluctant to send him to the university, wishing Nikola would follow in his footsteps in the clergy. He also entertained fantasies of going to America and teaming up with the reigning leader of electrical invention, Thomas Edison, so that their combined forces might revolutionize the world.

Tesla was an extraordinary student who frequently enraged his professors, questioning the technological status quo with an insight that surpassed his instructors'. He rebelled most stringently against the acceptance of direct current as the sole means of delivering electrical power. It was plain to him that DC was inefficient and incapable of adequately transmitting power over long distances, and there had to be a better way. There was talk of a theoretical "alternating current" system, but no one had figured out how to make it work. AC was frowned upon as a fanciful dream by the scientific establishment, in much the same way as cold fusion is regarded today. Tesla's merest suggestion of AC brought scorn in his lecture halls, but he was never discouraged enough to abandon the enticing riddle.

In the middle of Tesla's sophomore year of college, his father was felled by a stroke. Nikola returned home, and his father died soon after. Tesla never returned to the Polytechnic Institute. Lacking funds for tuition, he took a job at a government telegraph office. Tesla despaired for his interrupted education, but held on to his dream of becoming an electrical pioneer.

It was at this time that Tesla endured his ordeal with hypersensitivity that reduced him to a bedridden invalid. Considering the depressing turns his life had just taken, the bizarre affliction could possibly have been psychosomatic in origin. Whatever its cause, when Tesla finally emerged from the prolonged fugue state, he was armed with a powerful new insight on how alternating current could be successfully attained.

His great mental leap was this: two coils positioned at right angles and supplied with alternating current $90°$ out of phase could make a magnetic field rotate, with no need for the cumbersome commutator used in direct current motors. Tesla knew it would work without even having to build it and test it. Constructing it mentally and letting it run in his mind was proof enough for him.

This was Tesla's method for developing inventions throughout his career: no journals, no blueprints, no prototypes. The propensity for turning ideas into concrete visualizations which had tormented him in his youth was now turned to Tesla's advantage. He

FIRE FROM THE SKY

believed his technique was not only a valid one, but actually superior to the common practice of getting everything down on paper and conducting tentative trials. "The moment one constructs a device to carry into practice a crude idea, he finds himself unavoidably engrossed with the details of the apparatus," Tesla wrote in his autobiography. "As he goes on improving and reconstructing, his force of concentration diminishes and he loses sight of the great underlying principle."

Tesla now possessed the answer, but the problem of putting it into practice remained. In 1882 he found employment with Continental Edison Company in Paris, distinguishing himself as a fine engineer. Two years later he traveled to New York to meet the company's president, Thomas Edison himself.

It was not the harmonious meeting of the minds Tesla had once dreamed of. Edison regarded the hotshot European with contempt, and assuredly held no intentions of collaborating with him on some harebrained AC scheme. Edison viewed AC as a pipe dream at best, or, at worst, a threat to usurp his DC-based empire.

Tesla tried to make the best of the situation by offering to improve Edison's existing technology to the highest level possible. He promised to increase the efficiency of the DC dynamos by 25%, within two months' time. The skeptical Edison said he would pay Tesla fifty thousand dollars if he succeeded.

Exerting a massive, virtually non-stop effort, Tesla accomplished the feat, enhancing the dynamos by an even better margin than he proposed. But when he asked for his fifty thousand dollars, Edison refused to honor the deal, claiming that he had only been joking. Infuriated, Tesla quit and never worked for Edison again.

Tesla was soon approached by a group of investors who wished to market the arc lamp he had developed. Thus was the Tesla Electric Company founded. Tesla was eager to seize this opportunity to bring AC into existence at last, but his investors wanted nothing to do with it — so Tesla found himself rejected by the company that bore his own name.

That company soon ran afoul of financial hardships, leaving Tesla's stock shares worthless and stripping him of his rights to the arc light. Penniless, his enterprising spirit finally broken, one of the world's most brilliant men was reduced to shoveling in a labor crew for a dollar a day. He planned on committing suicide on his upcoming thirtieth birthday, at the stroke of midnight.

Before that could happen, A. K. Brown of Western Union learned of Tesla's plight. Aghast, Brown was determined to restore the genius to a worthy place, and offered to furnish him with a laboratory of his own. And what's more, Brown wanted Tesla to pursue the possibilities of alternating current.

Granted a blessed salvation, Tesla immediately went to work assembling his AC dynamo at last. It functioned in reality precisely as it had all those years inside his head. Tesla demonstrated his invention in a heavily publicized lecture, and instantly became the toast of the engineering community.

Among the AC converts in the lecture's audience was George Westinghouse, who negotiated with Tesla to manufacture the dynamos. The first application of the new technology: Niagara Falls. Westinghouse won the coveted contract to harness Niagara, bidding half of what Edison bid for the installation of a DC system. In 1895, the Niagara AC power system enjoyed a flawless inauguration, transmitting electricity to Buffalo twenty-

FIRE FROM THE SKY

two miles away — a complete impossibility in the suddenly outmoded world of direct current. No longer a curious luxury reserved for the urban upper class, electric power in the home would now be commonplace.

For the first time in his life, Nikola Tesla was an indisputable success.

THREE
YEARS OF "CONTINUOUS RAPTURE,"

From the beginning of A. K. Brown's and George Westinghouse's fortuitous partnerships with Tesla, the inventor was at work on other projects above and beyond the AC dynamo. Able to devote himself to the unhindered realization of his countless ideas, he would later recall these years of his life as "little short of continuous rapture."

Tesla's New York laboratory was a hive of continuous activity, with a small staff of as-

FIRE FROM THE SKY

sistants working solely from their employer's verbal instructions. His distaste for putting ideas down on paper, coupled with his tendency to get bored with a completed invention and move on to the next challenge, led Tesla to toss aside a large number of creations that he never even bothered to patent. Once, when exhaustion left Tesla in a state of temporary amnesia, his assistant filed for patents on many of the unregistered inventions on Tesla's behalf, and had the master sign the papers while still incapacitated. Tesla's shunning of documentation was of some benefit when fire destroyed the lab in 1895, right after the success at Niagara. The loss was a setback, but not a catastrophic one, since the most valuable of the laboratory's assets remained intact in Tesla's brain.

In 1891, Tesla developed the invention by which his name is most commonly known today: the Tesla coil. Simple enough for today's hobbyists and science-fair entrants to construct in fully functional homemade models, it was nonetheless a remarkable innovation which remains the basis for radios, televisions and other modern means of wireless communication.

Tesla became known for the lectures at which he demonstrated his inventions and concepts with a theatrical flair. Many attendees were laymen who had little comprehension of what Tesla said, but were mesmerized by the bolts of lightning that leapt from his ominously humming coils, and the unwired light bulbs that lit at the touch of Tesla's hand. These spectacular displays led Tesla to be popularly regarded as some sort of magician — a title that was bestowed not in ridicule, but in awe.

The wireless transmission of energy would become the ultimate pursuit of Tesla's career. He discovered that a vacuum tube held in proximity to a Tesla coil would burst into illumination, without wires, without even a filament inside the glowing tube. Electrical resonance was the key to this discovery. By determining the frequency of the needed electrical current, Tesla was able to turn a series of different lights on and off selectively, from yards away. He had just become an American citizen in 1891, and this new technology was to be his gift of thanks to his adoptive country: a means of transmitting energy instantly, across any distance, through thin air. Free energy for everyone.

One of Tesla's assistants reportedly questioned the implications of putting such an energy distribution plan into practice. He wondered what incentive there would be for the electrical power establishment to begin giving away its goods for free, and whether Tesla could possibly be "allowed" to introduce such an arrangement. The presence of such doubts enraged Tesla, who was convinced, somewhat naively, that his plan would be accepted simply because it was the right thing to do.

FIRE FROM THE SKY

As the years passed, Tesla's vision of wireless energy grew even grander in scope. He solved one of the problems implicit in his first theory, which was that transmission of power through air over long distances would result in a significant loss of energy. Rather than using air as a medium, he decided to send energy through the ground. This makes little sense in conventional electrical terms, whereby the earth's surface is regarded as, literally, "the ground" — a sinkhole used for discharging excess current from a conductor. But Tesla found that if it were charged highly enough, the ground could become the conductor itself. In this way, the entire planet could be transformed into a colossal electric transmitter.

In 1899, as logistics prevented him from conducting the necessary experiments within the confines of New York City, Tesla headed west. A Colorado attorney named Leonard Curtis, who had previously defended Tesla in court, offered to help Tesla set up a testing facility in Colorado Springs. Curtis was also an officer of the local power company, and provided electricity to Tesla at no cost.

Tesla and his assistants built a one-of-a-kind laboratory on the outskirts of town, which looked like a large barn topped by a 180-foot metal tower. This was Tesla's "magnifying transformer," which he called the greatest of his inventions.

The townspeople of Colorado Springs were naturally curious about what this great inventor was up to, and respected the signs around the perimeter of the compound reading "KEEP OUT — GREAT DANGER!" Still, they soon felt the effects of Tesla's apparatus. Sparks leapt from the ground as people walked the streets, singeing their feet through their shoes. The grass around the Tesla building glowed with a faint blue light. Metal objects held near fire hydrants would draw miniature lightning bolts from several inches away. Switched-off light bulbs within 100 feet of the tower spontaneously lit.

And Tesla was only tuning up his equipment. These were the side effects of adjusting the magnifying transformer into perfect resonance with the earth. Once it was properly calibrated, Tesla was ready to conduct his career's boldest symphony, using the entire planet as his orchestra.

Late one night in the fall of 1899, Tesla fired up his machine at full blast, in hopes of producing a phenomenon he called resonant rise. His tower pumped ten million volts into the earth's surface. The current raced through the earth at the speed of light, powerful enough to keep from dying out over the course of its journey. When it reached the opposite side of the planet, it bounced back, like ripples of water returning to their origin. Upon returning, the current was greatly weakened; but Tesla was sending out a series of pulses which reinforced one another, resulting in a tremendous cumulative effect.

At ground zero, where Tesla and his assistant stood bedazzled, the resonant rise manifested itself in an unearthly display of lightning that still stands as the most powerful man-made electrical surge in history. The returning current formed an arc of lightning that stretched skyward from Tesla's tower and progressively grew to an incredible 130 feet long. Apocalyptic crashes of thunder were heard twenty-two miles away. Tesla had been concerned that there might be an upper limit to generating resonant surges, but now he believed the potential was limitless. The demonstration did come to an unexpected halt, but that was because the power surge caused the overloaded Colorado Springs power generator to burst into flames. Tesla received no further free power from

FIRE FROM THE SKY

the plant's furious owners.

He returned to New York in search of backing for the global implementation of a resonant energy system. Now cognizant of the business world's inevitable reluctance to support giving away free energy, Tesla pitched his new project as a means of transmitting communication, rather than electrical power. Decades before the birth of the Internet, Tesla was envisioning an information superhighway that was a far more sophisticated communication network than the one we use today.

George Westinghouse passed on the idea. Tesla next proposed it to J. P. Morgan, the wealthiest man in America, who had previously declined to finance the inventor. The idea of a monopoly on world communications intrigued Morgan, and he enabled Tesla to build a new laboratory on Long Island. Named Wardenclyffe, it was to be a bigger and better version of his Colorado facility.

While Tesla worked on the project, a string of accidents and bad luck struck Wardenclyffe, and he was beginning to run out of money. Morgan's funds and enthusiasm seemed to evaporate. In a last-ditch effort to keep his investor from deserting him, Tesla revealed to Morgan that his true goal was not to replace the telegraph, but to replace the conventional transmission of electricity. Morgan responded by withdrawing his support entirely.

Tesla would never get another opportunity to bring free energy to the world.

FOUR

TESLA'S MILITARY INVENTIONS, INCLUDING THE OMINOUS DEATH RAY.

Given that Tesla's inventions generally possessed an element of social conscience, of doing good for humanity, it may seem surprising that he created a number of devices with military applications. And the notion of Tesla harnessing his mind for purposes of war may seem immensely frightening. After all, this is the man who boasted that with his resonance generator he could split the earth in two... and no one was ever quite sure

FIRE FROM THE SKY

whether he was joking.

The first Tesla invention with a proposed military use was his automaton technology, with which the labor of human beings could be performed by machines. Specifically, Tesla produced remote-controlled boats and submarines. He demonstrated the wireless ship at an exposition in Madison Square Garden in 1898. The automaton apparatus was so advanced, it used a form of voice recognition to respond to the verbal commands of Tesla and volunteers from the audience.

In public, Tesla spoke only of the humanitarian virtues of the invention: it would lessen the toils and drudgery of mankind and keep human lives out of harm's way. But Tesla actually had his hopes on a contract with the U.S. military. In a presentation before the War Department, Tesla argued that his unmanned torpedo craft could obliterate the Spanish Armada and end the war with Spain in an afternoon. The government never took Tesla up on his offer.

Tesla then decided to pitch the automated submarine to private industry, and submitted it for the approval of J. P. Morgan. According to some accounts, Morgan offered to manufacture Tesla's vessels, but only if Tesla would agree to marry Morgan's daughter. Such a deal was of course anathema to Tesla, and he and Morgan would not work together until Wardenclyffe, a couple of years later.

Tesla eventually landed a successful military contract — with the German Marine High Command. The product here was not unmanned sea craft, but sophisticated turbines which Admiral von Tirpitz used to great success in his fleet of warships. After J. P. Morgan cut off his support of Wardenclyffe, this foreign contract was Tesla's only substantial source of income. Upon the outbreak of World War I, Tesla chose to forfeit his German royalties, lest he be charged with treason.

Nearly broke, and finding the United States on the brink of war, Tesla dreamed up a new invention that might interest the military: the death ray.

The mechanism behind Tesla's death ray is not well understood. It was apparently some sort of particle accelerator. Tesla said it was an outgrowth of his magnifying transformer, which focused its energy output into a thin beam so concentrated it would not scatter, even over huge distances. He promoted the device as a purely defensive weapon, intended to knock down incoming attacks — making the death ray the great-great grandfather of the Strategic Defense Initiative.

It is not certain if Tesla ever used the death ray, or indeed if he even succeeded in building one. But the following is the often-related story of what happened one night in

FIRE FROM THE SKY

1908 when Tesla tested the foreboding weapon.

At the time, Robert Peary was making his second attempt to reach the North Pole. Cryptically, Tesla had notified the expedition that he would be trying to contact them somehow. They were to report to him the details of anything unusual they might witness on the open tundra. On the evening of June 30, accompanied by his associate George Scherff atop Wardenclyffe tower, Tesla aimed his death ray across the Atlantic towards the arctic, to a spot which he calculated was west of the Peary expedition.

Tesla switched on the device. At first, it was hard to tell if it was even working. Its extremity emitted a dim light that was barely visible. Then an owl flew from its perch on the tower's pinnacle, soaring into the path of the beam. The bird disintegrated instantly.

That concluded the test. Tesla watched the newspapers and sent telegrams to Peary in hopes of confirming the death ray's effectiveness. Nothing turned up. Tesla was ready to admit failure when news came of a strange event in Siberia.

On June 30, a massive explosion had devastated Tunguska, a remote area in the Siberian wilderness. Five hundred thousand square acres of land had been instantly destroyed. Equivalent to ten to fifteen megatons of TNT, the Tunguska incident is the most powerful explosion to have occurred in human history — not even subsequent thermonuclear detonations have surpassed it. The explosion was audible from 620 miles away. Scientists believe it was caused by either a meteorite or a fragment of a comet, although no obvious impact site or mineral remnants of such an object were ever found.

Nikola Tesla had a different explanation. It was plain that his death ray had overshot its intended target and destroyed Tunguska. He was thankful beyond measure that the explosion had — miraculously — killed no one. Tesla dismantled the death ray at once, deeming it too dangerous to remain in existence.

Six years later, the onset of the First World War caused Tesla to reconsider. He wrote to President Wilson, revealing his secret death ray test. He offered to rebuild the weapon for the War Department, to be used purely as a deterrent. The mere threat of such destructive force, he claimed, would cause the warring nations to agree at once to establish lasting peace.

The only response to Tesla's proposal was a form letter of appreciation from the president's secretary. The death ray was never reconstructed, and for that we should probably all be thankful.

Tesla made one one further attempt to aid in his country's war effort. In 1917, he conceived of a sending station that would emit exploratory waves of energy, enabling its operators to determine the precise location of distant enemy craft. The War Department rejected Tesla's "exploring ray" as a laughing stock. A generation later, a new invention exactly like this helped the Allies win World War II. It was called radar.

FIVE:
TESLA'S WILDEST DREAMS

Forever restless, and untethered by concerns of practicality and marketability, Tesla's mind spawned a vast miscellany of odd inventions. Many of these were never developed beyond the concept stage, and the ideas seemed to grow markedly weirder in the final years of Tesla's life.

Invention was normally a deliberate process for Tesla, his every intention and goal

FIRE FROM THE SKY

fully formed before he and his crew lifted a finger. But there were times when he stumbled upon a new discovery by mistake. Tesla performed his first experiments with resonance technology at his New York laboratory by firing up a small oscillator, which caused a minor amount of vibration. Suddenly, an alarmed squad of police officers stormed into the lab, demanding that Tesla stop at once. Manhattan was shaking for miles around. Tesla had not taken into account how resonance waves grow stronger the further they travel from their source. He had unintentionally created what became known as Tesla's earthquake machine.

Tesla also applied his resonance engines in bizarre forms of physical therapy. He created machines that flooded the human body with electrical currents and strong vibrations, intended to soothe aches and promote healing. And Tesla wasn't just the inventor of the "electrotherapeutic" device — he was also a client. He reportedly became somewhat addicted to administering the treatment to himself, insisting that a session with the machine rejuvenated him on his long stretches of work without food or sleep. Tesla once let his friend Samuel Clemens try out the healing machine. The author is said to have enjoyed the experience tremendously — until the vibrations brought him a case of spontaneous diarrhea. Tesla marketed this invention, and the Tesla Electrotherapeutic Company was one of the few commercial enterprises of his old age that was marginally successful.

Tesla gained another accidental revelation during his testing of the magnifying transformer in Colorado Springs. One evening during the construction of the device, the apparatus began to sound out a series of precise clicks, similar to Morse code. Tesla was convinced that these were signals being sent by extraterrestrial life. Tesla had expressed his belief in life on Mars, and now he thought he had proof. He later conceived of transmitters for communicating with Martians, espousing his view that the establishment of peaceful relations with our neighbors from outer space was among the most pressing duties that lay before humanity.

In his later years, Tesla was fascinated with the idea of light as both a particle and a wave — the fundamental proposition of what would become quantum physics. This field of inquiry led to the development of his death ray. Tesla also had the idea of creating a "wall of light" by manipulating electromagnetic waves in a certain pattern. This mysterious wall of light would enable time, space, gravity and matter to be altered at will, and engendered an array of Tesla proposals that seem to leap straight out of science fiction, including anti-gravity airships, teleportation and time travel.

FIRE FROM THE SKY

The single weirdest invention Tesla ever proposed was probably the "thought photography" machine. He reasoned that a thought formed in the mind created a corresponding image in the retina, and the electrical data of this neural transmission could be read and recorded in a machine. The stored information could then be processed through an artificial optic nerve and played back as visual patterns on a viewscreen.

It's a pity Tesla never made this last invention a reality. With the dearth of written notes and documentation he left behind for modern science to study, we can only conclude that Tesla's weirdest ideas were misconceived fantasies — maybe even symptoms of madness. Nothing less than a comprehensive recorded catalog of his brain waves could prove otherwise.

SIX:
THE FORGOTTEN GENIUS

Tesla has been excluded from the pages of history and the popular consciousness. Did he earn his obscurity, or was it thrust upon him?

On January 7, 1943, Nikola Tesla died in New York City at the age of 87. He was virtually penniless, living at the dilapidated Hotel New Yorker in a room that he shared with a flock of pigeons, which he considered his only friends.

FIRE FROM THE SKY

The thriving industries he had built had long since turned their backs on him. The scientific community shunned him and his eccentric views. To the general public, he was either unknown or an object of ridicule, a lunatic whose ravings were fit only for sensational tabloids. The popular Max Fleischer "Superman" cartoons of the 1940s pitted the Man of Steel against the death rays and electromagnetic terrors of a scheming mad scientist, whose name was Tesla.

How could this have happened? Whatever his flaws, however far afield he may have strayed at times, Tesla surely deserved better than this. Modern society owes him just as much as the people of his time did, if not more, and yet we have forgotten him.

There are several schools of thought on the question of Tesla's fall into obscurity. The first, and probably the most irrefutable, is that Tesla failed to make the history books because he failed as a businessman. The most successful people aren't necessarily the most brilliant, but those who can play the game to reach the top. Tesla was a disciple of the pure sciences as opposed to applied science, with little facility at figuring out how to profit from his ideas. His business associates often did not act on behalf of his best interests, and Tesla himself made scores of bad financial decisions.

For example, in the wake of Tesla's successful implementation of AC, he stood to collect an enormous amount of wealth. He had signed a contract with Westinghouse which could conceivably have put him among the richest men in America. But when George Westinghouse told Tesla that the financial drain of the arrangement would put his company's future in jeopardy, Tesla ripped the contract to shreds, as a gesture of friendship. Had he held Westinghouse to the deal, or at least negotiated for a fraction of it, Tesla would have died in luxury, and may have preserved his notoriety much more fittingly.

Other analysts take the blame off Tesla's shoulders, and propose that big business and the U.S. government conspired to suppress the inventor's genius. At the top of the suspected conspirator list is Thomas Edison. Edison despised his former employee's success with AC, and it is known that he set out on a campaign to smear Tesla's name. He held demonstrations at which animals were lethally electrocuted with AC-powered devices, in a deceptive and inhumane effort to warn the public of the danger posed by Tesla and Westinghouse's "unsafe" new electrical system. Edison also sat on the War Department advisory board that rejected Tesla's proposals of the death ray and his radar-like device.

J. P. Morgan is also implicated in the anti-Tesla cover-up. Morgan counted on increas-

FIRE FROM THE SKY

ing his already monumental wealth by exploiting Tesla's ideas, until he learned that Tesla was considering the free distribution of energy — a terrifying idea to any self-respecting capitalist. He ended his funding of Tesla's experiments at once, and some think he used his considerable clout to ensure that no one else would bankroll Tesla's threatening schemes.

The government, which had always held Tesla at arm's length when he attempted to pitch a proposal, became suddenly fascinated with his work as soon as he died. The FBI ordered the Office of Alien Property to seize all of Tesla's papers and possessions. This confiscation was unequivocally illegal, since Tesla had been an American citizen since 1891.

The records of Tesla's work were judged to pose no threat to national security, and the FBI's file on Tesla was closed in 1943. It was reopened in 1957 in the wake of reports that the Russians were performing mysterious Tesla technology experiments. Many are convinced the Pentagon has followed suit with top-secret Tesla-based projects of its own, the most infamous being HAARP, the High-frequency Active Auroral Research Program. Reminiscent of Tesla's giant magnifying transmitter, only pointed in the opposite direction, the $30-million experiment is designed to pump enormous quantities of energy into the atmosphere over Alaska. The purposes of HAARP are unclear, although researchers probing the project have called it everything from a communications and surveillance network to a mass mind-control device.

A final theory is that Tesla ruined his reputation with his own outlandish inventions and claims. Some claim that Tesla went wrong as soon as he struck upon his quest for wireless energy. Others believe that he descended into insanity or senility when he began to speak of death rays and Martians. Tesla never accepted the work of Albert Einstein, which he criticized as being vague and incoherent. Given his adherence to these beliefs, many question how great a scientist Tesla could have been.

Strictly speaking, such arguments are probably correct. To the best of modern scientific knowledge, Tesla's free energy system simply would not work, there are no signals broadcast from Mars, and the theory of relativity is sound. But there are two things left to consider.

First, even if Tesla's later ideas were dead wrong, they by no means diminish the immense quantity of very right ideas that he contributed to our world. And second, it bears remembering that alternating current was also perceived as unrealistic Tesla gibberish for quite some time before its true brilliance was finally proven. There is the possibility, however remote, that Tesla's most bizarre concepts will be validated at some point in the future, when science finally catches up with him. Only time will tell.

For now, Tesla's true legacy is increasingly being recognized, bit by bit. The Supreme Court ruled shortly after his death that Tesla was the legal inventor of radio, not Guglielmo Marconi. Similarly, Tesla has been rightfully acknowledged as the inventor of the fluorescent bulb, the vacuum tube amplifier and the X-ray machine. History books are now starting to include these facts. Finding exposure in our current so-called "information age," in which technology is king and strange new ideas are tolerated more and more, Tesla is becoming something of a folk hero. This may run the risk of reducing Tesla and his work to an Internet fad, but any effort that keeps his name alive is worthwhile.

The final fate of Tesla's Wardenclyffe laboratory was strangely fraught with meaning.

FIRE FROM THE SKY

In 1917, it was consigned to demolition. Tesla's money for its upkeep had run dry, and its meager remaining contents were reportedly coveted by German spies. As a preemptive move, it was dynamited. But the proud steel tower of Wardenclyffe remained. The demolition crew blasted the site repeatedly, but the tower would not collapse. They had to return at a later date and dynamite it once more. It fell to the ground, but did not explode, nor did it shatter into pieces upon its thunderous impact.

History has succeeded in toppling Tesla's achievements, but not in destroying them. We can right the fallen tower to its due eminence again.

SOURCES:

Grateful acknowledgement is given to the following sources:
- "My Inventions: The Autobiography of Nikola Tesla," Nikola Tesla, Hart Bros., 1982.
- "Tesla," Tad Wise, Turner Publishing, Inc., 1994.
- "The Fantastic Inventions of Nikola Tesla," Nikola Tesla (additional material by David H. Childress), Adventures Unlimited, 1993.
- "The Greatest Hacker of All Time," Dave Small, "Current Notes" magazine, 1987.
- "Tesla: Man Out of Time," Margaret Cheney, 1981.
- "Return of the Straight Dope," Cecil Adams, Ballantine, 1994.
- IGGY: Phil Hamilton's InfoGeek GatewaY:
http://www.nashville.com/~phil.hamilton
- Science Hobbyist web site:
http://www.eskimo.com/~billb/tesla/tesla.html
- Bogdan R. Kosanovic's Tesla web site:
http://www.neuronet.pitt.edu/~bogdan/tesla
- The International Tesla Society:
http://rainbow.rmi.net/~its/
- Nikola Tesla Museum:
http://www.yurope.com/org/tesla/
- "Bust the Smithsonian!" web site:
http://www.concentric.net/~jwwagner/
- The 50 Greatest Conspiracies of All Time:
http://www.conspire.com/haarp.html
- The Discovery Channel Online:
http://www.discovery.com/DCO/doc/1012/world/inventors/inventors040696/inventors.html
- Special thanks to the invaluable contributions of Shea Tisdale.

NIKOLA TESLA: THE GREATEST HACKER OF ALL TIME
by Dave Small
(c) 1987 Reprinted from Current Notes magazine.
KeelyNet BBS (214) 324-3501
Sponsored by Vangard Sciences
PO BOX 1031
Mesquite, TX 75150

FIRE FROM THE SKY

This material may be reproduced and distributed freely as long as it is complete and unabridged.

The question comes up from time to time. "Who's the greatest hacker ever? "Well, there's a lot of different opinions on this. Some say Steve Wozniak of Apple II fame. Maybe Andy Hertzfeld of the Mac operating system. Richard Stallman, say others, of MIT. Yet at such times when I mention who I think the greatest hacker is, everyone agrees (provided they know of him), and there's no further argument. So, let me introduce you to him, and his greatest hack. I'll warn you right up front that it's mind numbing. By the way, everything I'm going to tell you is true and verifiable down at your local library. Don't worry — we're not heading off into a Shirley MacLaine UFO-land story. Just some classy electrical engineering...

THE SCENE: COLORADO SPRINGS, CO.

Colorado Springs is in southern Colorado, about 70 mile south of Denver. These days it is known as the home of several optical disk research corporations and of NORAD, the missile defense command under Cheyenne Mountain. (I have a personal interest in Colorado Springs; my wife Sandy grew up there.) These events took place some time ago in Colorado Springs. A scientist had moved into town and set up a laboratory on Hill Street, on the southern outskirts. The lab had a two hundred foot copper antenna sticking up out of it, looking something like a HAM radio enthusiast's antenna. He moved in and started work. And strange electrical things happened near that lab. People would walk near the lab, and sparks would jump up from the ground to their feet, through the soles of their shoes. One boy took a screwdriver, held it near a fire hydrant, and drew a four inch electrical spark from the hydrant. Sometimes the grass around his lab would glow with an eerie blue corona, St. Elmo's Fire. What they didn't know was this was small stuff. The man in the lab was merely tuning up his apparatus. He was getting ready to run it wide open in an experiment that ranks as among the greatest, and most spectacular, of all time. One side effect of his experiment was the setting of the record for man-made lightning: some 42 meters in length (130 feet).

THE MAN: NIKOLA TESLA.

His name was Nikola Tesla. He was an immigrant from what is now Yugoslavia; there's a museum of his works in Belgrade. He's a virtual unknown in the United States, despite his accomplishments. I'm not sure why. Some people feel it's a dark plot, the same people who are into conspiracy theories. I feel it's more that Tesla, while a brilliant inventor, was

FIRE FROM THE SKY

also an awful businessman; he ended up going broke. Businessmen who go broke fade out of the public eye; we see this in the computer industry all the time. Edison, who wasn't near the inventor Tesla was, but who was a better businessman, is well remembered as is his General Electric. Still, let me list a few of Tesla's works just so you'll understand how bright he was. He invented the AC motor and transformer. (Think of every motor in your house.) He invented 3-phase electricity and popularized alternating current, the electrical distribution system used all over the world. He invented the Tesla Coil, which makes the high voltage that drives the picture tube in your computer's CRT. He is now credited with inventing modern radio as well; the Supreme Court overturned Marconi's patent in 1943 in favor of Tesla.

Tesla, in short, invented much of the equipment that gets power to your home every day from miles away, and many that use that power inside your home. His inventions made George Westinghouse (Westinghouse Corp.) a wealthy man. Finally, the unit of magnetic flux in the metric system is the "tesla". Other units include the "faraday" and the "henry", so you'll understand this is an honor given to few. So we're not talking about an unknown here, but rather a solid electrical engineer. Tesla whipped through a number of inventions early in his life. He found himself increasingly interested in resonance, and in particular, electrical resonance. Tesla found out something fascinating. If you set an electrical circuit to resonating, it does strange things indeed. Take for instance his Tesla Coil. This high frequency step-up transformer would kick out a few hundred thousand volts at radio frequencies. The voltage would come off the top of his coil as a "corona", or brush discharge. The little ones put out a six-inch spark; the big ones throw sparks many feet long. Yet Tesla could draw the sparks to his fingers without being hurt — the high frequency of the electricity keeps it on the surface of the skin, and prevents the current from doing any harm. Tesla got to thinking about resonance on a large scale. He'd already pioneered the electrical distribution system we use today, and that's not small thinking; when you think of Tesla, think big. He thought, let's say I send an electrical charge into the ground. What happens to it? Well, the ground is an excellent conductor of electricity.

Let me spend a moment on this so you understand, because topsoil doesn't seem very conductive to most. The ground makes a wonderful sinkhole for electricity. This is why you "ground" power tools; the third (round) pin in every AC outlet in your house is wired straight to, literally, the ground.

Typically, the handle of your power tool is hooked to ground; this way, if something shorts out in the tool and the handle gets electrified, the current ruches to the ground instead of into you. The ground has long been used in this manner, as a conductor.

Tesla generates a powerful pulse of electricity, and drains it into the ground. Because the ground is conductive, it doesn't stop. Rather, it spreads out like a radio wave, traveling at the speed of light, 186,000 miles per second. And it keeps going, because it's a powerful wave; it doesn't peter out after a few miles. It passes through the iron core of the earth with little trouble. After all, molten iron is very conductive. When the wave reaches the far side of the planet, it bounces back, like a wave in water bounces when it reaches an obstruction. Since it bounces, it makes a return trip; eventually, it returns to the point of origin. Now, this idea might seem wild. But it isn't science fiction. We bounced radar beams off the moon in the 1950's, and we mapped Venus by radar in the 1970's.

FIRE FROM THE SKY

Those planets are millions of miles away. The earth is a mere 3000 miles in diameter; sending an electromagnetic wave through it is a piece of cake. We can sense earthquakes all the way across the planet by the vibrations they set up that travel all that distance. So, while at first thought it seems amazing, it's really pretty straight forward. But, as I said, it's a typical example of how Tesla thought. And then he had one of his typically Tesla ideas.

He thought, when the wave returns to me (about 1/30th of a second after he sends it in), it's going to be considerably weakened by the trip. Why doesn't he send in another charge at this point, to strengthen the wave? The two will combine, go out, and bounce again. And then he'll reinforce it again, and again. The wave will build up in power. It's like pushing a swingset. You give a series of small pushes each time the swing goes out. And you build up a lot of power with a series of small pushes; ever tried to stop a swing when it's going full tilt? He wanted to find out the upper limit of resonance. And he was in for a surprise.

THE HACK: THE TESLA COIL

So Tesla moved into Colorado Springs, where one of his generators and electrical systems had been installed, and set up his lab. Why Colorado Springs? Well, his lab in New York had burned down, and he was depressed about that. And as fate would have it, a friend in Colorado Springs who directed the power company, Leonard Curtis, offered him free electricity. Who could resist that? After setting up his lab, he tuned his gigantic Tesla coil through that year, trying to get it to resonate perfectly with the earth below. And the townspeople noticed those weird effects; Tesla was electrifying the ground beneath their feet on the return bounce of the wave. Eventually, he got it tuned, keeping things at low power. But in the spirit of a true hacker, just once he decided to run it wide open, just to see what would happen. Just what was the upper limit of the wave he would build up, bouncing back and forth in the planet below? He had his Coil hooked to the ground below it, the 200 foot antenna above it, and getting as much electricity as he wanted right off the city power supply mains. Tesla went outside to watch (wearing three inch rubber soles for insulation) and had his assistant, Kolman Czito, turn the Coil on. There was a buzz from rows of oil capacitors, and a roar from the spark gap as wrist-thick arcs jumped across it. Inside the lab the noise was deafening. But Tesla was outside, watching the antenna. Any surge that returned to the area would run up the antenna and jump off as lightning. Off the top of the antenna shot a six foot lightning bolt. The bolt kept going in a steady arc, though, unlike a single lightning flash. And here Tesla watched carefully, for he wanted to see if the power would build up, if his wave theory would work. Soon the lightning was twenty feet long, then fifty. The surges were growing more powerful. Eighty feet — now thunder was following each lightning bolt. A hundred feet, a hundred twenty feet; the lightning shot upwards off the antenna. Thunder was heard booming around Tesla now (it was heard 22 miles away, in the town of Cripple Creek). The meadow Tesla was standing in was lit up with an electrical discharge very much like St. Elmo's Fire, casting a blue glow. His theory had worked! There didn't seem to be an upper limit to the surges; he was creating the most powerful electrical surges ever created by man. That moment he set the record, which he still holds, for manmade lightning. Then everything halted. The lightning discharges stopped, the thunder quit. He ran in, found the power company had turned off his power feed. He called them, shouted

FIRE FROM THE SKY

at them — they were interrupting his experiment! The foreman replied that Tesla had just overloaded the generator and set it on fire, his lads were busy putting out the fire in the windings, and it would be a cold day in hell before Tesla got any more free power from the Colorado Springs power company!

All the lights in Colorado Springs had gone out. And that, readers, is to me the greatest hack in history. I've seen some amazing hacks. The 8-bit Atari OS. The Mac OS. The phone company computers — well, lots of computers. But I've never seen anyone set the world's lightning record and shut off the power to an entire town, "just to see what would happen". For a few moments, there in Colorado Springs, he achieved something never before done. He had used the entire planet as a conductor, and sent a pulse through it. In that one moment in the summer of 1899, he made electrical history. That's right, in 1899 — darn near a hundred years ago. Well, you may say to yourself, that's a nice story, and I'm sure George Lucas could make a hell of a movie about it, special effects and all. But it's not relevant today. Or isn't it? Hang on to your hat.

THE SDI AND THE TESLA COIL

Let me lay a little political groundwork. Last October I attended Hackercon 2.0, another gathering of computer hackers from all over. It was an informal weekend at a camp in the hills west of Santa Clara. One of the more interesting memories of Hackers 2.0 were the numerous diatribes against the Strategic Defense Initiative. Most speakers claimed it was impossible, citing technical problems. So many people felt obligated to complain about SDI that the conference was jokingly called "SDIcon 2.0". Probably the high(?) point of the conference was Jerry Pournelle and Timothy Leary up on stage debating SDI. I'll leave the description to your imagination — it was everything you can think of and more. Personally, I was disturbed to see how many gifted hackers adopting the attitude of "let's not even try". That's not how micros got started. I mentioned to one Time magazine journalist that if anyone could make SDI go, it was the hackers gathered there. I also believe that the greatest hacker of them all, Nikola Tesla, solved the SDI technical problem back in 1899. The event was so long ago, and so amazing, that it's pretty much been forgotten; I described it last issue. Let me present my case for the Tesla Coil and SDI.

SOVIET USE OF THE TESLA COIL

You will recall I said that Tesla was born in Yugoslavia (although back then, it was "Serbo-Croatia"). He is not unknown there; he is regarded as a national hero. Witness the Nikola Tesla museum in Belgrade, for instance. There's been interferences picked up, on this side of the planet, which is causing problems in the ham radio bands. Direction finding equipment has traced the interference in the SW band to two sources in the Soviet Union, which are apparently two high powered Tesla Coils. Why on earth are the Soviets playing with Tesla Coils? There's one odd theory that they're subjecting Canada to low level electrical interference to cause attitude change. Sigh. Moving right along, there's another theory, more credible, that they are conducting research in "over the horizon" radar using Tesla's ideas. (The Soviets are certainly not saying what they're doing.) When I read about this testing, it worried me. I don't think they're playing with attitude control or radar. I think they're doing exactly what Tesla did in Colorado Springs.

COMPUTERS AND GROUNDING

Time for another discussion of grounding. Consider your computer equipment. You've

FIRE FROM THE SKY

doubtlessly been warned about static electricity, always been told to ground yourself (thus discharging the static into the ground, an electrical sinkhole) before touching your computer. Companies make anti-static spray for your rugs. Static is in the 20,000 to 50,000 volt range. Computer chips run on five to twelve volts. The internal insulation is built for that much voltage. When they get a shot of static in the multiple thousand volt range, the insulation is punctured, and the chip ruined. Countless computers have been damaged this way. Read any manual on inserting memory chips to a PC, and you'll see warnings about static; it's a big problem. Now Tesla was working in the millions of volts range. And his special idea — that the ground itself could be the conductor — now comes into relevance, nearly a hundred years after his dramatic demonstration in Colorado Springs. For, you see, in our wisdom we've grounded our many computers, to protect them from static. We've always assumed the ground is an electrical sinkhole. So, with our three-pin plugs we ground everything — the two flat pins in your wall go to electricity (hot and neutral); the third, round pin, goes straight to ground. That third pin is usually hooked with a thick wire to a cold water pipe, which grounds it effectively. Tesla proved that you can give that ground a terrific charge, millions of volts of high frequency electricity. (Tesla ran his large coil at 33 Khz). Remember, the lightning surging off his Coil was coming from the wave bouncing back and forth in the planet below. In short, he was modifying the ground's electrical potential, changing it from an electrical sinkhole to an electrical source. Tesla did his experiment in 1899. There weren't any home computers with delicate chips hooked up to grounds then. If there had been, he'd have fried everything in Colorado Springs. There was, however, one piece of electrical equipment grounded at the time of the experiment, the city power generator. It caught fire and ended Tesla's experiment. The cause of its failure is interesting as well. It died from "high frequency kickback", something most electrical engineers know about. Tesla forgot that as the generator fed him power, he was feeding it high frequency from his Coil. High frequency quickly heats insulation; a microwave oven works on the same principle. In a few minutes, the insulation inside that generator grew so hot that the generator caught fire. When the lights went out all over Colorado Springs, there was the first proof that Tesla's idea has strategic possibilities.

It gets scarier. Imagine Tesla's Coil, busily pumping an electrical wave in the Earth. On his side of the planet, he was getting 130 foot sparks, which is a hell of a lot of voltage and current. And simple wave theory will show you that those sort of potentials exist on the far side of the planet as well. Remember, the wave was bouncing back and forth, being reinforced on every trip. The big question is how focused the opposite electrical pole will be. No one knows. But it seems probable that the far side of the planet's ground target area could be subjected to considerable electrical interference. And if computer equipment is plugged into that ground, faithfully assuming the ground will never be a source of electricity, it's just too bad for that equipment. This sort of electrical interference makes static look tiny by comparison. It doesn't take much difference in ground potential to kill a computer connected across it. Lightning strikes cause a temporary flare in ground voltage; I remember replacing driver chips on a network on all computers that had been caught by one lightning strike, when I lived in Austin. Imagine the effect on relatively delicate electronics if someone fires up a Tesla Coil on the far side of the planet, and subjects the grounds to steep electrical swings. The military applications

FIRE FROM THE SKY

are pretty obvious — those ICBM's in North Dakota, for instance. It's possible they could be damaged in their silos, and from thousands of miles away. Running two or more Coils, you don't have to be exactly on the far side of the planet, either. Interference effects can give you high points where you need with varied tunings. Maybe, just maybe, the Soviets aren't doing "over the horizon" radar. Maybe they just bothered to read Tesla's notes. And maybe they are tuning up a real big surprise with their twin Coils.

"STAR WARS" AND THE TESLA COIL

You've heard of the Strategic Defense Initiative, or "Star Wars". We're searching for a way to stop a nuclear attack. Right now, we've got all sorts of high powered research projects, with the emphasis on "new technology". Excimer laser, kinetic kill techniques, and even more exotic ideas. As any of you know who have written computer programs, it's darned hard to get something "new" to work. Maybe it's an error to focus on "new" exclusively. Wouldn't it be something if the solution to SDI lies a hundred years ago, in the forgotten brilliance of Nikola Tesla? For right now we can immobilize the electronics of installations half a planet away. The technology to do it was achieved in 1899, and promptly forgotten. Remember, we're not talking vague, unproven theories here. We're talking the world's record for lightning, and the inventor whose power system lights up your house at night.

THE TESLA COIL WORKS.

All we'd have to do is build it. You might not believe the story about Tesla in Colorado Springs, and what he did. It's pretty amazing. It has a way of being forgotten because of that. And I'm not sure you want to hear about the SDI connection. Still, as you work on a computer, remember Tesla. His Tesla Coil supplies the high voltage for the picture tube you use. The electricity for your computer comes from a Tesla design AC generator, is sent through a Tesla transformer, and gets to your house through 3-phase Tesla power. Tesla's inventions... they have a way of working.

If we can be of service, you may contact
Jerry at (214) 324-8741 or Ron at (214) 242-9346

Nicola Tesla's Autobiography

This text has been entered by John R.H. Penner from a small booklet found in a used bookstore for $2.50. The only form of date identification is the name of the original purchaser, Arthua Daine (?), dated April 29, 1978.

The book appears to be considerably older, made with typewriters, and then photocopied and stapled. The booklet contained four photocopied photographs of Tesla, and was originally forty pages long.

FIRE FROM THE SKY

The book has no Copyright identification, nor any means of contacting the publishers. As far as I am aware, this autobiography is no longer available in printed form anywhere.

In the interest of making this important text available to the wider public, I have retyped the entire text word-for-word as it originally appears into this electronic format. I have exactly maintained page numbers as they appear in the original — including the somewhat odd artifact of Chapter 1 starting on page two.

If anyone knows how to reach the original publisher, please contact me at the below address, so proper credit may be given where it is due.

Introduction
Nikola Tesla was born in Croatia (then part of Austria-Hungary) on July 9, 1856, and died January 7, 1943. He was the electrical engineer who invented the AC (alternating current) induction motor, which made the universal transmission and distribution of electricity possible. Tesla began his studies in physics and mathematics at Graz Polytechnic, and then took philosophy at the University of Prague. He worked as an electrical engineer in Budapest, Hungary, and subsequently in France and Germany. In 1888 his discovery that a magnetic field could be made to rotate if two coils at right angles are supplied with AC current 90 degrees out of phase made possible the invention of the AC induction motor. The major advantage of this motor being its brushless operation, which many at the time believed impossible.

Tesla moved to the United States in 1884, where he worked for Thomas Edison who quickly became a rival - Edison being an advocate of the inferior DC power transmission system. During this time, Tesla was commissioned with the design of the AC generators installed at Niagara Falls. George Westinghouse purchased the patents to his induction motor, and made it the basis of the Westinghouse power system which still underlies the modern electrical power industry today.

He also did notable research on high-voltage electricity and wireless communication; at one point creating an earthquake which shook the ground for several miles around his New York laboratory. He also devised a system which anticipated worldwide wireless communications, fax machines, radar, radio- guided missiles and aircraft.

NIKOLA TESLA IS THE TRUE UNSUNG PROPHET OF THE ELECTRIC AGE; without whom our radio, auto ignition, telephone, alternating current power generation and transmission, radio and television would all have been impossible. Yet his life and times have vanished largely from public access. This AUTOBIOGRAPHY is released to remedy this situation, and to fill this "BLACK HOLE" in information space.
+Kolmogorov- Smirnov Publishing.
The Autobiography of Nicola Tesla
Chapter 1, My Early Life
The progressive development of man is vitally dependent on invention. It is the most important product of his creative brain. Its ultimate purpose is the complete mastery of mind over the material world, the harnessing of the forces of nature to human needs. This is the difficult task of the inventor who is often misunderstood and unrewarded. But he finds ample compensation in the pleasing exercises of his powers and in the knowl-

FIRE FROM THE SKY

edge of being one of that exceptionally privileged class without whom the race would have long ago perished in the bitter struggle against pitiless elements. Speaking for myself, I have already had more than my full measure of this exquisite enjoyment; so much, that for many years my life was little short of continuous rapture. I am credited with being one of the hardest workers and perhaps I am, if thought is the equivalent of labour, for I have devoted to it almost all of my waking hours. But if work is interpreted to be a definite performance in a specified time according to a rigid rule, then I may be the worst of idlers.

Every effort under compulsion demands a sacrifice of life-energy. I never paid such a price. On the contrary, I have thrived on my thoughts. In attempting to give a connected and faithful account of my activities in this story of my life, I must dwell, however reluctantly, on the impressions of my youth and the circumstances and events which have been instrumental in determining my career. Our first endeavours are purely instinctive promptings of an imagination vivid and undisciplined. As we grow older reason asserts itself and we become more and more systematic and designing. But those early impulses, though not immediately productive, are of the greatest moment and may shape our very destinies.

Indeed, I feel now that had I understood and cultivated instead of suppressing them, I would have added substantial value to my bequest to the world. But not until I had attained manhood did I realise that I was an inventor.

This was due to a number of causes. In the first place I had a brother who was gifted to an extraordinary degree; one of those rare phenomena of mentality which biological investigation has failed to explain. His premature death left my earth parents disconsolate. (I will explain my remark about my "earth parents" later.) We owned a horse which had been presented to us by a dear friend. It was a magnificent animal of Arabian breed, possessed of almost human intelligence, and was cared for and petted by the whole family, having on one occasion saved my dear father's life under remarkable circumstances.

My father had been called one winter night to perform an urgent duty and while crossing the mountains, infested by wolves, the horse became frightened and ran away, throwing him violently to the ground. It arrived home bleeding and exhausted, but after the alarm was sounded, immediately dashed off again, returning to the spot, and before the searching party were far on the way they were met by my father, who had recovered consciousness and remounted, not realising that he had been lying in the snow for several hours. This horse was responsible for my brother's injuries from which he died. I witnessed the tragic scene and although so many years have elapsed since, my visual impression of it has lost none of its force. The recollection of his attainments made every effort of mine seem dull in comparison. Anything I did that was creditable merely caused my parents to feel their loss more keenly. So I grew up with little confidence in myself.

But I was far from being considered a stupid boy, if I am to judge from an incident of which I have still a strong remembrance. One day the Aldermen were passing through a street where I was playing with other boys. The oldest of these venerable gentlemen, a wealthy citizen, paused to give a silver piece to each of us. Coming to me, he suddenly stopped and commanded, "Look in my eyes." I met his gaze, my hand outstretched to receive the much valued coin, when to my dismay, he said, "No, not much; you can get nothing from me. You are too smart."

They used to tell a funny story about me. I had two old aunts with wrinkled faces, one of them having two teeth protruding like the tusks of an elephant, which she buried in my cheek every time she kissed me.

Nothing would scare me more then the prospects of being by these affectionate, unattractive relatives. It happened that while being carried in my mother's arms, they asked who was the prettier of the two. After examining their faces intently, I answered thoughtfully, pointing to one of them, "This here is not as ugly as the other."

Then again, I was intended from my very birth, for the clerical profession and this thought constantly oppressed me. I longed to be an engineer, but my father was inflexible. He was the son of an officer who served in the army of the Great Napoleon and in common with his brother, professor of mathematics in a prominent institution, had received a military education; but, singularly enough, later embraced the clergy in which vocation he achieved eminence. He was a very erudite man, a veritable natural philosopher, poet and writer and his sermons were said to be as eloquent as those of Abraham a-Sancta-Clara. He had a prodigious memory and frequently recited at length from works in several languages. He often remarked playfully that if some of the classics were lost he could restore them. His style of writing was much admired. He penned sentences short and terse and full of wit and satire. The humorous remarks he made were always peculiar and characteristic. Just to illustrate, I may mention one or two instances.

Among the help, there was a cross-eyed man called Mane, employed to do work around the farm. He was chopping wood one day. As he swung the axe, my father, who stood nearby and felt very uncomfortable, cautioned him, "For God's sake, Mane, do not strike at what you are looking but at what you intend to hit."

On another occasion he was taking out for a drive, a friend who carelessly permitted his costly fur coat to rub on the carriage wheel. My father reminded him of it saying, "Pull in your coat; you are ruining my tire."

He had the odd habit of talking to himself and would often carry on an animated conversation and indulge in heated argument, changing the tone of his voice. A casual listener might have sworn that several people were in the room.

Although I must trace to my mother's influence whatever inventiveness I possess, the training he gave me must have been helpful. It comprised all sorts of exercises - as, guessing one another's thoughts, discovering the defects of some form of expression, repeating long sentences or performing mental calculations. These daily lessons were

FIRE FROM THE SKY

intended to strengthen memory and reason, and especially to develop the critical sense, and were undoubtedly very beneficial.

My mother descended from one of the oldest families in the country and a line of inventors. Both her father and grandfather originated numerous implements for household, agricultural and other uses. She was a truly great woman, of rare skill, courage and fortitude, who had braved the storms of life and passed through many a trying experience. When she was sixteen, a virulent pestilence swept the country. Her father was called away to administer the last sacraments to the dying and during his absence she went alone to the assistance of a neighbouring family who were stricken by the dread disease. She bathed, clothed and laid out the bodies, decorating them with flowers according to the custom of the country and when her father returned he found everything ready for a Christian burial.

My mother was an inventor of the first order and would, I believe, have achieved great things had she not been so remote from modern life and its multifold opportunities. She invented and constructed all kinds of tools and devices and wove the finest designs from thread which was spun by her. She even planted seeds, raised the plants and separated the fibres herself. She worked indefatigably, from break of day till late at night, and most of the wearing apparel and furnishings of the home were the product of her hands. When she was past sixty, her fingers were still nimble enough to tie three knots in an eyelash.

There was another and still more important reason for my late awakening. In my boyhood I suffered from a peculiar affliction due to the appearance of images, often accompanied by strong flashes of light, which marred the sight of real objects and interfered with my thoughts and action. They were pictures of things and scenes which i had really seen, never of those imagined. When a word was spoken to me the image of the object it designated would present itself vividly to my vision and sometimes I was quite unable to distinguish weather what I saw was tangible or not. This caused me great discomfort and anxiety. None of the students of psychology or physiology whom i have consulted, could ever explain satisfactorily these phenomenon. They seem to have been unique although I was probably predisposed as I know that my brother experienced a similar trouble.

The theory I have formulated is that the images were the result of a reflex action from the brain on the retina under great excitation. They certainly were not hallucinations such as are produced in diseased and anguished minds, for in other respects i was normal and composed. To give an idea of my distress, suppose that I had witnessed a funeral or some such nerve-wracking spectacle.

The, inevitably, in the stillness of night, a vivid picture of the scene would thrust itself before my eyes and persist despite all my efforts to banish it. If my explanation is correct, it should be possible to project on a screen the image of any object one conceives and make it visible. Such an advance would revolutionise all human relations. I am convinced that this wonder can and will be accomplished in time to come. I may add that I have devoted much thought to the solution of the problem.

I have managed to reflect such a picture, which i have seen in my mind, to the mind of another person, in another room. To free myself of these tormenting appearances, I tried to concentrate my mind on something else I had seen, and in this way I would often obtain temporary relief; but in order to get it I had to conjure continuously new images. It was not long before I found that I had exhausted all of those at my command; my 'reel'

FIRE FROM THE SKY

had run out as it were, because I had seen little of the world — only objects in my home and the immediate surroundings. As I performed these mental operations for the second or third time, in order to chase the appearances from my vision, the remedy gradually lost all its force. Then I instinctively commenced to make excursions beyond the limits of the small world of which I had knowledge, and I saw new scenes. These were at first very blurred and indistinct, and would flit away when I tried to concentrate my attention upon them. They gained in strength and distinctness and finally assumed the concreteness of real things. I soon discovered that my best comfort was attained if I simply went on in my vision further and further, getting new impressions all the time, and so I began to travel; of course, in my mind. Every night, (and sometimes during the day), when alone, I would start on my journeys — see new places, cities and countries; live there, meet people and make friendships and acquaintances and, however unbelievable, it is a fact that they were just as dear to me as those in actual life, and not a bit less intense in their manifestations.

This I did constantly until I was about seventeen, when my thoughts turned seriously to invention. Then I observed to my delight that I could visualise with the greatest facility. I needed no models, drawings or experiments. I could picture them all as real in my mind. Thus I have been led unconsciously to evolve what I consider a new method of materialising inventive concepts and ideas, which is radially opposite to the purely experimental and is in my opinion ever so much more expeditious and efficient.

The moment one constructs a device to carry into practice a crude idea, he finds himself unavoidably engrossed with the details of the apparatus. As he goes on improving and reconstructing, his force of concentration diminishes and he loses sight of the great underlying principle. Results may be obtained, but always at the sacrifice of quality. My method is different. I do not rush into actual work. When I get an idea, I start at once building it up in my imagination. I change the construction, make improvements and operate the device in my mind. It is absolutely immaterial to me whether I run my turbine in thought or test it in my shop. I even note if it is out of balance. There is no difference whatever; the results are the same. In this way I am able to rapidly develop and perfect a conception without touching anything. When I have gone so far as to embody in the invention every possible improvement I can think of and see no fault anywhere, I put into concrete form this final product of my brain. Invariably my device works as I conceived that it should, and the experiment comes out exactly as I planned it. In twenty years there has not been a single exception. Why should it be otherwise? Engineering, electrical and mechanical, is positive in results. There is scarcely a subject that cannot be examined beforehand, from the available theoretical and practical data. The carrying out into practice of a crude idea as is being generally done, is, I hold, nothing but a waste of energy, money, and time.

My early affliction had however, another compensation. The incessant mental exertion developed my powers of observation and enabled me to discover a truth of great importance. I had noted that the appearance of images was always preceded by actual vision of scenes under peculiar and generally very exceptional conditions, and I was impelled on each occasion to locate the original impulse. After a while this effort grew to be almost automatic and I gained great facility in connecting cause and effect. Soon I became aware, to my surprise, that every thought I conceived was suggested by an

FIRE FROM THE SKY

external impression. Not only this but all my actions were prompted in a similar way. In the course of time it became perfectly evident to me that I was merely an automation endowed with power OF MOVEMENT RESPONDING TO THE STIMULI OF THE SENSE ORGANS AND THINKING AND ACTING ACCORDINGLY. The practical result of this was the art of teleautomatics which has been so far carried out only in an imperfect manner. Its latent possibilities will, however be eventually shown. I have been years planning self-controlled automata and believe that mechanisms can be produced which will act as if possessed of reason, to a limited degree, and will create a revolution in many commercial and industrial departments. I was about twelve years of age when I first succeeded in banishing an image from my vision by wilful effort, but I never had any control over the flashes of light to which I have referred. They were, perhaps, my strangest and [most] inexplicable experience. They usually occurred when I found myself in a dangerous or distressing situations or when i was greatly exhilarated. In some instances i have seen all the air around me filled with tongues of living flame. Their intensity, instead of diminishing, increased with time and seemingly attained a maximum when I was about twenty-five years old.

While in Paris in 1883, a prominent French manufacturer sent me an invitation to a shooting expedition which I accepted. I had been long confined to the factory and the fresh air had a wonderfully invigorating effect on me. On my return to the city that night, I felt a positive sensation that my brain had caught fire. I was a light as though a small sun was located in it and I passed the whole night applying cold compressions to my tortured head. Finally the flashes diminished in frequency and force but it took more than three weeks before they wholly subsided. When a second invitation was extended to me, my answer was an emphatic NO!

These luminous phenomena still manifest themselves from time to time, as when a new idea opening up possibilities strikes me, but they are no longer exciting, being of relatively small intensity. When I close my eyes I invariably observe first, a background of very dark and uniform blue, not unlike the sky on a clear but starless night. In a few seconds this field becomes animated with innumerable scintillating flakes of green, arranged in several layers and advancing towards me. Then there appears, to the right, a beautiful pattern of two systems of parallel and closely spaced lines, at right angles to one another, in all sorts of colours with yellow, green, and gold predominating.

Immediately thereafter, the lines grow brighter and the whole is thickly sprinkled with dots of twinkling light. This picture moves slowly across the field of vision and in about ten seconds vanishes on the left, leaving behind a ground of rather unpleasant and inert grey until the second phase is reached.

Every time, before falling asleep, images of persons or objects flit before my view. When I see them I know I am about to lose consciousness. If they are absent and refuse to come, it means a sleepless night. To what an extent imagination played in my early life, I may illustrate by another odd experience.

Like most children, I was fond of jumping and developed an intense desire to support myself in the air. Occasionally a strong wind richly charged with oxygen blew from the mountains, rendering my body light as cork and then I would leap and float in space for a long time. It was a delightful sensation and my disappointment was keen when later I undeceived myself. During that period I contracted many strange likes, dislikes and

FIRE FROM THE SKY

habits, some of which I can trace to external impressions while others are unaccountable. I had a violent aversion against the earrings of women, but other ornaments, as bracelets, pleased me more or less according to design. The sight of a pearl would almost give me a fit, but I was fascinated with the glitter of crystals or objects with sharp edges and plane surfaces. I would not touch the hair of other people except, perhaps at the point of a revolver. I would get a fever by looking at a peach and if a piece of camphor was anywhere in the house it caused me the keenest discomfort.

Even now I am not insensible to some of these upsetting impulses. When I drop little squares of paper in a dish filled with liquid, I always sense a peculiar and awful taste in my mouth. I counted the steps in my walks and calculated the cubical contents of soup plates, coffee cups and pieces of food, otherwise my meal was unenjoyable. All repeated acts or operations I performed had to be divisible by three and if I missed I felt impelled to do it all over again, even if it took hours. Up to the age of eight years, my character was weak and vacillating. I had neither courage or strength to form a firm resolve. My feelings came in waves and surges and variated unceasingly between extremes. My wishes were of consuming force and like the heads of the hydra, they multiplied.

I was oppressed by thoughts of pain in life and death and religious fear. I was swayed by superstitious belief and lived in constant dread of the spirit of evil, of ghosts and ogres and other unholy monsters of the dark. Then all at once, there came a tremendous change which altered the course of my whole existence.

Of all things I liked books best. My father had a large library and whenever I could manage I tried to satisfy my passion for reading. He did not permit it and would fly in a rage when he caught me in the act. He hid the candles when he found that I was reading in secret. He did not want me to spoil my eyes. But I obtained tallow, made the wicking and cast the sticks into tin forms, and every night I would bush the keyhole and the cracks and read, often till dawn, when all others slept and my mother started on her arduous daily task.

On one occasion I came across a novel entitled 'Aoafi,' (the son of Aba), a Serbian translation of a well known Hungarian writer, Josika. This work somehow awakened my dormant powers of will and I began to practice self-control. At first my resolutions faded like snow in April, but in a little while I conquered my weakness and felt a pleasure I never knew before — that of doing as I willed.

In the course of time this vigorous mental exercise became second to nature. At the outset my wishes had to be subdued but gradually desire and will grew to be identical. After years of such discipline I gained so complete a mastery over myself that I toyed with passions which have meant destruction to some of the strongest men. At a certain age I contracted a mania for gambling which greatly worried my parents. To sit down to a game of cards was for me the quintessence of pleasure. My father led an exemplary life and could not excuse the senseless waste of my time and money in which I indulged. I had a strong resolve, but my philosophy was bad. I would say to him, 'I can stop whenever I please, but it is worth while to give up that which I would purchase with the joys of paradise?'

On frequent occasions he gave vent to his anger and contempt, but my mother was different. She understood the character of men and knew that one's salvation could only be brought about through his own efforts. One afternoon, I remember, when I had lost all my money and was craving for a game, she came to me with a roll of bills and said, 'Go and enjoy yourself. The sooner you lose all we possess, the better it will be. I know that you will get over it.' She was right. I conquered my passion then and there and only regretted that it had not been a hundred times as strong. I not only vanquished but tore it from my heart so as not to leave even a trace of desire.

Ever since that time I have been as indifferent to any form of gambling as to picking teeth. During another period I smoked excessively, threatening to ruin my health. Then my will asserted itself and I not only stopped but destroyed all inclination. Long ago I suffered from heart trouble until I discovered that it was due to the innocent cup of coffee I consumed every morning. I discontinued at once, though I confess it was not an easy task. In this way I checked and bridled other habits and passions, and have not only preserved my life but derived an immense amount of satisfaction from what most men would consider privation and sacrifice.

After finishing the studies at the Polytechnic Institute and University, I had a complete nervous breakdown and while the malady lasted I observed many phenomena, strange and unbelievable...

Chapter 2

I shall dwell briefly on these extraordinary experiences, on account of their possible interest to students of psychology and physiology and also because this period of agony was of the greatest consequence on my mental development and subsequent labours. But it is indispensable to first relate the circumstances and conditions which preceded them and in which might be found their partial explanation.

From childhood I was compelled to concentrate attention upon myself. This caused

FIRE FROM THE SKY

me much suffering, but to my present view, it was a blessing in disguise for it has taught me to appreciate the inestimable value of introspection in the preservation of life, as well as a means of achievement. The pressure of occupation and the incessant stream of impressions pouring into our consciousness through all the gateways of knowledge make modern existence hazardous in many ways. Most persons are so absorbed in the contemplation of the outside world that they are wholly oblivious to what is passing on within themselves. The premature death of millions is primarily traceable to this cause. Even among those who exercise care, it is a common mistake to avoid imaginary, and ignore the real dangers. And what is true of an individual also applies, more or less, to a people as a whole.

Abstinence was not always to my liking, but I find ample reward in the agreeable experiences I am now making. Just in the hope of converting some to my precepts and convictions I will recall one or two.

A short time ago I was returning to my hotel. It was a bitter cold night, the ground slippery, and no taxi to be had. Half a block behind me followed another man, evidently as anxious as myself to get under cover. Suddenly my legs went up in the air. At the same instant there was a flash in my brain. The nerves responded, the muscles contracted. I swung 180 degrees and landed on my hands. I resumed my walk as though nothing had happened when the stranger caught up with me. "How old are you?" he asked, surveying me critically.

"Oh, about fifty-nine," I replied, "What of it?"

"Well," said he, "I have seen a cat do this but never a man." About a month ago I wanted to order new eye glasses and went to an oculist who put me through the usual tests. He looked at me incredulously as I read off with ease the smallest print at considerable distance. But when I told him I was past sixty he gasped in astonishment. Friends of mine often remark that my suits fit me like gloves but they do not know that all my clothing is made to measurements which were taken nearly fifteen years ago and never changed. During this same period my weight has not varied one pound. In this connection I may tell a funny story.

One evening, in the winter of 1885, Mr. Edison, Edward H. Johnson, the President of the Edison Illuminating Company, Mr. Batchellor, Manager of the works, and myself, entered a little place opposite 65 Firth Avenue, where the offices of the company were located. Someone suggested guessing weights and I was induced to step on a scale. Edison felt me all over and said: "Tesla weighs 152 lbs. to an ounce," and he guessed it

FIRE FROM THE SKY

exactly. Stripped I weighed 142 pounds, and that is still my weight. I whispered to Mr. Johnson; "How is it possible that Edison could guess my weight so closely?"

"Well," he said, lowering his voice. "I will tell you confidentially, but you must not say anything. He was employed for a long time in a Chicago slaughterhouse where he weighed thousands of hogs every day. That's why."

My friend, the Hon. Chauncey M. Dupew, tells of an Englishman on whom he sprung one of his original anecdotes and who listened with a puzzled expression, but a year later, laughed out loud. I will frankly confess it took me longer than that to appreciate Johnson's joke. Now, my well-being is simply the result of a careful and measured mode of living and perhaps the most astonishing thing is that three times in my youth I was rendered by illness a hopeless physical wreck and given up by physicians. MORE than this, through ignorance and lightheartedness, I got into all sorts of difficulties, dangers and scrapes from which I extricated myself as by enchantment. I was almost drowned, entombed, lost and frozen. I had hairbreadth escapes from mad dogs, hogs, and other wild animals. I passed through dreadful diseases and met with all kinds of odd mishaps and that I am whole and hearty today seems like a miracle. But as I recall these incidents to my mind I feel convinced that my preservation was not altogether accidental, but was indeed the work of divine power. An inventor's endeavour is essentially life saving. Whether he harnesses forces, improves devices, or provides new comforts and conveniences, he is adding to the safety of our existence. He is also better qualified than the average individual to protect himself in peril, for he is observant and resourceful. If I had no other evidence that I was, in a measure, possessed of such qualities, I would find it in these personal experiences. The reader will be able to judge for himself if I mention one or two instances.

On one occasion, when about fourteen years old, I wanted to scare some friends who were bathing with me. My plan was to dive under a long floating structure and slip out quietly at the other end. Swimming and diving came to me as naturally as to a duck and I was confident that I could perform the feat.

Accordingly I plunged into the water and, when out of view, turned around and proceeded rapidly towards the opposite side. Thinking that I was safely beyond the structure, I rose to the surface but to my dismay struck a beam. Of course, I quickly dived and forged ahead with rapid strokes until my breath was beginning to give out. Rising for the second time, my head came again in contact with a beam. Now I was becoming desperate. However, summoning all my energy, I made a third frantic attempt but the result was the same. The torture of suppressed breathing was getting unendurable, my brain was reeling and I felt myself sinking. At that moment, when my situation seemed absolutely hopeless, I experienced one of those flashes of light and the structure above me appeared before my vision. I either discerned or guessed that there was a little space between the surface of the water and the boards resting on the beams and, with consciousness nearly gone, I floated up, pressed my mouth close to the planks and managed to inhale a little air, unfortunately mingled with a spray of water which nearly choked me. Several times I repeated this procedure as in a dream until my heart, which was racing at a terrible rate, quieted down, and I gained composure. After that I made a number of unsuccessful dives, having completely lost the sense of direction, but finally succeeded in getting out of the trap when my friends had already given me up and were fishing for

FIRE FROM THE SKY

my body. That bathing season was spoiled for me through recklessness but I soon forgot the lesson and only two years later I fell into a worse predicament.

There was a large flour mill with a dam across the river near the city where I was studying at the time. As a rule the height of the water was only two or three inches above the dam and to swim to it was a sport not very dangerous in which I often indulged. One day I went alone to the river to enjoy myself as usual. When I was a short distance from the masonry, however, I was horrified to observe that the water had risen and was carrying me along swiftly. I tried to get away but it was too late. Luckily, though, I saved myself from being swept over by taking hold of the wall with both hands. The pressure against my chest was great and I was barely able to keep my head above the surface. Not a soul was in sight and my voice was lost in the roar of the fall. Slowly and gradually

I became exhausted and unable to withstand the strain longer. Just as I was about to let go, to be dashed against the rocks below, I saw in a flash of light a familiar diagram illustrating the hydraulic principle that the pressure of a fluid in motion is proportionate to the area exposed and automatically I turned on my left side. As if by magic, the pressure was reduced and I found it comparatively easy in that position to resist the force of the stream. But the danger still confronted me. I knew that sooner or later I would be carried down, as it was not possible for any help to reach me in time, even if I had attracted attention. I am ambidextrous now, but then I was left-handed and had comparatively little strength in my right arm. For this reason I did not dare to turn on the other side to rest and nothing remained but to slowly push my body along the dam. I had to get away from the mill towards which my face was turned, as the current there was much swifter and deeper. It was a long and painful ordeal and I came near to failing at its very end, for I was confronted with a depression in the masonry. I managed to get over with the last ounce of my strength and fell in a swoon when I reached the bank, where I was found. I had torn virtually all the skin from my left side and it took several weeks before the fever had subsided and I was well. These are only two of many instanced, but they may be sufficient to show that had it not been for the inventor's instinct, I would not have lived to tell the tale.

Interested people have often asked me how and when I began to invent. This I can only answer from my present recollection in the light of which, the first attempt I recall was rather ambitious for it involved the invention of an apparatus and a method. In the former I was anticipated, but the later was original. It happened in this way. One of my playmates had come into the possession of a hook and fishing tackle which created quite an excitement in the village, and the next morning all started out to catch frogs. I was left alone and deserted owing to a quarrel with this boy. I had never seen a real hook and pictured it as something wonderful, endowed with peculiar qualities, and was despairing not to be one of the party. Urged by necessity, I somehow got hold of a piece of soft iron wire, hammered the end to a sharp point between two stones, bent it into shape, and fastened it to a strong string. I then cut a rod, gathered some bait, and went down to the brook where there were frogs in abundance. But I could not catch any and was almost discouraged when it occurred to me dangle the empty hook in front of a frog sitting on a stump. At first he collapsed but by and by his eyes bulged out and became bloodshot, he swelled to twice his normal size and made a vicious snap at the hook. Immediately I pulled him up. I tried the same thing again and again and the method proved infallible. When my comrades, who in spite of their fine outfit had caught nothing, came to me, they were green with envy. For a long time I kept my secret and enjoyed the monopoly but finally yielded to the spirit of Christmas. Every boy could then do the same and the following summer brought disaster to the frogs.

In my next attempt, I seem to have acted under the first instinctive impulse which later dominated me, — to harness the energies of nature to the service of man. I did this through the medium of May bugs, or June bugs as they are called in America, which were a veritable pest in that country and sometimes broke the branches of trees by the sheer weight of their bodies. The bushes were black with them. I would attach as many as four of them to a crosspiece, rotably arranged on a thin spindle, and transmit the motion of the same to a large disc and so derive considerable 'power.' These creatures were remarkably efficient, for once they were started, they had no sense to stop and continued whirling for hours and hours and the hotter it was, the harder they worked. All went well until a strange boy came to the place. He was the son of a retired officer in the Austrian army. That urchin ate May-bugs alive and enjoyed them as though they were the finest bluepoint oysters. That disgusting sight terminated my endeavours in this promising field and I have never since been able to touch a May-bug or any other insect for that matter.

After that, I believe, I undertook to take apart and assemble the clocks of my grandfather. In the former operation I was always successful, but often failed in the latter. So it came that he brought my work to a sudden halt in a manner not too delicate and it took thirty years before I tackled another clockwork again.

Shortly thereafter, I went into the manufacture of a kind of pop-gun which comprised a hollow tube, a piston, and two plugs of hemp. When firing the gun, the piston was pressed against the stomach and the tube was pushed back quickly with both hands. The air between the plugs was compressed and raised to a high temperature and one of them was expelled with a loud report. The art consisted in selecting a tube of the proper taper from the hollow stalks which were found in our garden. I did very well with that gun, but my activities interfered with the window panes in our house and met with painful discouragement.

If I remember rightly, I then took to carving swords from pieces of furniture which I could conveniently obtain. At that time I was under the sway of the Serbian national poetry and full of admiration for the feats of the heroes. I used to spend hours in mowing down my enemies in the form of cornstalks which ruined the crops and netted me several spankings from my mother. Moreover, these were not of the formal kind but the genuine article.

I had all this and more behind me before I was six years old and had passed through one year of elementary school in the village of Smiljan where my family lived. At this juncture we moved to the little city of Gospic nearby. This change of residence was like a calamity to me. It almost broke my heart to part from our pigeons, chickens and sheep, and our magnificent flock of geese which used to rise to the clouds in the morning and return from the feeding grounds at sundown in battle formation, so perfect that it would have put a squadron of the best aviators of the present day to shame. In our new house I was but a prisoner, watching the strange people I saw through my window blinds. My bashfulness was such that I would rather have faced a roaring lion than one of the city dudes who strolled about. But my hardest trial came on Sunday when I had to dress up

FIRE FROM THE SKY

and attend the service. There I met with an accident, the mere thought of which made my blood curdle like sour milk for years afterwards. It was my second adventure in a church. Not long before, I was entombed for a night in an old chapel on an inaccessible mountain which was visited only once a year. It was an awful experience, but this one was worse.

There was a wealthy lady in town, a good but pompous woman, who used to come to the church gorgeously painted up and attired with an enormous train and attendants. One Sunday I had just finished ringing the bell in the belfry and rushed downstairs, when this grand dame was sweeping out and I jumped on her train. It tore off with a ripping noise which sounded like a salvo of musketry fired by raw recruits. My father was livid with rage. He gave me a gentle slap on the cheek, the only corporal punishment he ever administered to me, but I almost feel it now. The embarrassment and confusion that followed are indescribably. I was practically ostracised until something else happened which redeemed me in the estimation of the community.

An enterprising young merchant had organised a fire department. A new fire engine was purchased, uniforms provided and the men drilled for service and parade. The engine was beautifully painted red and black. One afternoon, the official trial was prepared for and the machine was transported to the river.

The entire population turned out to witness the great spectacle. When all the speeches and ceremonies were concluded, the command was given to pump, but not a drop of water came from the nozzle. The professors and experts tried in vain to locate the trouble. The fizzle was complete when I arrived at the scene. My knowledge of the mechanism was nil and I knew next to nothing of air pressure, but instinctively I felt for the suction hose in the water and found that it had collapsed. When I waded in the river and opened it up, the water rushed forth and not a few Sunday clothes were spoiled. Archimedes running naked through the streets of Syracuse and shouting Eureka at the top of his voice did not make a greater impression than myself. I was carried on the shoulders and was hero of the day.

Upon settling in the city I began a four years course in the so-called Normal School preparatory to my studies at the College or Real-Gymnasium. During this period my boyish efforts and exploits as well as troubles, continued.

Among other things, I attained the unique distinction of champion crow catcher in the country. My method of procedure was extremely simple. I would go into the forest, hide in the bushes, and imitate the call of the birds. Usually I would get several answers and in a short while a crow would flutter down into the shrubbery near me. After that, all I needed to do was to throw a piece of cardboard to detract its attention, jump up and grab it before it could extricate itself from the undergrowth. In this way I would capture as many as I desired. But on one occasion something occurred which made me respect them. I had caught a fine pair of birds and was returning home with a friend. When we left the forest, thousands of crows had gathered making a frightful racket. In a few minutes they rose in pursuit and soon enveloped us. The fun lasted until all of a sudden I received a blow on the back of my head which knocked me down. Then they attacked me viciously. I was compelled to release the two birds and was glad to join my friend who had taken refuge in a cave.

In the school room there were a few mechanical models which interested me and turned my attention to water turbines. I constructed many of these and found great plea-

FIRE FROM THE SKY

sure in operating them. How extraordinary was my life an incident may illustrate. My uncle had no use for this kind of pastime and more than once rebuked me. I was fascinated by a description of Niagara Falls I had perused, and pictured in my imagination a big wheel run by the falls. I told my uncle that I would go to America and carry out this scheme. Thirty years later I was my ideas carried out at Niagara and marvelled at the unfathomable mystery of the mind.

I made all kinds of other contrivances and contraptions but among those, the arbalests I produced were the best. My arrows, when short, disappeared from sight and at close range traversed a plank of pine one inch thick. Through the continuous tightening of the bows I developed a skin on my stomach much like that of a crocodile and I am often wondering whether it is due to this exercise that I am able even now to digest cobblestones! Nor can I pass in silence my performances with the sling which would have enabled me to give a stunning exhibit at the Hippodrome. And now I will tell of one of my feats with this unique implement of war which will strain to the utmost the credulity of the reader.

I was practising while walking with my uncle along the river. The sun was setting, the trout were playful and from time to time one would shoot up into the air, its glistening body sharply defined against a projecting rock beyond. Of course any boy might have hit a fish under these propitious conditions but I undertook a much more difficult task and I foretold to my uncle, to the minutest detail, what I intended doing. I was to hurl a stone to meet the fish, press its body against the rock, and cut it in two. It was no sooner said than done. My uncle looked at me almost scared out of his wits and exclaimed "Vade retra Satanae!" and it was a few days before he spoke to me again. Other records, however great, will be eclipsed but I feel that I could peacefully rest on my laurels for a thousand years.

Chapter 3
How Tesla Conceived The Rotary Magnetic Field

At the age of ten I entered the Real gymnasium which was a new and fairly well equipped institution. In the department of physics were various models of classical scientific apparatus, electrical and mechanical. The demonstrations and experiments performed from time to time by the instructors fascinated me and were undoubtedly a powerful incentive to invention. I was also passionately fond of mathematical studies and

FIRE FROM THE SKY

often won the professor's praise for rapid calculation. This was due to my acquired facility of visualising the figures and performing the operation, not in the usual intuitive manner, but as in actual life. Up to a certain degree of complexity it was absolutely the same to me whether I wrote the symbols on the board or conjured them before my mental vision. But freehand drawing, to which many hours of the course were devoted, was an annoyance I could not endure. This was rather remarkable as most of the members of the family excelled in it. Perhaps my aversion was simply due to the predilection I found in undisturbed thought. Had it not been for a few exceptionally stupid boys, who could not do anything at all, my record would have been the worst.

It was a serious handicap as under the then existing educational regime drawing being obligatory, this deficiency threatened to spoil my whole career and my father had considerable trouble in railroading me from one class to another.

In the second year at that institution I became obsessed with the idea of producing continuous motion through steady air pressure. The pump incident, of which I have been told, had set afire my youthful imagination and impressed me with the boundless possibilities of a vacuum. I grew frantic in my desire to harness this inexhaustible energy but for a long time I was groping in the dark.

Finally, however, my endeavours crystallised in an invention which was to enable me to achieve what no other mortal ever attempted. Imagine a cylinder freely rotatable on two bearings and partly surrounded by a rectangular trough which fits it perfectly. The open side of the trough is enclosed by a partition so that the cylindrical segment within the enclosure divides the latter into two compartments entirely separated from each other by airtight sliding joints. One of these compartments being sealed and once for all exhausted, the other remaining open, a perpetual rotation of the cylinder would result. At least, so I thought.

A wooden model was constructed and fitted with infinite care and when I applied the pump on one side and actual observed that there was a tendency to turning, I was delirious with joy. Mechanical flight was the one thing I wanted to accomplish although still under the discouraging recollection of a bad fall I sustained by jumping with an umbrella from the top of a building. Every day I used to transport myself through the air to distant regions but could not understand just how I managed to do it. Now I had something concrete, a flying machine with nothing more than a rotating shaft, flapping wings, and; - a vacuum of unlimited power! From that time on I made my daily aerial excursions in a vehicle of comfort and luxury as might have befitted King Solomon. It took years

FIRE FROM THE SKY

before I understood that the atmospheric pressure acted at right angles to the surface of the cylinder and that the slight rotary effort I observed was due to a leak! Though this knowledge came gradually it gave me a painful shock.

I had hardly completed my course at the Real Gymnasium when I was prostrated with a dangerous illness or rather, a score of them, and my condition became so desperate that I was given up by physicians. During this period I was permitted to read constantly, obtaining books from the Public Library which had been neglected and entrusted to me for classification of the works and preparation of catalogues.

One day I was handed a few volumes of new literature unlike anything I had ever read before and so captivating as to make me utterly forget me hopeless state. They were the earlier works of Mark Twain and to them might have been due the miraculous recovery which followed. Twenty-five years later, when I met Mr. Clements and we formed a friendship between us, I told him of the experience and was amazed to see that great man of laughter burst into tears...

My studies were continued at the higher Real Gymnasium in Carlstadt, Croatia, where one of my aunts resided. She was a distinguished lady, the wife of a Colonel who was an old war-horse having participated in many battles, I can never forget the three years I passed at their home. No fortress in time of war was under a more rigid discipline. I was fed like a canary bird. All the meals were of the highest quality and deliciously prepared, but short in quantity by a thousand percent. The slices of ham cut by my aunt were like tissue paper. When the Colonel would put something substantial on my plate she would snatch it away and say excitedly to him; "Be careful. Niko is very delicate."

I had a voracious appetite and suffered like Tantalus. But I lived in an atmosphere of refinement and artistic taste quite unusual for those times and conditions. The land was low and marshy and malaria fever never left me while there despite the enormous amounts of quinine I consumed.

Occasionally the river would rise and drive an army of rats into the buildings, devouring everything, even to the bundles of fierce paprika. These pests were to me a welcome diversion. I thinned their ranks by all sorts of means, which won me the unenviable distinction of rat-catcher in the community. At last, however, my course was completed, the misery ended, and I obtained the certificate of maturity which brought me to the crossroads.

During all those years my parents never wavered in their resolve to make me embrace the clergy, the mere thought of which filled me with dread. I had become intensely interested in electricity under the stimulating influence of my Professor of Physics, who was an ingenious man and often demonstrated the principles by apparatus of his own invention. Among these I recall a device in the shape of a freely rotatable bulb, with tinfoil coating, which was made to spin rapidly when connected to a static machine. It is impossible for me to convey an adequate idea of the intensity of feeling I experienced in witnessing his exhibitions of these mysterious phenomena. Every impression produced a thousand echoes in my mind. I wanted to know more of this wonderful force; I longed for experiment and investigation and resigned myself to the inevitable with aching heart. Just as I was making ready for the long journey home I received word that my father wished me to go on a shooting expedition. It was a strange request as he had been always strenuously opposed to this kind of sport.

FIRE FROM THE SKY

But a few days later I learned that the cholera was raging in that district and, taking advantage of an opportunity, I returned to Gospic in disregard to my parent's wishes. It is incredible how absolutely ignorant people were as to the causes of this scourge which visited the country in intervals of fifteen to twenty years. They thought that the deadly agents were transmitted through the air and filled it with pungent odours and smoke. In the meantime they drank infested water and died in heaps. I contracted the dreadful disease on the very day of my arrival and although surviving the crisis, I was confined to bed for nine months with scarcely any ability to move. My energy was completely exhausted and for the second time I found myself at Death's door.

In one of the sinking spells which was thought to be the last, my father rushed into the room. I still see his pallid face as he tried to cheer me in tones belying his assurance. "Perhaps," I said, "I may get well if you will let me study engineering." "You will go to the best technical institution in the world," he solemnly replied, and I knew that he meant it. A heavy weight was lifted from my mind but the relief would have come too late had it not been for a marvellous cure brought through a bitter decoction of a peculiar bean. I came to life like Lazarus to the utter amazement of everybody.

My father insisted that I spend a year in healthful physical outdoor exercise to which I reluctantly consented. For most of this term I roamed in the mountains, loaded with a hunter's outfit and a bundle of books, and this contact with nature made me stronger in body as well as in mind. I thought and planned, and conceived many ideas almost as a rule delusive. The vision was clear enough but the knowledge of principles was very limited.

In one of my invention I proposed to convey letters and packages across the seas, through a submarine tube, in spherical containers of sufficient strength to resist the hydraulic pressure. The pumping plant, intended to force the water through the tube, was accurately figured and designed and all other particulars carefully worked out. Only one trifling detail, of no consequence, was lightly dismissed. I assumed an arbitrary velocity of the water and, what is more, took pleasure in making it high, thus arriving at a stupendous performance supported by faultless calculations. Subsequent reflections, however, on the resistance of pipes to fluid flow induced me to make this invention public property.

Another one of my projects was to construct a ring around the equator which would, of course, float freely and could be arrested in its spinning motion by reactionary forces, thus enabling travel at a rate of about one thousand miles an hour, impracticable by rail. The reader will smile. The plan was difficult of execution, I will admit, but not nearly so bad as that of a well known New York professor, who wanted to pump the air from the torrid to temperate zones, entirely forgetful of the fact that the Lord had provided a gigantic machine for this purpose.

Still another scheme, far more important and attractive, was to derive power from the rotational energy of terrestrial bodies. I had discovered that objects on the earth's surface owing to the diurnal rotation of the globe, are carried by the same alternately in and against the direction of translatory movement.

From this results a great change in momentum which could be utilised in the simplest imaginable manner to furnish motive effort in any habitable region of the world. I cannot find words to describe my disappointment when later I realised that I was in the predica-

FIRE FROM THE SKY

ment of Archimedes, who vainly sought for a fixed point in the universe.

At the termination of my vacation I was sent to the Poly-Technic School in Gratz, Styria (Austria), which my father had chosen as one of the oldest and best reputed institutions. That was the moment I had eagerly awaited and I began my studies under good auspices and firmly resolved to succeed. My previous training was above average, due to my father's teaching and opportunities afforded. I had acquired the knowledge of a number of languages and waded through the books of several libraries, picking up information more or less useful. Then again, for the first time, I could choose my subjects as I liked, and freehand drawing was to bother me no more.

I had made up my mind to give my parents a surprise, and during the whole first year I regularly started my work at three o'clock in the morning and continued until eleven at night, no Sundays or holidays excepted. As most of my fellow-students took things easily, naturally I eclipsed all records. In the course of the year I passed through nine exams and the professors thought I deserved more than the highest qualifications. Armed with their flattering certificated, I went home for a short rest, expecting triumph, and was mortified when my father made light of these hard-won honours.

That almost killed my ambition; but later, after he had died, I was pained to find a package of letters which the professors had written to him to the effect that unless he took me away from the Institution I would be killed through overwork. Thereafter I devoted myself chiefly to physics, mechanics and mathematical studies, spending the hours of leisure in the libraries.

I had a veritable mania for finishing whatever I began, which often got me into difficulties. On one occasion I started to read the works of Voltaire, when I learned, to my dismay that there were close to one hundred large volumes in small print which that monster had written while drinking seventy-two cups of black coffee per diem. It had to be done, but when I laid aside that last book I was very glad, and said, "Never more!"

My first year's showing had won me the appreciation and friendship of several professors. Among these, Professor Rogner, who was teaching arithmetical subjects and geometry; Professor Poeschl, who held the chair of theoretical and experimental physics, and Dr. Alle, who taught integral calculus and specialised in differential equations. This scientist was the most brilliant lecturer to whom I ever listened. He took a special interest in my progress and would frequently remain for an hour or two in the lecture room, giving me problems to solve, in which I delighted. To him I explained a flying machine I had conceived, not an illusory invention, but one based on sound, scientific principles, which has become realisable through my turbine and will soon be given to the world. Both Professors Rogner and Poeschl were curious men. The former had peculiar ways of expressing himself and whenever he did so, there was a riot, followed by a long embarrassing pause. Professor Poeschl was a methodical and thoroughly grounded German. He had enormous feet, and hands like the paws of a bear, but all of his experiments were skilfully performed with clock-like precision and without a miss. It was in the second year of my studies that we received a Gramoe Dyname from Paris, having the horseshoe form of a laminated field magnet, and a wire wound armature with a commutator. It was connected up and various effects of the currents were shown. While Professor Poeschl was making demonstrations, running the machine was a motor, the brushes gave trouble, sparking badly, and I observed that it might be possible to operate a mo-

FIRE FROM THE SKY

tor without these appliances. But he declared that it could not be done and did me the honour of delivering a lecture on the subject, at the conclusion he remarked, "Mr. Tesla may accomplish great things, but he certainly will never do this. It would be equivalent to converting a steadily pulling force, like that of gravity into a rotary effort. It is a perpetual motion scheme, an impossible idea." But instinct is something which transcends knowledge. We have, undoubtedly, certain finer fibres that enable us to perceive truths when logical deduction, or any other wilful effort of the brain, is futile.

For a time I wavered, impressed by the professor's authority, but soon became convinced I was right and undertook the task with all the fire and boundless confidence of my youth. I started by first picturing in my mind a direct-current machine, running it and following the changing flow of the currents in the armature. Then I would imagine an alternator and investigate the progresses taking place in a similar manner. Next I would visualise systems comprising motors and generators and operate them in various ways.

The images I saw were to me perfectly real and tangible. All my remaining term in Gratz was passed in intense but fruitless efforts of this kind, and I almost came to the conclusion that the problem was insolvable.

In 1880 I went to Prague, Bohemia, carrying out my father's wish to complete my education at the University there. It was in that city that I made a decided advance, which consisted in detaching the commutator from the machine and studying the phenomena in this new aspect, but still without result. In the year following there was a sudden change in my views of life.

I realised that my parents had been making too great sacrifices on my account and resolved to relieve them of the burden. The wave of the American telephone had just reached the European continent and the system was to be installed in Budapest, Hungary. It appeared an ideal opportunity, all the more as a friend of our family was at the head of the enterprise.

It was here that I suffered the complete breakdown of the nerves to which I have referred. What I experienced during the period of the illness surpasses all belief. My sight and hearing were always extraordinary. I could clearly discern objects in the distance when others saw no trace of them. Several times in my boyhood I saved the houses of our neighbours from fire by hearing the faint crackling sounds which did not disturb their sleep, and calling for help. In 1899, when I was past forty and carrying on my experiments in Colorado, I could hear very distinctly thunderclaps at a distance of 550 miles. My ear was thus over thirteen times more sensitive, yet at that time I was, so to speak, stone deaf in comparison with the acuteness of my hearing while under the nervous strain.

In Budapest I could hear the ticking of a watch with three rooms between me and the timepiece. A fly alighting on a table in the room would cause a dull thud in my ear. A carriage passing at a distance of a few miles fairly shook my whole body. The whistle of a locomotive twenty or thirty miles away made the bench or chair on which I sat, vibrate so strongly that the pain was unbearable. The ground under my feet trembled continuously. I had to support my bed on rubber cushions to get any rest at all. The roaring noises from near and far often produced the effect of spoken words which would have frightened me had I not been able to resolve them into their accumulated components. The sun rays, when periodically intercepted, would cause blows of such force on my brain that they would stun me. I had to summon all my will power to pass under a bridge

FIRE FROM THE SKY

or other structure, as I experienced the crushing pressure on the skull. In the dark I had the sense of a bat, and could detect the presence of an object at a distance of twelve feet by a peculiar creepy sensation on the forehead. My pulse varied from a few to two hundred and sixty beats and all the tissues of my body with twitchings and tremors, which was perhaps hardest to bear. A renowned physician who have me daily large doses of Bromide of Potassium, pronounced my malady unique and incurable.

It is my eternal regret that I was not under the observation of experts in physiology and psychology at that time. I clung desperately to life, but never expected to recover. Can anyone believe that so hopeless a physical wreck could ever be transformed into a man of astonishing strength and tenacity; able to work thirty-eight years almost without a day's interruption, and find himself still strong and fresh in body and mind? Such is my case. A powerful desire to live and to continue the work and the assistance of a devoted friend, an athlete, accomplished the wonder. My health returned and with it the vigour of mind.

In attacking the problem again, I almost regretted that the struggle was soon to end. I had so much energy to spare. When I understood the task, it was not with a resolve such as men often make. With me it was a sacred vow, a question of life and death. I knew that I would perish if I failed. Now I felt that the battle was won. Back in the deep recesses of the brain was the solution, but I could net yet give it outward expression.

One afternoon, which is ever present in my recollection, I was enjoying a walk with my friend in the City Park and reciting poetry. At that age, I knew entire books by heart, word for word. One of these was Goethe's "Faust." The sun was just setting and reminded me of the glorious passage, *"Sie ruckt und weicht, der Tag ist uberlebt, Dort eilt sie hin und fordert neues Leben. Oh, dañ kein Flugel mich vom Boden hebt Ihr nach und immer nach zu streben! Ein sch√ner Traum indessen sie entweicht, Ach, au des Geistes Fl+gein wird so leicht Kein korperlicher Flugel sich gesellen!"* As I uttered these inspiring words the idea came like a flash of lightening and in an instant the truth was revealed. I drew with a stick on the sand, the diagram shown six years later in my address before the American Institute of Electrical Engineers, and my companion understood them perfectly. The images I saw were wonderfully sharp and clear and had the solidity of metal and stone, so much so that I told him, "See my motor here; watch me reverse it." I cannot begin to describe my emotions. Pygmalion seeing his statue come to life could not have been more deeply moved. A thousand secrets of nature which I might have stumbled upon accidentally, I would have given for that one which I had wrested from her against all odds and at the peril of my existence...

Chapter 4
The Discovery of the Tesla Coil and Transformer
(The Basic Part of Every Radio and T.V.)

For a while I gave myself up entirely to the intense enjoyment of picturing machines and devising new forms. It was a mental state of happiness about as complete as I have ever known in life. Ideas came in an uninterrupted stream and the only difficulty I had was to hold them fast. The pieces of apparatus I conceived were to me absolutely real

FIRE FROM THE SKY

and tangible in every detail, even to the minutest marks and signs of wear. I delighted in imagining the motors constantly running, for in this way they presented to the mind's eye a fascinating sight.

When natural inclination develops into a passionate desire, one advances towards his goal in seven-league boots. In less than two months I evolved virtually all the types of motors and modifications of the system which are now identified with my name, and which are used under many other names all over the world. It was, perhaps, providential that the necessities of existence commanded a temporary halt to this consuming activity of the mind.

I came to Budapest prompted by a premature report concerning the telephone enterprise and, as irony of fate willed it, I had to accept a position as draughtsman in the Central Telegraph Office of the Hungarian Government at a salary which I deem it my privilege not to disclose. Fortunately, I soon won the interest of the Inspector-in-Chief and was thereafter employed on calculations, designs and estimates in connection with new installations, until the Telephone exchange started, when I took charge of the same. The knowledge and practical experience I gained in the course of this work, was most valuable and the employment gave me ample opportunities for the exercise of my inventive faculties. I made several improvements in the Central Station apparatus and perfected a telephone repeater or amplifier which was never patented or publicly described but would be creditable to me even today. In recognition of my efficient assistance the organiser of the undertaking, Mr. Puskas, upon disposing of his business in Budapest, offered me a position in Paris which I gladly accepted.

I never can forget the deep impression that magic city produced on my mind. For several days after my arrival, I roamed through the streets in utter bewilderment of the new spectacle. The attractions were many and irresistible, but, alas, the income was spent as soon as received. When Mr. Puskas asked me how I was getting along in the new sphere, I described the situation accurately in the statement that "The last twenty-nine days of the month are the toughest."

I led a rather strenuous life in what would now be termed "Rooseveltian fashion." Every morning, regardless of the weather, I would go from the Boulevard St. Marcel, where I resided, to a bathing house on the Seine; plunge into the water, loop the circuit twenty-seven times and then walk an hour to reach Ivry, where the Company's factory was located. There I would have a woodchopper's breakfast at half-past seven o'clock and then eagerly await the lunch hour, in the meanwhile cracking hard nuts for the Manager of the Works, Mr. Charles Batchellor, who was an intimate friend and assistant of Edison. Here I was thrown in contact with a few Americans who fairly fell in love with my because of my proficiency in Billiards! To these men I explained my invention and one of them, Mr. D. Cunningham, foreman of the Mechanical Department, offered to form a stock company. The proposal seemed to me comical in the extreme. I did not have the faintest conception of what he meant, except that it was an American way of doing things. Nothing came of it, however, and during the next few months I had to travel from one place to another in France and Germany to cure the ills of the power plants.

On my return to Paris, I submitted to one of the administrators of the Company, Mr. Rau, a plan for improving their dynamos and was given an opportunity. My success was complete and the delighted directors accorded me the privilege of developing automatic regulators which were much desired. Shortly after, there was some trouble with the lighting plant which had been installed at the new railroad station in Strañburg, Alsace. The wiring was defective and on the occasion of the opening ceremonies, a large part of a wall was blown out through a short-circuit, right in the presence of old Emperor William I. The German Government refused to take the plant and the French Company was facing a serious loss. On account of my knowledge of the German language and past experience, I was entrusted with the difficult task of straightening out matters and early in 1883, I went to Strañburg on that mission.

Some of the incidents in that city have left an indelible record on my memory. By a curious coincidence, a number of the men who subsequently achieve fame, lived there about that time. In later life I used to say, "There were bacteria of greatness in that old town." Others caught the disease, but I escaped!" The practical work, correspondence, and conferences with officials kept me preoccupied day and night, but as soon as I was able to manage, I undertook the construction of a simple motor in a mechanical shop opposite the railroad station, having brought with me from Paris some material for that purpose. The consummation of the experiment was, however, delayed until the summer of that year, when I finally had the satisfaction of seeing the rotation effected by alternating currents of different phase, and without sliding contacts or commutator, as I had conceived a year before. It was an exquisite pleasure but not to compare with the delirium of joy following the first revelation.

Among my new friends was the former Mayor of the city, Mr. Sauzin, whom I had already, in a measure, acquainted with this and other inventions of mine and whose support I endeavoured to enlist. He was sincerely devoted to me and put my project before several wealthy persons, but to my mortification, found no response. He wanted to help me in every possible way and the approach of the first of July, 1917, happens to remind me of a form of "assistance" I received from that charming man, which was not financial, but none the less appreciated.

In 1870, when the Germans invaded the country, Mr. Sauzin had buried a good sized allotment of St. Estephe of 1801 and he came to the conclusion that he knew no worthier person than myself, to consume that precious beverage. This, I may say, is one of the unforgettable incidents to which I have referred. My friend urged me to return to Paris as soon as possible and seek support there.

This I was anxious to do, but my work and negotiations were protracted, owing to all sorts of petty obstacles I encountered, so that at times the situation seemed hopeless.

FIRE FROM THE SKY

Just to give an idea of German thoroughness and "efficiency," I may mention here a rather funny experience.

An incandescent lamp of 16 c.p. was to be placed in a hallway, and upon selected the proper location, I ordered the "monteur" to run the wires. After working for a while, he concluded that the engineer had to be consulted and this was done. The latter made several objections but ultimately agreed that the lamp should be placed two inches from the spot I had assigned, whereupon the work proceeded.

Then the engineer became worried and told me that Inspector Averdeck should be notified. That important person was called, he investigated, debated, and decided that the lamp should be shifted back two inches, which was the placed I had marked! It was not long, however, before Averdeck got cold feet himself and advised me that he had informed Ober-Inspector Hieronimus of the matter and that I should await his decision. It was several days before the Ober-Inspector was able to free himself of other pressing duties, but at last he arrived and a two hour debate followed, when he decided to move the lamp two inches further. My hopes that this was the final act, were shattered when the Ober-Inspector returned and said to me, "Regierungsrath Funke is particular that I would not dare to give an order for placing this lamp without his explicit approval."

Accordingly, arrangements for a visit from that great man were made. We started cleaning up and polishing early in the morning, and when Funke came with his retinue he was ceremoniously received. After two hours of deliberation, he suddenly exclaimed, "I must be going!," and pointing to a place on the ceiling, he ordered me to put the lamp there. It was the exact spot which I had originally chosen! So it went day after day with variations, but I was determined to achieve, at whatever cost, and in the end my efforts were rewarded.

By the spring of 1884, all the differences were adjusted, the plant formally accepted, and I returned to Paris with pleasing anticipation. One of the administrators had promised me a liberal compensation in case I succeeded, as well as a fair consideration of the improvements I had made to their dynamos and I hoped to realise a substantial sum. There were three administrators, whom I shall designate as A, B, and C for convenience. When I called on A, he told me that B had the say. This gentleman thought that only C could decide, and the latter was quite sure that A alone had the power to act. After several laps of this circulus viciousus, it dawned upon me that my reward was a castle in Spain.

The utter failure of my attempts to raise capital for development was another disappointment, and when Mr. Bachelor pressed me to go to America with a view of redesigning the Edison machines, I determined to try my fortunes in the Land of Golden Promise. But the chance was nearly missed. I liquefied my modest assets, secured accommodations and found myself at the railroad station as the train was pulling out. At that moment, I discovered that my money and tickets were gone. What to do was the question. Hercules had plenty of time to deliberate, but I had to decide while running alongside the train with opposite feeling surging in my brain like condenser oscillations. Resolve, helped by dexterity, won out in the nick of time and upon passing through the usual experience, as trivial and unpleasant, I managed to embark for New York with the remnants of my belongings, some poems and articles I had written, and a package of calculations relating to solutions of an unsolvable integral and my flying machine. During the

FIRE FROM THE SKY

voyage I sat most of the time at the stern of the ship watching for an opportunity to save somebody from a watery grave, without the slightest thought of danger.

Later, when I had absorbed some of the practical American sense, I shivered at the recollection and marvelled at my former folly. The meeting with Edison was a memorable event in my life. I was amazed at this wonderful man who, without early advantages and scientific training, had accomplished so much. I had studied a dozen languages, delved in literature and art, and had spent my best years in libraries reading all sorts of stuff that fell into my hands, from Newton's "Principia" to the novels of Paul de Kock, and felt that most of my life had been squandered. But it did not take long before I recognised that it was the best thing I could have done. Within a few weeks I had won Edison's confidence, and it came about in this way.

The S.S. Oregon, the fastest passenger steamer at that time, had both of its lighting machines disabled and its sailing was delayed. As the superstructure had been built after their installation, it was impossible to remove them from the hold. The predicament was a serious one and Edison was much annoyed. In the evening I took the necessary instruments with me and went aboard the vessel where I stayed for the night. The dynamos were in bad condition, having several short-circuits and breaks, but with the assistance of the crew, I succeeded in putting them in good shape. At five o'clock in the morning, when passing along Fifth Avenue on my way to the shop, I met Edison with Bachelor and a few others, as they were returning home to retire. "Here is our Parisian running around at night," he said. When I told him that I was coming from the Oregon and had repaired both machines, he looked at me in silence and walked away without another word. But when he had gone some distance I heard him remark, "Bachelor, this is a good man." And from that time on I had full freedom in directing the work. For nearly a year my regular hours were from 10:30 A.M. until 5 o'clock the next morning without a day's exception. Edison said to me, "I have had many hard working assistants, but you take the cake." During this period I designed twenty-four different types of standard machines with short cores and uniform pattern, which replaced the old ones. The Manager had promised me fifty thousand dollars on the completion of this task, but it turned out to be a practical joke. This gave me a painful shock and I resigned my position.

Immediately thereafter, some people approached me with the proposal of forming an arc light company under my name, to which I agreed. Here finally, was an opportunity to develop the motor, but when I broached the subject to my new associates they said, "No, we want the arc lamp. We don't care for this alternating current of yours." In 1886 my system of arc lighting was perfected and adopted for factory and municipal lighting, and I was free, but with no other possession than a beautifully engraved certificate of stock of hypothetical value. Then followed a period of struggle in the new medium for which I was not fitted, but the reward came in the end, and in April, 1887, the TESLA Electric Co. was organised, providing a laboratory and facilities. The motors I built there were exactly as I had imagined them. I made no attempt to improve the design, but merely reproduced the pictures as they appeared to my vision and the operation was always as I expected.

In the early part of 1888, an arrangement was made with the Westinghouse Company for the manufacture of the motors on a large scale. But great difficulties had still to be overcome. My system was based on the use of low frequency currents and the

FIRE FROM THE SKY

Westinghouse experts had adopted 133 cycles with the objects of securing advantages in transformation. They did not want to depart with their standard forms of apparatus and my efforts had to be concentrated upon adapting the motor to these conditions. Another necessity was to produce a motor capable of running efficiently at this frequency on two wire, which was not an easy accomplishment.

At the close of 1889, however, my services in Pittsburgh being no longer essential, I returned to New York and resumed experimental work in a Laboratory on Grand Street, where I began immediately the design of high-frequency machines. The problems of construction in this unexplored field were novel and quite peculiar, and I encountered many difficulties. I rejected the inductor type, fearing that it might not yield perfect sine waves, which were so important to resonant action. Had it not been for this, I could have saved myself a great deal of labour. Another discouraging feature of the high-frequency alternator seemed to be the inconstancy of speed which threatened to impose serious limitations to its use. I had already noted in my demonstrations before the American Institution of Electrical Engineers, that several times the tune was lost, necessitating re-adjustment, and did not yet foresee what I discovered long afterwards, - a means of operating a machine of this kind at a speed constant to such a degree as not to vary more than a small fraction of one revolution between the extremes of load. From many other considerations, it appeared desirable to invent a simpler device for the production of electric oscillations.

In 1856, Lord Kelvin had exposed the theory of the condenser discharge, but no practical application of that important knowledge was made. I saw the possibilities and undertook the development of induction apparatus on this principle. My progress was so rapid as to enable me to exhibit at my lecture in 1891, a coil giving sparks of five inches. On that occasion I frankly told the engineers of a defect involved in the transformation by the new method, namely, the loss in the spark gap. Subsequent investigation showed that no matter what medium is employed, -be it air, hydrogen, mercury vapour, oil, or a stream of electrons, the efficiency is the same. It is a law very much like the governing of the conversion of mechanical energy. We may drop a weight from a certain height vertically down, or carry it to the lower level along any devious path; it is immaterial insofar as the amount of work is concerned. Fortunately however, this drawback is not fatal, as by proper proportioning of the resonant, circuits of an efficiency of 85 percent is attainable. Since my early announcement of the invention, it has come into universal use and wrought a revolution in many departments, but a still greater future awaits it.

When in 1900 I obtained powerful discharges of 1,000 feet and flashed a current around the globe, I was reminded of the first tiny spark I observed in my Grand Street laboratory and was thrilled by sensations akin to those I felt when I discovered the rotating magnetic field.

Chapter 5.

As I review the events of my past life I realise how subtle are the influences that shape our destinies. An incident of my youth may serve to illustrate. One winter's day I managed to climb a steep mountain, in company with other boys.

The snow was quite deep and a warm southerly wind made it just suitable for our purpose. We amused ourselves by throwing balls which would roll down a certain distance, gathering more or less snow, and we tried to outdo one another in this sport. Sud-

FIRE FROM THE SKY

denly a ball was seen to go beyond the limit, swelling to enormous proportions until it became as big as a house and plunged thundering into the valley below with a force that made the ground tremble. I looked on spellbound incapable of understanding what had happened. For weeks afterward the picture of the avalanche was before my eyes and I wondered how anything so small could grow to such an immense size.

Ever since that time the magnification of feeble actions fascinated me, and when, years later, I took up the experimental study of mechanical and electrical resonance, I was keenly interested from the very start. Possibly, had it not been for that early powerful impression I might not have followed up the little spark I obtained with my coil and never developed my best invention, the true history of which I will tell.

Many technical men, very able in their special departments, but dominated by a pedantic spirit and nearsighted, have asserted that excepting the induction motor, I have given the world little of practical use. This is a grievous mistake. A new idea must not be judged by its immediate results. My alternating system of power transmission came at a psychological moment, as a long sought answer to pressing industrial questions, and although considerable resistance had to be overcome and opposing interests reconciled, as usual, the commercial introduction could not be long delayed. Now, compare this situation with that confronting my turbines, for example. One should think that so simple and beautiful an invention, possessing many features of an ideal motor, should be adopted at once and, undoubtedly, it would under similar conditions. But the prospective effect of the rotating field was not to render worthless existing machinery; on the contrary, it was to give it additional value. The system lent itself to new enterprise as well as to improvement of the old. My turbine is an advance of a character entirely different. It is a radical departure in the sense that its success would mean the abandonment of the antiquated types of prime movers on which billions of dollars have been spent. Under such circumstances, the progress must needs be slow and perhaps the greatest impediment is encountered in the prejudicial opinions created in the minds of experts by organised opposition.

Only the other day, I had a disheartening experience when I met my friend and former assistant, Charles F. Scott, now professor of Electric Engineering at Yale. I had not seen him for a long time and was glad to have an opportunity for a little chat at my office. Our conversation, naturally enough, drifted on my turbine and I became heated to a high degree. "Scott," I exclaimed, carried away by the vision of a glorious future, "My turbine will scrap all the heat engines in the world." Scott stroked his chin and looked away

FIRE FROM THE SKY

thoughtfully, as though making a mental calculation. "That will make quite a pile of scrap," he said, and left without another word!

These and other inventions of mine, however, were nothing more than steps forward in a certain directions. In evolving them, I simply followed the inborn instinct to improve the present devices without any special thought of our far more imperative necessities. The "Magnifying Transmitter" was the product of labours extending through years, having for their chief object, the solution of problems which are infinitely more important to mankind than mere industrial development.

If my memory serves me right, it was in November, 1890, that I performed a laboratory experiment which was one of the most extraordinary and spectacular ever recorded in the annal of Science. In investigating the behaviour of high frequency currents, I had satisfied myself that an electric field of sufficient intensity could be produced in a room to light up electrodeless vacuum tubes. Accordingly, a transformer was built to test the theory and the first trial proved a marvellous success. It is difficult to appreciate what those strange phenomena meant at the time. We crave for new sensations, but soon become indifferent to them. The wonders of yesterday are today common occurrences. When my tubes were first publicly exhibited, they were viewed with amazement impossible to describe. From all parts of the world, I received urgent invitations and numerous honours and other flattering inducements were offered to me, which I declined. But in 1892 the demand became irresistible and I went to London where I delivered a lecture before the institution of Electrical Engineers.

It has been my intention to leave immediately for Paris in compliance with a similar obligation, but Sir James Dewar insisted on my appearing before the Royal Institution. I was a man of firm resolve, but succumbed easily to the forceful arguments of the great Scotchman. He pushed me into a chair and poured out half a glass of a wonderful brown fluid which sparkled in all sorts of iridescent colours and tasted like nectar. "Now," said he, "you are sitting in Faraday's chair and you are enjoying whiskey he used to drink." (Which did not interest me very much, as I had altered my opinion concerning strong drink). The next evening I have a demonstration before the Royal Institution, at the termination of which, Lord Rayleigh addressed the audience and his generous words gave me the first start in these endeavours. I fled from London and later from Paris, to escape favours showered upon me, and journeyed to my home, where I passed through a most painful ordeal and illness.

Upon regaining my health, I began to formulate plans for the resumption of work in America. Up to that time I never realised that I possessed any particular gift of discovery, but Lord Rayleigh, whom I always considered as an ideal man of science, had said so and if that was the case, I felt that I should concentrate on some big idea.

At this time, as at many other times in the past, my thoughts turned towards my Mother's teaching. The gift of mental power comes from God, Divine Being, and if we concentrate our minds on that truth, we become in tune with this great power. My Mother had taught me to seek all truth in the Bible; therefore I devoted the next few months to the study of this work.

One day, as I was roaming the mountains, I sought shelter from an approaching storm. The sky became overhung with heavy clouds, but somehow the rain was delayed until, all of a sudden, there was a lightening flash and a few moments after, a deluge. This

FIRE FROM THE SKY

observation set me thinking. It was manifest that the two phenomena were closely related, as cause and effect, and a little reflection led me to the conclusion that the electrical energy involved in the precipitation of the water was inconsiderable, the function of the lightening being much like that of a sensitive trigger. Here was a stupendous possibility of achievement.

If we could produce electric effects of the required quality, this whole planet and the conditions of existence on it could be transformed. The sun raises the water of the oceans and winds drive it to distant regions where it remains in a state of most delicate balance. If it were in our power to upset it when and wherever desired, this might life sustaining stream could be at will controlled.

We could irrigate arid deserts, create lakes and rivers, and provide motive power in unlimited amounts. This would be the most efficient way of harnessing the sun to the uses of man. The consummation depended on our ability to develop electric forces of the order of those in nature.

It seemed a hopeless undertaking, but I made up my mind to try it and immediately on my return to the United States in the summer of 1892, after a short visit to my friends in Watford, England; work was begun which was to me all the more attractive, because a means of the same kind was necessary for the successful transmission of energy without wires.

At this time I made a further careful study of the Bible, and discovered the key in Revelation. The first gratifying result was obtained in the spring of the succeeding year, when I reached a tension of about 100,000,000 volts — one hundred million volts — with my conical coil, which I figured was the voltage of a flash of lightening. Steady progress was made until the destruction of my laboratory by fire, in 1895, as may be judged from an article by T.C. Martin which appeared in the April number of the Century Magazine. This calamity set me back in many ways and most of that year had to be devoted to planning and reconstruction. However, as soon as circumstances permitted, I returned to the task.

Although I knew that higher electric-motive forces were attainable with apparatus of larger dimensions, I had an instinctive perception that the object could be accomplished by the proper design of a comparatively small and compact transformer. In carrying on tests with a secondary in the form of flat spiral, as illustrated in my patents, the absence of streamers surprised me, and it was not long before I discovered that this was due to the position of the turns and their mutual action. Profiting from this observation, I resorted to the use of a high tension conductor with turns of considerable diameter, sufficiently separated to keep down the distributed capacity, while at the same time preventing undue accumulation of the charge at any point. The application of this principle enabled me to produce pressures of over 100,000,000 volts, which was about the limit obtainable without risk of accident. A photograph of my transmitter built in my laboratory at Houston Street, was published in the Electrical Review of November, 1898.

In order to advance further along this line, I had to go into the open, and in the spring of 1899, having completed preparations for the erection of a wireless plant, I went to Colorado where I remained for more than one year. Here I introduced other improvements and refinements which made it possible to generate currents of any tension that may be desired. Those who are interested will find some information in regard to the

FIRE FROM THE SKY

experiments I conducted there in my article, "The Problem of Increasing Human Energy," in the Century Magazine of June 1900, to which I have referred on a previous occasion.

I will be quite explicit on the subject of my magnifying transformer so that it will be clearly understood. In the first place, it is a resonant transformer, with a secondary in which the parts, charged to a high potential, are of considerable area and arranged in space along ideal enveloping surfaces of very large radii of curvature, and at proper distances from one another, thereby insuring a small electric surface density everywhere, so that no leak can occur even if the conductor is bare. It is suitable for any frequency, from a few to many thousands of cycles per second, and can be used in the production of currents of tremendous volume and moderate pressure, or of smaller amperage and immense electromotive force. The maximum electric tension is merely dependent on the curvature of the surfaces on which the charged elements are situated and the area of the latter. Judging from my past experience there is no limit to the possible voltage developed; any amount is practicable. On the other hand, currents of many thousands of amperes may be obtained in the antenna. A plant of but very moderate dimensions is required for such performances. Theoretically, a terminal of less than 90 feet in diameter is sufficient to develop an electromotive force of that magnitude, while for antenna currents of from 2,000-4,000 amperes at the usual frequencies, it need not be larger than 30 feet in diameter. In a more restricted meaning, this wireless transmitter is one in which the Hertzwave radiation is an entirely negligible quantity as compared with the whole energy, under which condition the damping factor is extremely small and an enormous charge is stored in the elevated capacity. Such a circuit may then be excited with impulses of any kind, even of low frequency and it will yield sinusoidal and continuous oscillations like those of an alternator. Taken in the narrowest significance of the term, however, it is a resonant transformer which, besides possessing these qualities, is accurately proportioned to fit the globe and its electrical constants and properties, by virtue of which design it becomes highly efficient and effective in the wireless transmission of energy.

Distance is then *ABSOLUTELY ELIMINATED, THERE BEING NO DIMINUATION IN THE INTENSITY* of the transmitted impulses. It is even possible to make the actions increase with the distance from the plane, according to an exact mathematical law. This invention was one of a number comprised in my "World System" of wireless transmission which I undertook to commercialise on my return to New York. As to the immediate purposes of my enterprise, they were clearly outlined in a technical statement of that period from which I quote, "The world system has resulted from a combination of several original discoveries made by the inventor in the course of long continued research and experimentation. It makes possible not only the instantaneous and precise wireless transmission of any kind of signals, messages or characters, to all parts of the world, but also the interconnection of the existing telegraph, telephone, and other signal stations without any change in their present equipment. By its means, for instance, a telephone subscriber here may call up and talk to any other subscriber on the Earth. An inexpensive receiver, not bigger than a watch, will enable him to listen anywhere, on land or sea, to a speech delivered or music played in some other place, however distant."

These examples are cited merely to give an idea of the possibilities of this great sci-

FIRE FROM THE SKY

entific advance, which annihilates distance and makes that perfect natural conductor, the Earth, available for all the innumerable purposes which human ingenuity has found for a line-wire. One far-reaching result of this is that any device capable of being operated through one or more wires (at a distance obviously restricted) can likewise be actuated, without artificial conductors and with the same facility and accuracy, at distances to which there are no limits other than those imposed by the physical dimensions of the earth.

Thus, not only will entirely new fields for commercial exploitation be opened up by this ideal method of transmission, but the old ones vastly extended. The World System is based on the application of the following import and inventions and discoveries:

1) The Tesla Transformer: This apparatus is in the production of electrical vibrations as revolutionary as gunpowder was in warfare. Currents many times stronger than any ever generated in the usual ways and sparks over one hundred feet long, have been produced by the inventor with an instrument of this kind.

2) The Magnifying Transmitter: This is Tesla's best invention, a peculiar transformer specially adapted to excite the earth, which is in the transmission of electrical energy when the telescope is in astronomical observation. By the use of this marvellous device, he has already set up electrical movements of greater intensity than those of lightening and passed a current, sufficient to light more than two hundred incandescent lamps, around the Earth.

3) The Tesla Wireless System: This system comprises a number of improvements and is the only means known for transmitting economically electrical energy to a distance without wires. Careful tests and measurements in connection with an experimental station of great activity, erected by the inventor in Colorado, have demonstrated that power in any desired amount can be conveyed, clear across the Globe if necessary, with a loss not exceeding a few per cent.

4) The Art of Individualisation: This invention of Tesla is to primitive Tuning, what refined language is to unarticulated expression. It makes possible the transmission of signals or messages absolutely secret and exclusive both in the active and passive aspect, that is, non-interfering as well as non-interferable.

Each signal is like an individual of unmistakable identity and there is virtually no limit to the number of stations or instruments which can be simultaneously operated without the slightest mutual disturbance.

5) The Terrestrial Stationary Waves: This wonderful discovery, popularly explained, means that the Earth is responsive to electrical vibrations of definite pitch, just as a tuning fork to certain waves of sound. These particular electrical vibrations, capable of powerfully exciting the Globe, lend themselves to innumerable uses of great importance commercially and in many other respects. The "first World System" power plant can be put in operation in nine months. With this power plant, it will be practicable to attain electrical activities up to ten million horsepower and it is designed to serve for as many technical achievements as are possible without due expense. Among these are the following:

1) The interconnection of existing telegraph exchanges or offices all over the world;
2) The establishment of a secret and non-interferable government telegraph service;
3) The interconnection of all present telephone exchanges or offices around the Globe;

FIRE FROM THE SKY

4) The universal distribution of general news by telegraph or telephone, in conjunction with the Press;

5) The establishment of such a "World System" of intelligence transmission for exclusive private use;

6) The interconnection and operation of all stock tickers of the world;

7) The establishment of a World system — of musical distribution, etc.;

8) The universal registration of time by cheap clocks indicating the hour with astronomical precision and requiring no attention whatever;

9) The world transmission of typed or handwritten characters, letters, checks, etc.;

10) The establishment of a universal marine service enabling the navigators of all ships to steer perfectly without compass, to determine the exact location, hour and speak; to prevent collisions and disasters, etc.;

11) The inauguration of a system of world printing on land and sea;

12) The world reproduction of photographic pictures and all kinds of drawings or records..."

I also proposed to make demonstration in the wireless transmission of power on a small scale, but sufficient to carry conviction. Besides these, I referred to other and incomparably more important applications of my discoveries which will be disclosed at some future date. A plant was built on Long Island with a tower 187 feet high, having a spherical terminal about 68 feet in diameter. These dimensions were adequate for the transmission of virtually any amount of energy.

Originally, only from 200 to 300 K.W. were provided, but I intended to employ later several thousand horsepower. The transmitter was to emit a wave-complex of special characteristics and I had devised a unique method of telephonic control of any amount of energy. The tower was destroyed two years ago (1917) but my projects are being developed and another one, improved in some features will be constructed.

On this occasion I would contradict the widely circulated report that the structure was demolished by the Government, which owing to war conditions, might have created prejudice in the minds of those who may not know that the papers, which thirty years ago conferred upon me the honour of American citizenship, are always kept in a safe, while my orders, diplomas, degrees, gold medals and other distinctions are packed away in old trunks. If this report had a foundation, I would have been refunded a large sum of money which I expended in the construction of the tower. On the contrary, it was in the interest of the Government to preserver it, particularly as it would have made possible, to mention just one valuable result, the location of a submarine in any part of the world. My plant, services, and all my improvements have always been at the disposal of the officials and ever since the outbreak of the European conflict, I have been working at a sacrifice on several inventions of mine relating to aerial navigation, ship propulsion and wireless transmission, which are of the greatest importance to the country. Those who are well informed know that my ideas have revolutionised the industries of the United States and I am not aware that there lives an inventor who has been, in this respect, as fortunate as myself, — especially as regards the use of his improvements in the war.

I have refrained from publicly expressing myself on this subject before, as it seemed improper to dwell on personal matters while all the world was in dire trouble. I would add further, in view of various rumours which have reached me, that Mr. J. Pierpont Morgan did not interest himself with me in a business way, but in the same large spirit in which he has assisted many other pioneers. He carried out his generous promise to the letter and it would have been most unreasonable to expect from him anything more. He had the highest regard for my attainments and gave me every evidence of his complete faith in my ability to ultimately achieve what I had set out to do. I am unwilling to accord to some small-minded and jealous individuals the satisfaction of having thwarted my efforts. These men are to me nothing more than microbes of a nasty disease. My project was retarded by laws of nature. The world was not prepared for it. It was too far ahead of time, but the same laws will prevail in the end and make it a triumphal success.

Chapter 6.

No subject to which I have ever devoted myself has called for such concentration of mind, and strained to so dangerous a degree the finest fibres of my brain, as the systems of which the Magnifying transmitter is the foundation. I put all the intensity and vigour of youth in the development of the rotating field discoveries, but those early labours were of a different character. Although strenuous in the extreme, they did not involve that keen and exhausting discernment which had to be exercised in attacking the many prob-

FIRE FROM THE SKY

lems of the wireless.

Despite my rare physical endurance at that period, the abused nerves finally rebelled and I suffered a complete collapse, just as the consummation of the long and difficult task was almost in sight. Without doubt I would have paid a greater penalty later, and very likely my career would have been prematurely terminated, had not providence equipped me with a safety device, which seemed to improve with advancing years and unfailingly comes to play when my forces are at an end. So long as it operates I am safe from danger, due to overwork, which threatens other inventors, and incidentally, I need no vacations which are indispensable to most people. When I am all but used up, I simply do as the darkies who "naturally fall asleep while white folks worry."

To venture a theory out of my sphere, the body probably accumulates little by little a definite quantity of some toxic agent and I sink into a nearly lethargic state which lasts half an hour to the minute. Upon awakening I have the sensation as though the events immediately preceding had occurred very long ago, and if I attempt to continue the interrupted train of thought I feel veritable nausea. Involuntarily, I then turn to other and am surprised at the freshness of the mind and ease with which I overcome obstacles that had baffled me before. After weeks or months, my passion for the temporarily abandoned invention returns and I invariably find answers to all the vexing questions, with scarcely any effort. In this connection, I will tell of an extraordinary experience which may be of interest to students of psychology.

I had produced a striking phenomenon with my grounded transmitter and was endeavouring to ascertain its true significance in relation to the currents propagated through the earth. It seemed a hopeless undertaking, and for more than a year I worked unremittingly, but in vain. This profound study so entirely absorbed me, that I became forgetful of everything else, even of my undermined health. At last, as I was at the point of breaking down, nature applied the preservative inducing lethal sleep. Regaining my senses, I realised with consternation that I was unable to visualise scenes from my life except those of infancy, the very first ones that had entered my consciousness. Curiously enough, these appeared before my vision with startling distinctness and afforded me welcome relief. Night after night, when retiring, I would think of them and more and more of my previous existence was revealed. The image of my mother was always the principal figure in the spectacle that slowly unfolded, and a consuming desire to see her again gradually took possession of me. This feeling grew so strong that I resolved to drop all work and satisfy my longing, but I found it too hard to break away from the laboratory, and

FIRE FROM THE SKY

several months elapsed during which I had succeeded in reviving all the impressions of my past life, up to the spring of 1892. In the next picture that came out of the mist of oblivion, I saw myself at the Hotel de la Paix in Paris, just coming to from one of my peculiar sleeping spells, which had been caused by prolonged exertion of the brain. Imagine the pain and distress I felt, when it flashed upon my mind that a dispatch was handed to me at that very moment, bearing the sad news that my mother was dying. I remembered how I made the long journey home without an hour of rest and how she passed away after weeks of agony.

It was especially remarkable that during all this period of partially obliterated memory, I was fully alive to everything touching on the subject of my research. I could recall the smallest detail and the least insignificant observations in my experiments and even recite pages of text and complex mathematical formulae.

My belief is firm in a law of compensation. The true rewards are ever in proportion to the labour and sacrifices made. This is one of the reasons why I feel certain that of all my inventions, the magnifying Transmitter will prove most important and valuable to future generations. I am prompted to this prediction, not so much by thoughts of the commercial and industrial revolution which it will surely bring about, but of the humanitation consequences of the many achievements it makes possible. Considerations of mere utility weigh little in the balance against the higher benefits of civilisation. We are confronted with portentous problems which can not be solved just by providing for our material existence, however abundantly. On the contrary, progress in this direction is fraught with hazards and perils not less menacing than those born from want and suffering. If we were to release the energy of atoms or discover some other way of developing cheap and unlimited power at any point on the globe, this accomplishment, instead of being a blessing, might bring disaster to mankind in giving rise to dissension and anarchy, which would ultimately result in the enthronement of the hated regime of force. The greatest good will come from technical improvements tending to unification and harmony, and my wireless transmitter is preeminently such. By its means, the human voice and likeness will be reproduced everywhere and factories driven thousands of miles from waterfalls furnishing power. Aerial machines will be propelled around the earth without a stop and the sun's energy controlled to create lakes and rivers for motive purposes and transformation of arid deserts into fertile land. Its introduction for telegraphic, telephonic and similar uses, will automatically cut out the statics and all other interferences which at present, impose narrow limits to the application of the wireless. This is a timely topic on which a few words might not be amiss.

During the past decade a number of people have arrogantly claimed that they had succeeded in doing away with this impediment. I have carefully examined all of the arrangements described and tested most of them long before they were publicly disclosed, but the finding was uniformly negative. Recent official statement from the U.S. Navy may, perhaps, have taught some beguilable news editors how to appraise these announcements at their real worth. As a rule, the attempts are based on theories so fallacious, that whenever they come to my notice, I can not help thinking in a light vein. Quite recently a new discovery was heralded, with a deafening flourish of trumpets, but it proved another case of a mountain bringing forth a mouse. This reminds me of an exciting incident which took place a year ago, when I was conducting my experiments with currents of

FIRE FROM THE SKY

high frequency.

Steve Brodie had just jumped off the Brooklyn Bridge. The feat has been vulgarised since by imitators, but the first report electrified New York. I was very impressionable then and frequently spoke of the daring printer. On a hot afternoon I felt the necessity of refreshing myself and stepped into one of the popular thirty thousand institutions of this great city, where a delicious twelve per cent beverage was served, which can now be had only by making a trip to the poor and devastated countries of Europe. The attendance was large and not over-distinguished and a matter was discussed which gave me an admirable opening for the careless remark, "This is what I said when I jumped off the bridge." No sooner had I uttered these words, than I felt like the companion of Timothens, in the poem of Schiller. In an instant there was pandemonium and a dozen voices cried, "It is Brodie!" I threw a quarter on the counter and bolted for the door, but the crowd was at my heels with yells, - "Stop, Steeve!", which must have been misunderstood, for many persons tried to hold me up as I ran frantically for my haven of refuge. By darting around corners I fortunately managed, through the medium of a fire escape, to reach the laboratory, where I threw off my coat, camouflaged myself as a hard-working blacksmith and started the forge. But these precautions proved unnecessary, as I had eluded my pursuers. For many years afterward, at night, when imagination turns into spectres the trifling troubles of the day, I often thought, as I tossed on the bed, what my fate would have been, had the mob caught me and found out that I was not Steve Brodie!

Now the engineer who lately gave an account before a technical body of a novel remedy against statics based on a "heretofore unknown law of nature," seems to have been as reckless as myself when he contended that these disturbances propagate up and down, while those of a transmitter proceed along the earth. It would mean that a condenser as this globe, with its gaseous envelope, could be charged and discharged in a manner quite contrary to the fundamental teachings propounded in every elemental text book of physics. Such a supposition would have been condemned as erroneous, even in Franklin's time, for the facts bearing on this were then well known and the identity between atmospheric electricity and that developed by machines was fully established. Obviously, natural and artificial disturbances propagate through the earth and the air in exactly the same way, and both set up electromotive forces in the horizontal, as well as vertical sense. Interference can not be overcome by any such methods as were proposed. The truth is this: In the air the potential increases at the rate of about fifty volts per foot of elevation, owing to which there may be a difference of pressure amounting to twenty, or even forty thousand volts between the upper and lower ends of the antenna. The masses of the charged atmosphere are constantly in motion and give up electricity to the conductor, not continuously, but rather disruptively, this producing a grinding noise in a sensitive telephonic receiver. The higher the terminal and the greater the space encompast by the wires, the more pronounced is the effect, but it must be understood that it is purely local and has little to do with the real trouble.

In 1900, while perfecting my wireless system, one form of apparatus compressed four antennae. These were carefully calibrated in the same frequency and connected in multiple with the object of magnifying the action in receiving from any direction. When I desired to ascertain the origin of the transmitted impulse, each diagonally situated pair was put in series with a primary coil energising the detector circuit. In the former case,

FIRE FROM THE SKY

the sound was loud in the telephone; in the latter it ceased, as expected, - the two antennae neutralising each other, but the true statics manifested themselves in both instances and I had to devise special preventives embodying different principles. By employing receivers connected to two points of the ground, as suggested by me long ago, this trouble caused by the charged air, which is very serious in the structures as now built, is nullified and besides, the liability of all kinds of interference is reduced to about one-half because of the directional character of the circuit. This was perfectly self-evident, but came as a revelation to some simple-minded wireless folks whose experience was confined to forms of apparatus that could have been improved with an axe, and they have been disposing of the bear's skin before killing him. If it were true that strays performed such antics, it would be easy to get rid of them by receiving without aerials. But, as a matter of fact, a wire buried in the ground which, conforming to this view, should be absolutely immune, is more susceptible to certain extraneous impulses than one placed vertically in the air. To state it fairly, a slight progress has been made, but not by virtue of any particular method or device. It was achieved simply by discerning the enormous structures, which are bad enough for transmission but wholly unsuitable for reception and adopting a more appropriate type of receiver. As I have said before, to dispose of this difficulty for good, a radical change must be made in the system and the sooner this is done the better.

It would be calamitous, indeed, if at this time when the art is in its infancy and the vast majority, not excepting even experts, have no conception of its ultimate possibilities, a measure would be rushed through the legislature making it a government monopoly. This was proposed a few weeks ago by Secretary Daniels and no doubt that distinguished official has made his appeal to the Senate and House of Representatives with sincere conviction. But universal evidence unmistakably shows that the best results are always obtained in healthful commercial competition. There are, however, exceptional reasons why wireless should be given the fullest freedom of development. In the first place, it offers prospects immeasurably greater and more vital to betterment of human life than any other invention or discovery in the history of man. Then again, it must be understood that this wonderful art has been, in its entirety, evolved here and can be called "American" with more right and propriety than the telephone, the incandescent lamp or the aeroplane.

Enterprising press agents and stock jobbers have been so successful in spreading misinformation, that even so excellent a periodical as the *Scientific American*, accords the chief credit to a foreign country. The Germans, of course, gave us the Hertz waves and the Russian, English, French and Italian experts were quick in using them for signalling purposes. It was an obvious application of the new agent and accomplished with the old classical and unimproved induction coil, scarcely anything more than another kind of heliography. The radius of transmission was very limited, the result attained of little value, and the Hertz oscillations, as a means for conveying intelligence, could have been advantageously replaced by sound waves, which I advocated in 1891. Moreover, all of these attempts were made three years after the basic principles of the wireless system, which is universally employed today, and its potent instrumentalities had been clearly described and developed in America.

No trace of those Hertzian appliances and methods remains today. We have proceeded

FIRE FROM THE SKY

in the very opposite direction and what has been done is the product of the brains and efforts of citizens of this country. The fundamental patents have expired and the opportunities are open to all. The chief argument of the Secretary is based on interference. According to his statement, reported in the New York Herald of July 29th, signals from a powerful station can be intercepted in every village in the world. In view of this fact, which was demonstrated in my experiments in 1900, it would be of little use to impose restrictions in the United States.

As throwing light on this point, I may mention that only recently an odd looking gentleman called on me with the object of enlisting my services in the construction of world transmitters in some distant land. "We have no money," he said, "but carloads of solid gold, and we will give you a liberal amount." I told him that I wanted to see first what will be done with my inventions in America, and this ended the interview. But I am satisfied that some dark forces are at work, and as time goes on the maintenance of continuous communication will be rendered more difficult. The only remedy is a system immune against interruption. It has been perfected, it exists, and all that is necessary is to put it in operation.

The terrible conflict is still uppermost in the minds and perhaps the greatest importance will be attached to the magnifying Transmitter as a machine for attack and defence, more particularly in connection with TELAUTAMATICS. This invention is a logical outcome of observations begun in my boyhood and continued throughout my life. When the first results were published, the Electrical Review stated editorially that it would become one of the "most potent factors in the advance of civilisation of mankind." The time is not distant when this prediction will be fulfilled. In 1898 and 1900, it was offered by me to the Government and might have been adopted, were I one of those who would go to Alexander's shepherd when they want a favour from Alexander!

At that time I really thought that it would abolish war, because of its unlimited destructiveness and exclusion of the personal element of combat. But while I have not lost faith in its potentialities, my views have changed since.

War can not be avoided until the physical cause for its recurrence is removed and this, in the last analysis, is the vast extent of the planet on which we live. Only though annihilation of distance in every respect, as the conveyance of intelligence, transport of passengers and supplies and transmission of energy will conditions be brought about some day, insuring permanency of friendly relations. What we now want most is closer contact and better understanding between individuals and communities all over the earth and the elimination of that fanatic devotion to exalted ideals of national egoism and pride, which is always prone to plunge the world into primeval barbarism and strife. No league or parliamentary act of any kind will ever prevent such a calamity. These are only new devices for putting the weak at the mercy of the strong.

I have expressed myself in this regard fourteen years ago, when a combination of a few leading governments, a sort of Holy alliance, was advocated by the late Andrew Carnegie, who may be fairly considered as the father of this idea, having given to it more publicity and impetus than anybody else prior to the efforts of the President. While it can not be denied that such aspects might be of material advantage to some less fortunate peoples, it can not attain the chief objective sought. Peace can only come as a natural consequence of universal enlightenment and merging of races, and we are still far

FIRE FROM THE SKY

from this blissful realisation, because few indeed, will admit the reality - that God made man in His image - in which case all earth men are alike. There is in fact but one race, of many colours. Christ is but one person, yet he is of all people, so why do some people think themselves better than some other people?

As I view the world of today, in the light of the gigantic struggle we have witnessed, I am filled with conviction that the interests of humanity would be best served if the United States remained true to its traditions, true to God whom it pretends to believe, and kept out of "entangling alliances." Situated as it is, geographically remote from the theatres of impending conflicts, without incentive to territorial aggrandisement, with inexhaustible resources and immense population thoroughly imbued with the spirit of liberty and right, this country is placed in a unique and privileged position. It is thus able to exert, independently, its colossal strength and moral force to the benefit of all, more judiciously and effectively, than as a member of a league.

I have dwelt on the circumstances of my early life and told of an affliction which compelled me to unremitting exercise of imagination and self-observation.

This mental activity, at first involuntary under the pressure of illness and suffering, gradually became second nature and led me finally to recognise that I was but an automaton devoid of free will in thought and action and merely responsible to the forces of the environment. Our bodies are of such complexity of structure, the motions we perform are so numerous and involved and the external impressions on our sense organs to such a degree delicate and elusive, that it is hard for the average person to grasp this fact. Yet nothing is more convincing to the trained investigator than the mechanistic theory of life which had been, in a measure, understood and propounded by Descartes three hundred years ago. In his time many important functions of our organisms were unknown and especially with respect to the nature of light and the construction and operation of the eye, philosophers were in the dark.

In recent years the progress of scientific research in these fields has been such as to leave no room for a doubt in regard to this view on which many works have been published. One of its ablest and most eloquent exponents is, perhaps, Felix le Dantec, formerly assistant of Pasteur. Professor Jacques Loeb has performed remarkable experiments in heliotropism, clearly establishing the controlling power of light in lower forms of organisms and his latest book, "Forced Movements," is revelatory. But while men of science accept this theory simply as any other that is recognised, to me it is a truth which I hourly demonstrate by every act and thought of mine. The consciousness of the external impression prompting me to any kind of exertion, - physical or mental, is ever present in my mind. Only on very rare occasions, when I was in a state of exceptional concentration, have I found difficulty in locating the original impulse. The by far greater number of human beings are never aware of what is passing around and within them and millions fall victims of disease and die prematurely just on this account. The commonest, everyday occurrences appear to them mysterious and inexplicable. One may feel a sudden wave of sadness and rack his brain for an explanation, when he might have noticed that it was caused by a cloud cutting off the rays of the sun. He may see the image of a friend dear to him under conditions which he construes as very peculiar, when only shortly before he has passed him in the street or seen his photograph somewhere. When he loses a collar button, he fusses and swears for an hour, being unable to visualise his

FIRE FROM THE SKY

previous actions and locate the object directly. Deficient observation is merely a form of ignorance and responsible for the many morbid notions and foolish ideas prevailing. There is not more than one out of every ten persons who does not believe in telepathy and other psychic manifestations, spiritualism and communion with the dead, and who would refuse to listen to willing or unwilling deceivers?

Just to illustrate how deeply rooted this tendency has become even among the clearheaded American population, I may mention a comical incident. Shortly before the war, when the exhibition of my turbines in this city elicited widespread comment in the technical papers, I anticipated that there would be a scramble among manufacturers to get hold of the invention and I had particular designs on that man from Detroit who has an uncanny faculty for accumulating millions. So confident was I, that he would turn up some day, that I declared this as certain to my secretary and assistants. Sure enough, one fine morning a body of engineers from the Ford Motor Company presented themselves with the request of discussing with me an important project. "Didn't I tell you?," I remarked triumphantly to my employees, and one of them said, "You are amazing, Mr. Tesla. Everything comes out exactly as you predict."

As soon as these hardheaded men were seated, I of course, immediately began to extol the wonderful features of my turbine, when the spokesman interrupted me and said, "We know all about this, but we are on a special errand. We have formed a psychological society for the investigation of psychic phenomena and we want you to join us in this undertaking." I suppose these engineers never knew how near they came to being fired out of my office.

Ever since I was told by some of the greatest men of the time, leaders in science whose names are immortal, that I am possessed of an unusual mind, I bent all my thinking faculties on the solution of great problems regardless of sacrifice. For many years I endeavoured to solve the enigma of death, and watched eagerly for every kind of spiritual indication. But only once in the course of my existence have I had an experience which momentarily impressed me as supernatural. It was at the time of my mother's death.

I had become completely exhausted by pain and long vigilance, and one night was carried to a building about two blocks from our home. As I lay helpless there, I thought that if my mother died while I was away from her bedside, she would surely give me a sign. Two or three months before, I was in London in company with my late friend, Sir William Crookes, when spiritualism was discussed and I was under the full sway of these thoughts. I might not have paid attention to other men, but was susceptible to his arguments as it was his epochal work on radiant matter, which I had read as a student, that made me embrace the electrical career. I reflected that the conditions for a look into the beyond were most favourable, for my mother was a woman of genius and particularly excelling in the powers of intuition. During the whole night every fibre in my brain was strained in expectancy, but nothing happened until early in the morning, when I fell in a sleep, or perhaps a swoon, and saw a cloud carrying angelic figures of marvellous beauty, one of whom gazed upon me lovingly and gradually assumed the features of my mother. The appearance slowly floated across the room and vanished, and I was awakened by an indescribably sweet song of many voices. In that instant a certitude, which no words can express, came upon me that my mother had just died. And that was true. I was unable to understand the tremendous weight of the painful knowledge I received in advance, and wrote a letter to Sir William Crookes while still under the domination of these impressions and in poor bodily health. When I recovered, I sought for a long time the external cause of this strange manifestation and, to my great relief, I succeeded after many months of fruitless effort.

I had seen the painting of a celebrated artist, representing allegorically one of the seasons in the form of a cloud with a group of angels which seemed to actually float in the air, and this had struck me forcefully. It was exactly the same that appeared in my dream, with the exception of my mother's likeness. The music came from the choir in the church nearby at the early mass of Easter morning, explaining everything satisfactorily in conformity with scientific facts.

This occurred long ago, and I have never had the faintest reason since to change my views on psychical and spiritual phenomena, for which there is no foundation. The belief in these is the natural outgrowth of intellectual development. Religious dogmas are no longer accepted in their orthodox meaning, but every individual clings to faith in a supreme power of some kind.

We all must have an ideal to govern our conduct and insure contentment, but it is immaterial whether it be one of creed, art, science, or anything else, so long as it fulfils the function of a dematerialising force. It is essential to the peaceful existence of humanity as a whole that one common conception should prevail. While I have failed to obtain any evidence in support of the contentions of psychologists and spiritualists, I have proved to my complete satisfaction the automatism of life, not only through continuous observations of individual actions, but even more conclusively through certain generalisations. These amount to a discovery which I consider of the greatest moment to human society, and on which I shall briefly dwell.

I got the first inkling of this astonishing truth when I was still a very young man, but for many years I interpreted what I noted simply as coincidences.

Namely, whenever either myself or a person to whom I was attached, or a cause to which I was devoted, was hurt by others in a particular way, which might be best popularly characterised as the most unfair imaginable, I experienced a singular and undefinable pain which, for the want of a better term, I have qualified as "cosmic" and shortly thereafter, and invariably, those who had inflicted it came to grief. After many such cases I confided this to a number of friends, who had the opportunity to convince themselves of the theory of which I have gradually formulated and which may be stated in the following few words: Our bodies are of

similar construction and exposed to the same external forces. This results in likeness of response and concordance of the general activities on which all our social and other rules and laws are based. We are automata entirely controlled by the forces of the medium, being tossed about like corks on the surface of the water, but mistaking the resultant of the impulses from the outside for the free will. The movements and other actions we perform are always life preservative and though seemingly quite independent from one another, we are connected by invisible links. So long as the organism is in perfect order, it responds accurately to the agents that prompt it, but the moment that there is some derangement in any individual, his self-preservative power is impaired.

Everybody understands, of course, that if one becomes deaf, has his eyes weakened, or his limbs injured, the chances for his continued existence are lessened. But this is also true, and perhaps more so, of certain defects in the brain which drive the automaton, more or less, of that vital quality and cause it to rush into destruction. A very sensitive and observant being, with his highly developed mechanism all intact, and acting with precision in obedience to the changing conditions of the environment, is endowed with a transcending mechanical sense, enabling him to evade perils too subtle to be directly perceived. When he comes in contact with others whose controlling organs are radically faulty, that sense asserts itself and he feels the "cosmic" pain.

The truth of this has been borne out in hundreds of instances and I am inviting other students of nature to devote attention to this subject, believing that through combined systematic effort, results of incalculable value to the world will be attained. The idea of constructing an automaton, to bear out my theory, presented itself to me early, but I did not begin active work until 1895, when I started my wireless investigations. During the succeeding two or three years, a number of automatic mechanisms, to be actuated from a distance, were constructed by me and exhibited to visitors in my laboratory.

In 1896, however, I designed a complete machine capable of a multitude of operations, but the consummation of my labours was delayed until late in 1897.

This machine was illustrated and described in my article in the Century Magazine of June, 1900; and other periodicals of that time and when first shown in the beginning of 1898, it created a sensation such as no other invention of mine has ever produced. In November, 1898, a basic patent on the novel art was granted to me, but only after the Examiner-in-Chief had come to New York and witnessed the performance, for what I claimed seemed unbelievable. I remember that when later I called on an official in Washington, with a view of offering the invention to the Government, he burst out in laughter upon my telling him what I had accomplished. Nobody thought then that there was the faintest prospect of perfecting such a device. It is unfortunate that in this patent, following the advice of my attorneys, I indicated the control as being affected through the medium of a single circuit and a well-known form of detector, for the reason that I had not yet secured protection on my methods and apparatus for individualisation. As a matter of fact, my boats were controlled through the joint action of several circuits and interference of every kind was excluded.

Most generally, I employed receiving circuits in the form of loops, including condensers, because the discharges of my high-tension transmitter ionised the air in the (laboratory) so that even a very small aerial would draw electricity from the surrounding atmosphere for hours.

Just to give an idea, I found, for instance, that a bulb twelve inches in diameter, highly exhausted, and with one single terminal to which a short wire was attached, would deliver well on to one thousand successive flashes before all charge of the air in the laboratory was neutralised. The loop form of receiver was not sensitive to such a disturbance and it is curious to note that it is becoming popular at this late date. In reality, it collects much less energy than the aerials or a long grounded wire, but it so happens that it does away with a number of defects inherent to the present wireless devices.

In demonstrating my invention before audiences, the visitors were requested to ask questions, however involved, and the automaton would answer them by signs.

This was considered magic at the time, but was extremely simple, for it was myself who gave the replies by means of the device.

FIRE FROM THE SKY

At the same period, another larger telautomatic boat was constructed, a photograph of which was shown in the October 1919 number of the Electrical Experimenter. It was controlled by loops, having several turns placed in the hull, which was made entirely watertight and capable of submergence. The apparatus was similar to that used in the first with the exception of certain special features I introduced as, for example, incandescent lamps which afforded a visible evidence of the proper functioning of the machine. These automata, controlled within the range of vision of the operator, were, however, the first and rather crude steps in the evolution of the art of Telautomatics as I had conceived it.

The next logical improvement was its application to automatic mechanisms beyond the limits of vision and at great distances from the centre of control, and I have ever since advocated their employment as instruments of warfare in preference to guns. The importance of this now seems to be recognised, if I am to judge from casual announcements through the press, of achievements which are said to be extraordinary but contain no merit of novelty, whatever. In an imperfect manner it is practicable, with the existing wireless plants, to launch an aeroplane, have it follow a certain approximate course, and perform some operation at a distance of many hundreds of miles. A machine of this kind can also be mechanically controlled in several ways and I have no doubt that it may prove of some usefulness in war. But there are to my best knowledge, no instrumentalities in existence today with which such an object could be accomplished in a precise manner. I have devoted years of study to this matter and have evolved means, making such and greater wonders easily realisable.

As stated on a previous occasion, when I was a student at college I conceived a flying machine quite unlike the present ones. The underlying principle was sound, but could not be carried into practice for want of a prime-mover of sufficiently great activity. In recent years, I have successfully solved this problem and am now planning aerial machines *devoid of sustaining planes, ailerons, propellers, and other external attachments*, which will be capable of immense speeds and are very likely to furnish powerful arguments for peace in the near future. Such a machine, sustained and propelled *entirely by reaction*, is shown on one of the pages of my lectures, and is supposed to be controlled either mechanically, or by wireless energy. By installing proper plants, it will be practicable to "project a missile of this kind into the air and drop it" almost on the very spot designated, which may be thousands of miles away.

But we're not going to stop at this. Telautomats will ultimately be produced capable of acting as if possessed of their own intelligence, and their advent will create a revolution. As early as 1898, I proposed to representatives of a large manufacturing concern the construction and public exhibition of an automobile carriage which, left to itself, would perform a great variety of operations involving something akin to judgement. But my proposal was deemed chimerical at the time and nothing came of it.

At present, many of the ablest minds are trying to devise expedients for preventing a repetition of the awful conflict which is only theoretically ended and the duration and main issues of which I have correctly predicted in an article printed in the Sun of December 20, 1914. The proposed League is not a remedy but, on the contrary, in the opinion of a number of competent men, may bring about results just the opposite.

It is particularly regrettable that a punitive policy was adopted in framing the terms of peace, because a few years hence, it will be possible for nations to fight without armies, ships or guns, by weapons far more terrible, to the destructive action and range of which there is virtually no limit.

Any city, at a distance, whatsoever, from the enemy, can be destroyed by him and no power on earth can stop him from doing so. If we want to avert an impending calamity and a state of things which may transform the globe into an inferno, we should push the development of flying machines and wireless transmission of energy without an instant's delay and with all the power and resources of the nation.

A NEW HYPOTHESIS OF ALIEN ABDUCTION
by Martin Cannon

Section I. Introduction
Section II. The Technology
Section III. Applications
Section IV. Abductions

FIRE FROM THE SKY

I. Introduction
One wag has dubbed the problem "Terra and the Pirates."
The pirates, ostensibly, are marauders from another solar system; their victims include a growing number of troubled human beings who insist that they've been shanghaied by these otherworldly visitors. An outlandish scenario - yet through the works of such authors as Budd Hopkins[1] and Whitley Strieber,[2] the "alien abduction" syndrome has seized the public imagination. Indeed, tales of UFO contact threaten to lapse into fashionability, even though, as I have elsewhere noted,[3] they may still inflict a formidable social price upon the claimant.

Some time ago, I began to research these claims, concentrating my studies on the social and political environment surrounding these events. As I studied, the project grew and its scope widened. Indeed, I began to feel as though I'd gone digging through familiar terrain only to unearth Gomorrah.

These excavations may have disgorged a solution.

The Problem
Among ufologists, the term "abduction" has come to refer to an infinitely confounding experience, or matrix of experiences, shared by a dizzying number of individuals, who claim that travellers from the stars have scooped them out of their beds, or snatched them from their cars, and subjected them to interrogations, quasi-medical examinations, and "instruction" periods.

Usually, these sessions are said to occur within alien spacecraft; frequently, the stories include terrifying details reminiscent of the tortures inflicted in Germany's death camps. The abductees often (though not always) lose all memory of these events; they find themselves back in their cars or beds, unable to account for hours of "missing time." Hypnosis, or some other trigger, can bring back these haunted hours in an explosion of recollection - and as the smoke clears, an abductee will often spot a trail of similar experiences, stretching all the way back to childhood.

Perhaps the oddest fact of these odd tales: Many abductees, for all their vividly-recollected agonies, claim to love their alien tormentors. That's the word I've heard repeatedly: love.

Within the community of "scientific ufologists" - those lonely, all too little-heard advocates of reasonable and open-minded debate on matters saucerological - these claims have elicited cautious interest and a commendable restraint from conclusion-hopping.

FIRE FROM THE SKY

Outside the higher realms of scientific ufology, the situation is, alas, quite different. In the popular press, in both the "straight" and sensationalist media, within that journalistic realm where issues are defined and public opinion solidified (despite a frequently superficial approach to matters of evidence and investigation) abduction scenarios have elicited two basic reactions: that of the Believer and the Skeptic.

The Believers - and here we should note that "Believers" and "abductees" are two groups whose memberships overlap but are in no way congruent - accept such stories at face value. They accept, despite the seeming absurdity of these tales, the internal contradictions, the askew logic of narrative construction, the severe discontinuity of emotional response to the actions described. The Believers believe, despite reports that their beloved "space brothers" use vile and inhuman tactics of medical examination - senseless procedures most of us (and certainly the vanguard of an advanced race) would be ashamed to inflict on an animal. The Believers believe, despite the difficulty of reconciling these unsettling tales with their own deliriums of benevolent off-worlders.

Occasionally, the rough notes of a rationalization are offered: "The aliens don't know what they are doing," we hear; or "Some aliens are bad." Yet the Believers confound their own reasoning when they insist on ascribing the wisdom of the ages and the beneficence of the angels to their beloved visitors. The aliens allegedly know enough about our society to go about their business undetected by the local authorities and the general public; they communicate with the abductees in human tongue; they concern themselves with details of the percipients' innermost lives - yet they remain so ignorant of our culture as to be unaware of the basic moral precepts concerning the dignity of the individual and the right to self-determination. Such dichotomies don't bother the Believers; they are the faithful, and faith is assumed to have its mysteries.

Sancta Simplicitas

Conversely, the Skeptics dismiss these stories out of hand. They dismiss, despite the intriguing confirmatory details: the multiple witness events, the physical traces left by the ufonauts, the scars and implants left on the abductees. The skeptics scoff, though the abductees tell stories similar in detail - even certain tiny details, not known to the general public.

Philip Klass is a debunker who, through his appearances on such television programs as NOVA and NIGHTLINE, has been in a position to affect much of the public debate on UFOs. In his interesting but poorly-documented work on abductions,4 Klass claims that "abduction" is a psychological disease, spread by those who write about it. This argument exactly resembles the professional press-basher's frequent assertion that terrorism metastasizes through media exposure. Yet for all the millions of words expectorated by newsfolk on the subject of terrorism, terrorist actions remain quite rare, as any statistician (though few politicians) will admit, and verifiable linkage between crimes and their coverage remains to be found. For that matter, there have been books - bestsellers, even - on unicorns and gnomes. People who claim to see those creatures are few. Abductees are plentiful.

Both Believer and Skeptic, in my opinion, miss the real story. Both make the same mistake: They connect the abduction phenomenon to the forty-year history of UFO sightings, and they apply their prejudices about the latter to the controversy about the former.

FIRE FROM THE SKY

At first sight, the link seems natural. Shouldn't our thoughts about UFOs color our thoughts about UFO abductions?

No.

They may well be separate issues. Or, rather, they are connected only in this: The myth of the UFO has provided an effective cover story for an entirely different sort of mystery. Remove yourself from the Believer/Skeptic dialectic, and you will see the third alternative.

As we examine this alternative, we will, of necessity, stray far from the saucers. We must turn our face from the paranormal and concentrate on the occult - if, by "occult," we mean secret.

I posit that the abductees have been abducted. Yet they are also spewing fantasy - or, more precisely, they have been given a set of lies to repeat and believe. If my hypothesis proves true, then we must accept the following: The kidnapping is real. The fear is real. The pain is real. The instruction is real. But the little grey men from Zeti Reticuli are not real; they are constructs, Halloween masks meant to disguise the real faces of the controllers. The abductors may not be visitors from Beyond; rather, they may be a symptom of the carcinoma which blackens our body politic.

The fault lies not in our stars, but in ourselves.

The Hypothesis

Substantial evidence exists linking members of this country's intelligence community (including the Central Intelligence Agency, the Defense Advanvced Research Projects Agency, and the Office of Naval Intelligence) with the esoteric technology of mind control. For decades, "spy-chiatrists" working behind the scenes - on college campuses, in CIA-sponsored institutes, and (most heinously) in prisons - have experimented with the erasure of memory, hypnotic resistance to torture, truth serums, post-hypnotic suggestion, rapid induction of hypnosis, electronic stimulation of the brain, non-ionizing radiation, microwave induction of intracerebral "voices," and a host of even more disturbing technologies. Some of the projects exploring these areas were ARTICHOKE, BLUEBIRD, PANDORA, MKDELTA, MKSEARCH and the infamous MKULTRA.

I have read nearly every available book on these projects, as well as the relevant congressional testimony[5]. I have also spent much time in university libraries researching relevant articles, contacting other researchers (who have graciously allowed me access to their files), and conducting interviews. Moreover, I traveled to Washington, DC to review the files John Marks compiled when he wrote THE SEARCH FOR "THE MANCHURIAN CANDIDATE."[6] These files include some 20,000 pages of CIA and Defense Department documents, interviews, scientific articles, letters, etc. The views presented here are the result of extensive and ongoing research.

As a result of this research, I have come to the following conclusions:

1. Although misleading (and occasionally perjured) testimony before Congress indicated that the CIA's "brainwashing" efforts met with little success,[7] striking advances were, in fact, made in this field. As CIA veteran Miles Copeland once admitted to a reporter, "The congressional subcommittee which went into this sort of thing got only the barest glimpse." [8]

2. Clandestine research into thought manipulation has NOT stopped, despite CIA protestations that it no longer sponsors such studies. Victor Marchetti, 14-year veteran of

the CIA and author of the renown expose, THE CIA AND THE CULT OF INTELLIGENCE, confirmed in a 1977 interview that the mind control research continues, and that CIA claims to the contrary are a "cover story." 9

3. The Central Intelligence Agency was not the only government agency involved in this research.10 Indeed, many branches of our government took part in these studies - including NASA, the Atomic Energy Commission, as well as all branches of the Defense Department.

To these conclusions I would append the following - not as firmly established historical fact, but as a working hypothesis and grounds for investigation:

4. The "UFO abduction" phenomenon might be a continuation of clandestine mind control operations.

I recognize the difficulties this thesis might present to those readers emotionally wedded to the extraterrestrial hypothesis, or to those whose political WELTANSHAUUNG disallows any such suspicions. Still, the openminded student of abductions should consider the possibilities. Certainly, we are not being narrow-minded if we ask researchers to exhaust ALL terrestrial explanations before looking heavenward.

Granted, this particular explanation may, at first, seem as bizarre as the phenomenon itself. But I invite the skeptical reader to examine the work of George Estabrooks, a seminal theorist on the use of hypnosis in warfare, and a veteran of Project MKULTRA. Estabrooks once amused himself during a party by covertly hypnotizing two friends, who were led to believe that the Prime Minister of England had just arrived; Estabrooks' victims spent an hour conversing with, and even serving drinks to, the esteemed visitor.11 For ufologists, this incident raises an inescapable question: If the Mesmeric arts can successfully evoke a non-existent Prime Minister, why can't a representative from the Pleiades be similarly induced?

But there is much more to the present day technology of mind control than mere hypnosis - and many good reasons to suspect that UFO abduction accounts are an artifact of continuing brainwashing/behavior modification experiments. Moreover, I intend to demonstrate that, by using UFO mythology as a cover story, the experimenters may have solved the major problem with the work conducted in the 1950s - "the disposal problem," i.e., the question of "What do we do with the victims?"

If, in these pages, I seem to stray from the subject of the saucers, I plead for patience. Before I attempt to link UFO abductions with mind control experiments, I must first show that this technology exists. Much of the forthcoming is an introduction to the topic of mind control - what it is, and how it works.

II. The Technology
A Brief Overview

In the early days of World War II, George Estabrooks, of Colgate University, wrote to the Department of War, describing in breathless terms the possible uses of hypnosis in warfare.12 The Army was intrigued; Estabrooks had a job. The true history of Estabrooks' wartime collaboration with the CID, FBI.13 and other agencies may never be told: After the war, he burned his diary pages covering the years 1940-45, and thereafter avoided

FIRE FROM THE SKY

discussing his continuing government work with anyone, even close members of the family.14 Occasionally, he strongly intimated that his work involved the creation of hypno-programmed couriers and hypnotically-induced split personalities, but whether he succeeded in these areas remains a controversial point. Nevertheless, the eccentric and flamboyant Estabrooks remains a pivotal figure in the early history of clandestine behavioral research.

Which is not to say that he worked alone. World War II was the first conflict in which the human brain became a field of battle, where invading forces were led by the most notable names in psychology and pharmacology. On both sides, the war spurred furious efforts to create a "truth drug" for use in interrogating prisoners. General William "Wild Bill" Donovan, director of the OSS, tasked his crack team - including Dr. Winifred Overhulser, Dr. Edward Strecker, Harry J. Anslinger and George White - to modify human perception and behavior through chemical means; their "medicine cabinet" included scopolamine, peyote, barbiturates, mescaline, and marijuana. (This research had its amusing side: Donovan's "psychic warriors" conducted many extensive and expensive trials before deciding that the best method of administering tetrahydrocannibinol, the active ingredient in marijuana, was via the cigarette. Any jazz musician could have told them as much.15)

Simultaneously, the notorious Nazi doctors at Dachau experimented with mescaline as a means of eliminating the victim's will to resist. Jews, slavs, gypsies, and other "Untermenschen" in the camp were surreptitiously slipped the drug; later, mescaline was combined with hypnosis.16 The results of these tests were made available to the United States after the War.

In 1947, the Navy conducted the first known post-war mind control program, Project CHAPTER, which continued the drug experiments. Decades later, journalists and investigators still haven't uncovered much information about this project - or, indeed, about any of the military's other excursions into this field. We know that the Army eventually founded operations THIRD CHANCE and DERBY HAT; other project names remain mysterious, though the existence of these programs is unquestionable.

The newly-formed CIA plunged into this cesspool in 1950, with Project BLUEBIRD, rechristened ARTICHOKE in 1951. To establish a "cover story" for this research, the CIA funded a propaganda effort designed to convince the world that the Communist Bloc had devised insidious new methods of re-shaping the human will; the CIA's own efforts could therefore, if exposed, be explained as an attempt to "catch up" with Soviet and

FIRE FROM THE SKY

Chinese work. The primary promoter of this "line" was one Edward Hunter, a CIA contract employee operating undercover as a journalist, and, later, a prominent member of the John Birch society. (Hunter was an OSS veteran of the China theatre - the same spawning grounds which produced Richard Helms, Howard Hunt, Mitch WerBell, Fred Chrisman, Paul Helliwell and a host of other noteworthies who came to dominate that strange land where the worlds of intelligence and right-wing extremism meet.17)

Hunter offered "brainwashing" as the explanation for the numerous confessions signed by American prisoners of war during the Korean War and (generally) UN-recanted upon the prisoners' repatriation. These confessions alleged that the United States used germ warfare in the Korean conflict, a claim which the American public of the time found impossible to accept. Many years later, however, investigative reporters discovered that Japan's germ warfare specialists (who had wreaked incalculable terror on the conquered Chinese during WWII) had been mustered into the American national security apparatus - and that the knowledge gleaned from Japan's horrifying germ warfare experiments probably WAS used in Korea, just as the "brainwashed" soldiers had indicated.18 Thus, we now know that the entire brainwashing scare of the 1950s constituted a CIA hoax perpetrated upon the American public: CIA deputy director Richard Helms admitted as much when, in 1963, he told the Warren Commission that Soviet mind control research consistently lagged years behind American efforts.19

When the CIA's mind control program was transferred from the Office of Security to the Technical Services Staff (TSS) in 1953, the name changed again - to MKULTRA.20 Many consider this wide-ranging "octopus" project - whose tentacles twined through the corridors of numerous universities and around the necks of an army of scientists - the most ominous operation in CIA's catalogue of atrocity. Through MKULTRA, the Agency created an umbrella program of a positively Joycean scope, designed to ferret out all possible means of invading what George Orwell once called "the space between our ears" (Later still, in 1962, mind control research was transferred to the Office of Research and Development; project cryptonyms remain unrevealed.21)

What was studied? Everything - including hypnosis, conditioning, sensory deprivation, drugs, religious cults, microwaves, psychosurgery, brain implants, and even ESP. When MKULTRA "leaked" to the public during the great CIA investigations of the 1970s, public attention focused most heavily on drug experimentation and the work with ESP.22 Mystery still shrouds another area of study, the area which seems to have most interested ORD: psychoelectronics. This research may prove key to our understanding of the UFO abduction phenomenon.

Implants

Perhaps the most interesting pieces of evidence surrounding the abduction phenomenon are the intracerebral implants allegedly visible in the X-rays and MRI scans of many abductees.23

Indeed, abductees often describe operations in which needles are inserted into the brain; more frequently still, they report implantation of foreign objects through the sinus cavities. Many abduction specialists assume that these intracranial incursions must be the handiwork of scientists from the stars. Unfortunately, these researchers have failed to familiarize themselves with certain little-heralded advances in terrestrial technology.

The abductees' implants strongly suggest a technological lineage which can be traced to a device known as a "stimoceiver," invented in the late '50s-early '60s by a neuroscientist named Jose Delgado. The stimoceiver is a miniature depth electrode which can receive and transmit electronic signals over FM radio waves. By stimulating a correctly-positioned stimoceiver, an outside operator can wield a surprising degree of control over the subject's responses.

The most famous example of the stimoceiver in action occurred in a Madrid bull ring. Delgado "wired" the bull before stepping into the ring, entirely unprotected. Furious for gore, the bull charged toward the doctor - then stopped, just before reaching him. The technician-turned-toreador had halted the animal by simply pushing a button on a black box, held in the hand.24

Delgado's PHYSICAL CONTROL OF THE MIND: TOWARD A PSYCHOCIVILISED SOCIETY 25 remains the sole, full-length, popularly-written work on intracerebral implants and electronic stimulation of the brain (ESB). (The book's ominous title and unconvincing philosophical rationales for mass mind control prompted an unfavorable public reaction - which may have deterred other researchers from publishing on this theme for a general audience.) While subsequent work has long since superceded the techniques described in this book, Delgado's achievements were seminal. His animal and human experiments clearly demonstrate that the experimenter can electronically induce emotions and behavior: Under certain conditions, the extremes of temperament - rage, lust, fatigue, etc. - can be elicited by an outside operator as easily as an organist might call forth a C-major chord.

Delgado writes: "Radio stimulation of different points in the amygdala and hippocampus in the four patients produced a variety of effects, including pleasant sensations, elation, deep, thoughtful concentration, odd feelings, super relaxation, colored visions, and other responses."26 The evocative phrase "colored vision" clearly indicates remotely-induced hallucination; we will detail later how these hallucinations may be "controlled" by an outside operator.

Speaking in 1966 - and reflecting research undertaken years previous - Delgado asserted that his experiments "support the distasteful conclusion that motion, emotion, and behavior can be directed by electrical forces and that humans can be controlled like robots by push buttons."27 He even prophesied a day when brain control could be turned over to non-human operators, by establishing two-way radio communication between the implanted brain and a computer.28

Of one experimental subject, Delgado notes that "the patient expressed the successive sensations of fainting, fright and floating around. These 'floating' feelings were repeatedly evoked on different days by stimulation of the same point..."29 Ufologists may recognize the similarity of this sequence of events to abductee reports of the opening minutes of their experiences.30 Under subsequent hypnosis, the abductee could be instructed to misremember the cause of this floating sensation.

In a fascinating series of experiments, Delgado attached the stimoceiver to the tympanic membrane, thereby transforming the ear into a sort of microphone. An assistant would whisper "How are you?" into the ear of a suitably "fixed" cat, and Delgado could hear the words over a loudspeaker in the next room. The application of this technology to the spy trade should be readily apparent. According to Victor Marchetti, The Agency once attempted a highly-sophisticated extension of this basic idea, in which radio im-

FIRE FROM THE SKY

plants were attached to a cat's cochlea, to facilitate the pinpointing of specific conversations, freed from extraneous surrounding noises.31 Such "advances" exacerbate the already-imposing level of Twentieth-Century paranoia: Not only can our phones be tapped and mail checked, but even tabby may be spying on us!

Yet the ramifications of this technology may go even deeper than Marchetti indicates. I presume that if a suitably-wired subject's inner ear can be made into a microphone, it can also be made into a loudspeaker - one possible explanation for the "voices" heard by abductees.32 Indeed, I have personally viewed a strange, opalescent implant within the ear canal of an abductee. I see no reason to ascribe this device to alien intrusion - more than likely, the "intruders" in this case were the technological inheritors of the Delgado legacy. Indeed, not many years after Delgado's experiments with the cat, Ralph Schwitzgebel devised a "bug-in-the-ear" via which the therapist - odd term, under the circumstances - can communicate with his subject.33

Other researchers have made notable contributions to this field.

Robert G. Heath, of Tulane University, who has implanted as many as 125 electrodes in his subjects, achieved his greatest notoriety by attempting to "cure" homosexuality through ESB. In his experiments, he discovered that he could control his patients' memory, (a feat which, applied in the ufological context, may account for the phenomenon of "missing time"); he could also induce sexual arousal, fear, pleasure, and hallucinations.34

Heath and another researcher, James Olds,35 have independently illustrated that areas of the brain in and near the hypothalamus have, when electronically stimulated, what has been described as "rewarding" and "aversive" effects. Both animals and men, when given the means to induce their own ESB of the brain's pleasure centers, will stimulate themselves at a tremendous rate, ignoring such basic drives as hunger and thirst.36 (Using fixed electrodes of his own invention, John C. Lilly had accomplished similar effects in the early 1950s.37) Anyone who has studied the abduction phenomenon will find himself on familiar territory here, for the abductee accounts are replete with stories of bewildering and inappropriate sexual response countered by extremely painful stimuli - operant conditioning, at its most extreme, and most insidious, for here we see a form of conditioning in which the manipulator renders himself invisible. Indeed, B.F. Skinner-esque aversive therapy, remotely appiled, was Heath's prescription for "healing" homosexuality.38

Ralph Schwitzgebel and his brother Robert have produced a panoply of devices for tracking individuals over long ranges; they may be considered the creators of the "electronic house arrest" devices recently approved by the courts.39 Schwitzgebel devices could be used for tracking all the physical and neurological signs of a "patient" within a quarter of a mile,40 thereby lifting the distance limitations which restricted Delgado.

In Ralph Schwitzgebel's initial work, application of this technology to ESB seems to have been limited to cumbersome brain implants with protruding wires. But the technology was soon miniaturized, and a scheme was proposed whereby radio receivers would be mounted on utility poles throughout a given city, thereby providing 24-hour-a-day monitoring capability[41]. Like Heath, Schwitzgebel was much exercised about homosexuality and the use of intracranial devices to combat sexual deviation. But he has also spoken ominously about applying his devices to "socially troublesome persons"... which, of course, could mean anyone.42

FIRE FROM THE SKY

Bryan Robinson, of the Yerkes primate laboratory has conducted fascinating simian research on the use of remote ESB in a social context. He could cause mothers to ignore their offspring, despite the babies' cries. He could turn submission into dominance, and vice-versa.43

Perhaps the most disturbing wanderer into this mind-field is Joseph A. Meyer, of the National Security Agency, the most formidable and secretive component of America's national security complex. Meyer has proposed implanting roughly half of all Americans arrested - not necessarily convicted - of any crime; the numbers of "subscribers" (his euphemism) would run into the tens of millions. "Subscribers" could be monitored continually by computer wherever they went. Meyer, who has carefully worked out the economics of his mass-implantation system, asserts that taxpayer liability should be reduced by forcing subscribers to "rent" the implant from the State. Implants are cheaper and more efficient than police, Meyer suggests, since the call to crime is relentless for the poor "urban dweller" - who, this spook-scientist admits in a surprisingly candid aside, is fundamentally unnecessary to a post-industrial economy. "Urban dweller" may be another of Meyer's euphemisms: He uses New York's Harlem as his model community in working out the details of his mind-management system.44

Abductee Implants

If we are to take seriously abductee accounts of brain implants, we must consider the possibility that the implanters, properly perceived, DON'T look much like the "greys" pictured on Strieber's dustjackets. Instead, the visitors may resemble Dr. Meyer and his brethren. We would thus have an explanation for both the reports of abductee brain implants and, as we shall see, the "scoop marks" and other scars visible on other parts of the abductees' bodies. We would also have an explanation for the reports of individuals suffering personality change after contact with the UFO phenomenon.

Skeptics might counter that the time factor of UFO abductions disallows this possibility. If estimates of "missing time" are correct, the abductions rarely take longer than one-to-three hours. Wouldn't a brain surgeon, operating under less-than-ideal conditions (perhaps in a mobile unit) need more time?

No - not if we accept the claims of a Florida doctor named Daniel Man. He recently proposed a draconian solution to the overblown "missing children problem," by suggesting a program wherein America's youngsters would be implanted with tiny transmitters in order to track the children continuously. Man brags that the operation can be done right in the office - and would take less than 20 minutes.45

Conceivably, it might take a tad longer in the field.

A Question of Timing

The history of brain implantation, as gleaned from the open literature, is certainly disquieting. Yet this history has almost certainly been censored, and the dates manipulated in a nigh-Orwellian fashion. When dealing with research funded by the engines of national security, one can never know the true origin date of any individual scientific advance. However, if we listen carefully to the scientists who have pioneered this research, we may hear whispers, faint but unmistakable, hinting that remotely-applied ESB originated earlier than published studies would indicate.

In his autobiography THE SCIENTIST John C. Lilly (who would later achieve a cultish reknown for his work with dolphins, drugs and sensory deprivation) records a conversation he had with the director of the National Institute of Mental Health - in 1953. The director asked Lilly to brief the CIA, FBI, NSA and the various military intelligence services on his work using electrodes to stimulate directly the pleasure and pain centers of the brain. Lilly refused, noting, in his reply:

Dr. Antoine Remond, using our techniques in Paris, has demonstrated that this method of stimulation of the brain can be applied to the human without the help of the neurosurgeon; he is doing it in his office in Paris without neurosurgical supervision.

*This means that anybody with the proper apparatus can carry this out on a person covertly, with no external signs that electrodes have been used on that person. I feel that if this technique got into the hands of a secret agency, they would have total control over a human being and be able to change his beliefs extremely quickly, leaving little evidence of what they had done.*46

Lilly's assertion of the moral high ground here is interesting. Despite his avowed phobia against secrecy, a careful reading of THE SCIENTIST reveals that he continued to do work useful to this country's national security apparatus. His sensory deprivation experiments expanded upon the work of ARTICHOKE's Maitland Baldwin, and even his dolphin research has - perhaps inadvertently proved useful in naval warfare.47 One should note that Lilly's work on monkeys carried a "secret" classification, and that NIMH was a common CIA funding conduit.48

But the most important aspect of Lilly's statement is its date. 1953? How far back does radio-controlled ESB go? Alas, I have not yet seen Remond's work - if it is available in the open literature. In the documents made available to Marks, the earliest reference to remotely-applied ESB is a 1959 financial document pertaining to MKULTRA subproject 94. The general subproject descriptions sent to the CIA's financial department rarely contain much information, and rarely change from year to year, leaving us little idea as to when this subproject began.

Unfortunately, even the Freedom of Information Act couldn't pry loose much information on electronic mind control techniques, though we know a great deal of study was done in these areas. We have, for example, only four pages on subproject 94 - by comparison, a veritable flood of documents were released on the use of drugs in mind control. (Whenever an author tells us that MKULTRA met with little success, the reference is to drug testing.) On this point, I must criticize John Marks: His book never mentions that roughly 20-25 percent of the subprojects are "dark" - i.e., little or no information was ever made available, despite lawyers and FOIA requests. Marks seems to feel that the only information worth having is the information he received. We know, however, that research into psychoelectronics was extensive indeed, statements of project goals dating from ARTICHOKE and BLUEBIRD days clearly identify this area as a high priority. Marks' anonymous informant, jocularly named "Deep Trance," even told a previous interviewer that, beginning in 1963, CIA and the military's mind control efforts strongly emphasized electronics.49 I therefore assume - not rashly, I hope - that the "dark" MKULTRA subprojects concerned matters such as brain implants, microwaves, ESB, and related technologies.

I make an issue of the timing and secrecy involved in this research to underscore three points:

1. We can never know with certainty the true origin dates of the various brainwashing methods - often, we discover that techniques which seem impossibly futuristic actually originated in the 19th century. (Pioneering ESB research was conducted in 1898, by J.R. Ewald, professor of physiology at Straussbourg.50)

2. The open literature almost certainly gives a bowdlerized view of the actual research.

3. Lavishly-funded clandestine researchers - unrestrained by peer review or the need for strict controls - can achieve far more rapid progress than scientists "on the outside."

Potential critics should keep these points in mind should they attempt to invalidate the "mind control" thesis of UFO abductions by citing an abduction account which antedates Delgado.

The Quandary

We have amply demonstrated, then, that as far back as the 1960s - and possibly earlier still - scientists have had the capability to create implants similar to those now purportedly visible in abductee MRI scans. Indeed, we have no notion just how advanced this technology has become, since the popular press stopped reporting on brain implantation in the 1970s. The research has no doubt continued, albeit in a less public fashion. In fact, scientists such as Delgado have cast their eye far beyond the implants; ESB effects can now be elicited with microwaves and other forms of electromagnetic radiation, used with and without electrodes.

So why - if we take UFO abduction accounts at face value - are the "advanced aliens" using an old technology, Earth technology, a technology which may soon be rendered obsolescent, if it hasn't been so rendered already? I am reminded of the charming anachronisms in the old Flash Gordon serials, where swords and spaceships clashed continually.

Do they also watch black-and-white television on Zeta Reticuli?

Remote Hypnosis

Hypnosis provides the (highly controversial) key which opens the door to many abduction accounts.51 And obviously, if my thesis is correct, hypnosis plays a large part in the abduction itself. One thing we know with certainty: Since the earliest days of project BLUEBIRD, the CIA's spy-chiatrists spent enormous sums mastering Mesmer's art.

I cannot here give even a brief summary of hypnosis, nor even of the CIA's studies in this area. (Fortunately, FOIA requests were rather more successful in shaking loose information on this topic than in the area of psycho-electronics.) Here, we will concentrate on a particularly intriguing allegation - one heard faintly, but persistently, for the past twenty years by those who would investigate the shadow side of politics.

If this allegation proves true, hypnosis is not necessarily a person-to-person affair.

The abductee - or the mind control victim - need not have physical contact with a hypnotist for hypnotic suggestion to take effect; trance could be induced, and suggestions made, via the intracerebral transmitters described above. The concept sounds like something out of Huxley's or Orwell's most masochistic fantasies. Yet remote hypnosis was first reported - using allegedly parapsychological means - in the early 1930s, by L.L. Vasilev, Professor of Physiology in the University of Leningrad.52 Later, other scientists attempted to accomplish the same goal, using less mystic means.

Over the years, certain journalists have asserted that the CIA has mastered a technol-

FIRE FROM THE SKY

ogy call RHIC-EDOM. RHIC means "Radio Hypnotic Intracerebral Control." EDOM stands for "Electronic Dissolution of Memory." Together, these techniques can - allegedly - remotely induce hypnotic trance, deliver suggestions to the subject, and erase all memory for both the instruction period and the act which the subject is asked to perform.

RHIC uses the stimoceiver, or a microminiaturized offspring of that technology to induce a hypnotic state. Interestingly, this technique is also reputed to involve the use of intramuscular implants, a detail strikingly reminiscent of the "scars" mentioned in Budd Hopkins' MISSING TIME. Apparently, these implants are stimulated to induce a post-hypnotic suggestion.

EDOM is nothing more than missing time itself - the erasure of memory from consciousness through the blockage of synaptic transmission in certain areas of the brain. By jamming the brain's synapses through a surfeit of acetocholine, neural transmission along selected pathways can be effectively stilled. According to the proponents of RHIC-EDOM, acetocholine production can be affected by electromagnetic means. (Modern research in the psycho-physiological effects of microwaves confirm this proposition.)

Does RHIC-EDOM exist? In our discussion of Delgado's work, I have already cited a strange little book (published in 1969) titled WERE WE CONTROLLED?, written by one Lincoln Lawrence, a former FBI agent turned journalist. (The name is a pseudonym; I know his real identity.) This work deals at length with RHIC-EDOM; a careful comparison of Lawrence's work with MKULTRA files declassified ten years later indicates a strong possibility that the writer did indeed have "inside" sources.

Here is how Lawrence describes RHIC in action:

It is the ultra-sophisticated application of post-hypnotic suggestion triggered at will [italics in original] by radio transmission. It is a recurring hypnotic state, re-induced automatically at intervals by the same radio control. An individual is brought under hypnosis. This can be done either with his knowledge - or without it by use of narco-hypnosis, which can be brought into play under many guises. He is then programmed to perform certain actions and maintain certain attitudes upon radio signal.53

Other authors have mentioned this technique - specifically Walter Bowart (in his book OPERATION MIND CONTROL) and journalist James Moore, who, in a 1975 issue of a periodical called MODERN PEOPLE, claimed to have secured a 350-page manual, prepared in 1963, on RHIC-EDOM.54 He received the manual from CIA sources, although - interestingly - the technique is said to have originated in the military.

The following quote by Moore on RHIC should prove especially intriguing to abduction researchers who have confronted odd "personality shifts" in abductees:

Medically, these radio signals are directed to certain parts of the brain. When a part of your brain receives a tiny electrical impulse from outside sources, such as vision, hearing, etc., an emotion is produced - anger at the sight of a gang of boys beating an old woman, for example. The same emotion of anger can be created by artificial radio signals sent to your brain by a controller. You could instantly feel the same white-hot anger without any apparent reason.55

Lawrence's sources imparted an even more tantalizing - and frightening - revelation:

...there is already in use a small EDOM generator-transmitter which can be concealed on the body of a person. Contact with this person - a casual handshake or even just a touch

FIRE FROM THE SKY

*- transmits a tiny electronic charge plus an ultra-sonic signal tone which for a short while will disturb the time orientation of the person affected.*56

If RHIC-EDOM exists, it goes a long way toward providing an earthbound rationale for alien abductions - or, at least, certain aspects of them. The phenomenon of "missing time" is no longer mysterious. Abductee implants, both intracerebral and otherwise, are explained. And note the reference to "recurring hypnotic state, reinduced automatically by the same radio command." This situation may account for "repeater" abductees who, after their initial encounter, have regular sessions of "missing time" and abduction - even while a bed-mate sleeps undisturbed.

At present, I cannot claim conclusively that RHIC-EDOM is real. To my knowledge, the only official questioning of a CIA represetative concerning these techniques occurred in 1977, during Senate hearings on CIA drug testing. Senator Richard Schweicker had the following interchange with Dr. Sidney Gottlieb, an important MKULTRA administrator:

SCHWEICKER: Some of the projects under MKULTRA involved hypnosis, is that correct?

GOTTLIEB: Yes.

SCHWEICKER: Did any of these projects involve something called radio hypnotic intracerebral control, which is a combination, as I understand it, in layman's terms, of radio transmissions and hypnosis.

GOTTLIEB: My answer is "No."

SCHWEICKER: None whatsoever?

GOTTLIEB: Well, I am trying to be responsive to the terms you used. As I remember it, there was a current interest, running interest, all the time in what effects people's standing in the field of radio energy have, and it could easily have been that somewhere in many projects, someone was trying to see if you could hypnotize someone easier if he was standing in a radio beam. That would seem like a reasonable piece of research to do.

Schweicker went on to mention that he had heard testimony that radar (i.e., microwaves) had been used to wipe out memory in animals; Gottlieb responded, "I can believe that, Senator."57

Gottlieb's blandishments do not comfort much. For one thing, the good doctor did not always provide thoroughly candid testimony. (During the same hearing he averred that 99 percent on the CIA's research had been openly published; if so, why are so many MKULTRA subprojects still "dark," and why does the Agency still go to great lengths to protect the identities of its scientists?58)

We should also recognize that the CIA's operations are compartmentalized on a "need-to-know" basis; Gottlieb may not have had access to the information requested by Schweicker. Note that the MKULTRA rubric circumscribed Gottlieb's statement: RHIC-EDOM might have been the focus of another program. (There were several others: MKNAOMI, MKACTION, MKSEARCH, etc.) Also keep in mind the revelation by "Deep Trance" that the CIA concentrated on psychoelectronics after the termination of MKULTRA in 1963. Most significantly: RHIC-EDOM is described by both Lawrence and Moore as a product of MILITARY research; Gottlieb spoke only of matters pertaining to CIA. He may thus have spoken truthfully - at least in a strictly technical sense - while still misleading

FIRE FROM THE SKY

the Congressional interlocutors.

Personally, I believe that the RHIC-EDOM story deserves a great deal of further research. I find it significant that when Dr. Petter Lindstrom examined X-rays of Robert Naesland, a Swedish victim of brain-implantation, the doctor authoritatively cited WERE WE CONTROLLED? in his letter of response.[59] This is the same Dr. Lindstrom noted for his pioneering use of ultrasonics in neurosurgery.[60] Lincoln Lawrence's book has received a strong endorsement indeed.

Bowart's OPERATION MIND CONTROL contains a significant interview with an intelligence agent knowledgeable in these areas. Granted, the reader has every right to adopt a skeptical attitude toward information culled from anonymous sources; still, one should note that this operative's statements confirm, in pertinent part, Lawrence's thesis.[61]

Most importantly: The open literature on brain-wave entrainment and the behavioral effects of electromagnetic radiation substantiates much of the RHIC-EDOM story - as we shall see.

That's Entrainment

Robert Anton Wilson, an author with a devoted cult following, recently has taken to promoting a new generation of "mind machines" designed to promote creativity, stimulate learning, and alter consciousness - i.e., provide a drug-less high. Interestingly, these machines can also induce "Out-of-Body Experiences," in which the percipient mentally "travels" to another location while his body remains at rest.[62] This rapidly-developing technology has spawned a technological equivalent to the drug culture; indeed, the aficionados of the electronic buzz even have their own magazine, REALITY HACKERS. I strongly suspect that we will hear much of these machines in the future.

One such device is called the "hemi-synch." This headphone-like invention produces slightly different frequences in each ear; the brain calculates the difference between these frequencies, resulting in a rhythm known as the "binaural beat." The brain "entrains" itself to this beat - that is, the subject's EEG slows down or speeds up to keep pace with its electronic running partner.[63]

The brain has a "beat" of its own.

This rhythm was first discovered in 1924 by the German psychiatrist Hans Berger, who recorded cerebral voltages as part of a telepathy study.[64] He noted two distinct frequencies: alpha (8-13 cycles per second), associated with a relaxed, alert state, and beta (14-30 cycles per second), produced during states of agitation and intense mental concentration. Later, other rhythms were noted, which are particularly important for our present purposes: theta (4-7 cycles per second), a hypnogogic state, and delta (.5 to 3.5 cycles per second), generally found in sleeping subjects.[65]

The hemi-synch - and related mind-machines - can produce alpha or theta waves, on demand, according to the operator's wishes. A suitably-entrained brain is much more responsive to suggestion, and is even likely to experience vivid hallucinations.

I have spoken to several UFO abductees who describe a "stereophonic sound" effect - exactly similar to that produced by the hemi-sync - preceding many "encounters." Of course, one usually administers the hemi-synch via headphones, but I see no reason why the effect cannot be transmitted via the above described stimoceiver. Again, I remind the reader of the abductee with an implant just inside her ear canal.

There's more than one way to entrain a brain. Michael Hutchison's excellent book

FIRE FROM THE SKY

MEGA BRAIN details the author's personal experiences with many such devices - the Alpha-stim, TENS, the Synchro-energizer, Tranquilite, etc. He recounts dazzling, Dali-esque hallucinations, as a result of using this mind-expanding technology; moreover, he offers a seductive argument that these devices may represent a true breakthrough in consciousness-control, thereby fulfilling the dashed dream of the hallucinogenic '60s.

I wish to avoid a knee-jerk Luddite response to these fascinating wonderboxes. At the same time, I recognize the dangers involved. What about the possibility of an outside operator literally "changing our minds" by altering our brainwaves without our knowledge or permission? If these machines can induce a hypnotic state, what's to stop a skilled hypnotist from making use of this state?

Granted, most of these devices require some physical interaction with the subject. But a tool called the Bio-Pacer can, according to its manufacturer, produce a number of mood altering frequencies - WITHOUT attachment to the subject. Indeed, the Bio-Pacer III (a high-powered version) can affect an entire room. This device costs $275, according to the most recent price sheet available.66 What sort of machine might $27,500 buy? Or $275,000? What effects, what ranges might a million-dollar machine be capable of?

The military certainly has that sort of money.

And they're certainly interested in this sort of technology, according to Michael Hutchison. His interview with an informant named Joseph Light elicited some particularly provocative revelations. According to Light:

*There are important elements in the scientific community, powerful people, who are very much interested in these areas... but they have to keep most of their work secret. Because as soon as they start to publish some of these sensitive things, they have problems in their lives. You see, they work on research grants, and if you follow the research being done, you find that as soon as these scientists publish something about this, their research funds are cut off. There are areas in bioelectric research where very simple techniques and devices can have mind-boggling effects. Conceivably, if you have a crazed person with a bit of a technical background, he can do a lot of damage.*67

This last statement is particularly evocative. In 1984, a violent neo-Nazi group called The Order (responsible for the murder of talk-show host Alan Berg) established contact with two government scientists engaged in clandestine research to project chemical imbalances and render targeted individuals docile via certain frequencies of electronic waves. For $100,000 the scientists were willing to deliver this information.68

Thus, at least one group of crazed individuals almost got the goods.

Wave Your Brain Goodbye

Every Senator and Congressional representative has a "wavie" file. So do many state representatives. Wavies have even pled their case to private institutions such as the Christic Institute.69

And who are the wavies?

They claim to be victims of clandestine bombardment with non-ionizing radiation - or microwaves. They report sudden changes in psychological states, alteration of sleep patterns, intracerebral voices and other sounds, and physiological effects. Most people never realize how many wavies there are in this country. I've spoken to a number of wavies myself.

Are these troubled individuals seeking an exterior rationale for their mental prob-

FIRE FROM THE SKY

lems? Maybe. Indeed, I'm sure that such is the case in many instances. But the fact is that the literature on the behavioral effects of microwaves, extra-low-frequencies (ELF) and ultra-sonics is such that we cannot blithely dismiss all such claims.

For decades, American science and industry tried to convince the population that microwaves could have no adverse effects on human beings at sub-thermal levels - in other words, the attitude was, "If it can't burn you, it can't hurt you." This approach became increasingly difficult to defend as reports mounted of microwave-induced physiological effects. Technicians described "hearing" certain radar installations; users of radar telescopes began developing cataracts at an appallingly high rate.[70] The Soviets had long recognized the strange and sometimes subtle effects of these radio frequencies, which is why their exposure standards have always been much stricter.

Soviet microwave bombardment of the U.S. Embassy in Moscow prompted the Defense Advanced Research Projects Agency's Project PANDORA (later renamed), whose ostensible goal was to determine whether these pulsations (reportedly 10 cycles per second, which puts them in the alpha range) could be used for the purposes of mind control. I suspect that the "war on Tchaikovsky Street," as I call it,[71] was used, at least in part, as a cover story for DARPA mind control research, and that the stories floated in the news (via, for example, Jack Anderson's column) about Soviet remote brainwashing served the same propaganda purposes as did the bleatings of Edward Hunter during the 1950s.[72]

What can low-level microwaves do to the mind?

According to a DIA report released under the Freedom of Information Act,[73] microwaves can induce metabolic changes, alter brain functions, and disrupt behavior patterns. PANDORA discovered that pulsed microwaves can create leaks in the blood/brain barrier, induce heart seizures, and create behavioral disorganization.[74] In 1970, a RAND Corporation scientist reported that microwaves could be used to promote insomnia, fatigue, irritability, memory loss, and hallucinations.[75]

Perhaps the most significant work in this area has been produced by Dr. W. Ross Adey at the University of Southern California. He determined that behavior and emotional states can be altered without electrodes - simply by placing the subject in an electromagnetic field. By directing a carrier frequency to stimulate the brain and using amplitude modulation to "shape" the wave into a mimicry of a desired EEG frequency, he was able to impose a 4.5 cps theta rhythm on his subjects - a frequency which he previously measured in the hippocampus during avoidance learning. Thus, he could externally condition the mind towards an aversive reaction.[76] (Adey has also done extensive work on the use of electrodes in animals.[77])

According to another prominent microwave scientist, Allen Frey, other frequencies could - in animal studies - induce docility.[78] The controversial researcher Andrijah Puharich asserts that "a weak (1mW) 4 Hz magnetic sine wave will modify human brain waves in 6 to 10 seconds. The psychological effects of a 4 Hz sine magnetic wave are negative - causing dizzyness, nausea, headache, and can lead to vomiting." Conversely, an 8 Hz magnetic sine wave has beneficial effects.[79] Though some writers question Puharich's integrity (perhaps correctly, considering his involvement in the confused tale of Uri Geller), his claims here seem in line with the findings of less-flamboyant experimenters.

FIRE FROM THE SKY

As investigative journalist Anne Keeler writes:

*Specific frequencies at low intensities can predictably influence sensory processes... pleasantness-unpleasantness, strain-relaxation, and excitement-quiescence can be created with the fields. Negative feelings and avoidance are strong biological phenomena and relate to survival. Feelings are the true basis of much "decision-making" and often occur as subthreshold impressions.... Ideas including names [my italics] can be synchronized with the feelings that the fields induce.*80

Adey and compatriots have compiled an entire library of frequencies and pulsation rates which can affect the mind and nervous system. Some of these effects can be extremely bizarre. For example, engineer Tom Jarski, in an attempt to replicate the seminal work of F. Cazzamali, found that a particular frequency caused a ringing sensation in the ears of his subjects - who felt strangely compelled to BITE the experimenters!81 On the other hand, the diet-conscious may be intrigued by the finding that rats exposed to ELF waves failed to gain weight normally.82

For our present purposes, the most significant electromagnetic research findings concern microwave signals modulated by hypnoidal EEG frequencies. Microwaves can act much like the "hemi-synch" device previously described - that is, they can entrain the brain to theta rhythms.83 I need not emphasize the implications of remotely synchronizing the brain to resonate at a frequency conducive to sleep, or to hypnosis.

Trance may be remotely induced - but can it be directed? Yes. Recall the intracerebral voices mentioned earlier in our discussion of Delgado. The same effect can be produced by "the wave." Frey demonstrated in the early 1960s that microwaves could produce booming, hissing, buzzing, and other intra-cerebral static (this phenomenon is now called "the Frey effect"); in 1973, Dr. Joseph Sharp, of the Walter Reed Army Institute of Research, expanded on Frey's work in an experiment where the subject - in this case, Sharp himself - "heard" and understood spoken words delivered via a pulsed-microwave analog of the speaker's sound vibrations.84

Dr. Robert Becker comments that "Such a device has obvious applications in covert operations designed to drive a target crazy with 'voices' or deliver undetectable instructions to a programmed assassin."85 In other words, we now have, at the push of a button, the technology either to inflict an electronic gaslight - or to create a true Manchurian Candidate. Indeed, the former capability could effectively disguise the latter. Who will listen to the victims, when electronically-induced hallucinations they recount exactly parallel the classical signals of paranoid schizophrenia and/or temporal lobe epilepsy?

Perhaps the most ominous revelations, however, concern the mysterious work of J.F. Schapitz, who in 1974 filed a plan to explore the interaction of radio frequencies and hypnosis. He proposed the following:

In this investigation it will be shown that the spoken word of the hypnotist may be conveyed by modulated electro-magnetic energy directly into the subconscious parts of the human brain [my italics] - i.e., without employing any technical devices for receiving or transcoding the messages and without the person exposed to such influence having a chance to control the information input consciously.

FIRE FROM THE SKY

He outlined an experiment, innocent in its immediate effects yet chilling in its implications, whereby subjects would be implanted with the subconscious suggestion to leave the lab and buy a particular item; this action would be triggered by a certain cue word or action. Schapitz felt certain that the subjects would rationalize the behavior - in other words, the subject would seize upon any excuse, however thin, to chalk up his actions to the working of free will.86 His instincts on this latter point coalesce perfectly with findings of professional hypnotists.87

Schapitz's work was funded by the Department of Defense. Despite FOIA requests, the results have never been publicly revealed.88

Final Thoughts on "The Wave"

I must again offer a caveat about possible disparities between the "official" record of electromagnetism's psychological effects and the hidden history. Once more, we face a question of timing. How long ago did this research REALLY begin?

In the eary years of this century, Nikola Tesla seems to have stumbled upon certain of the behavioral effects of electromagnetic exposure.89 Cazamalli, mentioned earlier, conducted his studies in the 1930s. In 1934, E.L. Chaffe and R.U. Light published a paper on "A Method for the Remote Control of Electrical Stimulation of the Nervous System."90 From the very beginning of their work with microwaves, the Soviets explored the more subtle physiological effects of electromagnetism - and despite the bleatings of certain right-wing alarmists91 that an "electromagnetic gap" separates us from Soviet advances, East European literature in this area has been closely monitored for decades by the West. ARTICHOKE/BLUEBIRD project outlines, dating from the early 1950s, prominently mention the need to explore all possible uses of the electromagnetic spectrum.

Another point worth mentioning concerns the combination of EMR and miniature brain electrodes. The father of the stimoceiver, Dr. J.M.R. Delgado, has recently conducted experiments in which monkeys are exposed to electromagnetic fields, thereby eliciting a wide range of behavioral effects - one monkey might fly into a volcanic rage while, just a few feet away, his simian partner begins to nod off. Fascinatingly, when monkeys with brain implants felt "the wave," the effects were greatly intensified. Apparently, these tiny electrodes can act as amplifiers of the electromagnetic effect.92

This last point is important to our "alien abduction" thesis. Critics might counter that any burst of microwave energy powerful enough to have truly remote effects would probably also create a thermal reaction. That is, if a clandestine operator propagated a "wave" from outside an abductee's bedroom (say, from a low-flying helicopter, or from a truck travelling alongside the subject's car), the power necessary to do the job might be such that the microwave would cook the target before it got a chance to launder his thoughts. Our abductee would end up like the victim of the microwave "hit" in the finale of Jerzy Kozinsky's COCKPIT.

It's a fair criticism. But Delgado's work may give us our solution. Once an abductee has been implanted - and if we are to trust hypnotic regression accounts of abductees at all, the first implanting session may occur in childhood - the chip-in-the-brain would act an an intensifier of the signal. Such an individual could have any number of "UFO" experiences while his or her bed partner dozes comfortably.

Furthermore, recent reports indicate that a "waver" can achieve pinpoint accuracy

FIRE FROM THE SKY

without the use of Delgado-style implants. In 1985, volunteers at the Midwest Research Institute in Kansas City, Missouri, were exposed to microwave beams as part of an experiment sponsored by the Department of Energy and the New York State Department of Health. As THE ARIZONA REPUBLIC[93] described the experiment, "A matched control group sat in the same room without being bombarded by *non-ionizing radiation*." [My italics.] Apparently, one can focus "the wave" quite narrowly - a fact which has wide implications for abductees.

III. Applications

So we now have some idea of the tools available to the "spy-chiatrists." How have these tools been used?

This question necessarily involves some detective work. The Central Intelligence Agency, under duress, provided some, though not enough, documentation of its efforts to commandeer "the space between our ears." We know that these efforts were extensive, long-term, and at least partially successful. We know also that these experiments

FIRE FROM THE SKY

used human subjects. But who? When?

One paradox of this line of inquiry is that, for many readers, the victims elicit sympathy only insofar as they remain anonymous. Intellectually, we realize that MKULTRA and its allied projects must have affected hundreds, probably thousands, of individuals. Yet we react with deep suspicion whenever one of these individuals steps forward and identifies himself, or whenever an independent investigator argues that mind control has directed some newsworthy person's otherwise inexplicable actions. Where, the skeptic may rightfully ask, is the documentation supporting such accusations? Most of the MKULTRA "paper trail" was (allegedly) burnt at Richard Helms' order; what's left has been censored, leaving black ink smudges wherever the names originally appeared. Claimed mind control victims can, for the most part, only give us testimony - and how reliable can such testimony be, especially in light of the fact that one purpose of MKULTRA was to induce insanity? Anyone asserting that he was victimized by the program might well be seeking an extrinsic excuse for his own psychopathology. If you say that you are a manufactured madman, you were probably mad to begin with: Catch 22.

When John Marks wrote THE SEARCH FOR "THE MANCHURIAN CANDIDATE." he received numerous letters from people insisting that they had been drugged, "waved," or otherwise abused by the CIA or the military. Most of these communications went directly into his crank file. Perhaps many deserved that destination; I know of at least one that did not.[94]

Marks did, however, devote much attention to Val Orlikov, a former "patient" of perhaps the most notorious figure in the annals of American medical crime: Dr. Ewen Cameron, a CIA-funded scientist heading the Allan Memorial Institute at McGill University, Montreal, Canada. Cameron, a highly-respected mental health researcher,[95] experimented with a technique he called "psychic driving," a brainwashing program which involved inflicting upon a subject an endless tape loop blaring selected messages, 16- to-24 hours a day, combined with massive electroshock and LSD. The project's "guinea pigs" were patients who had come to Allan Memorial with relatively minor psychological complaints. Cameron's experiments failed and his theories were discredited, which may explain why the CIA and its apologists now feel relatively comfortable discussing the Frankensteinian efforts at Allan Memorial, as opposed to more successful work elsewhere.

Orlikov's testimony has received much respectful attention from those writers who have examined MKULTRA, and correctly so. When I studied the files at the National Security Archives, I was particularly keen to read her original letters to John Marks, for these pages had led to the unmasking of an especially heinous CIA project. The letters, interestingly enough, proved just as vague, disjointed, and bizarre as similar correspondence which researchers routinely dismiss. Orlikov can't be blamed for the hazy nature of her recollections; a certain amount of fog is to be expected, given the nature of the crime perpetrated against her. The important point is that her story, ultimately, was found to be true. All of which leads me to wonder: Why did HER claims prompt investigation when those of others prompt only dismissal? Perhaps the answer lies in the fact that Orlikov's husband became a Canadian Member of Parliament. Any victims of CIA experimentation who wish to be taken seriously ought, perhaps, first make sure to marry well.

Of course, we can easily forgive previous writers and readers whose researches into MKULTRA have been biased in favor of complacency.[96] But we can't let this natural prejudice cripple our present investigation. Let us examine, then, a few of the "horror stories" from the mind control literature and highlight possible correlations to abductee testimony.

Palle Hardrup's "Guardian Angel"

As mentioned previously, I have not delved much into the subject of hypnosis in this paper - primarily because of space and time limitations, but also because discussions of the possibilities of hypnosis per se tend to cloud the issue of its use in conjunction with the above-mentioned electronic techniques. Obviously, however, hypnosis is a major weapon in the mind controller's armament; in a forthcoming full-length work, I intend to deal with this subject at much greater length.

Needless to say, one of the primary objectives of MKULTRA and related projects was to determine whether one could hypnotically induce someone to commit an anti-social act. This possibility remains one of the most hotly debated issues in hypnosis, for conventional wisdom asserts that no individual can be hypnotized to commit an action which violates his interior moral code. Martin Orne, editor of the presitigious INTERNATIONAL JOURNAL OF CLINICAL AND EXPERIMENTAL HYPNOSIS agrees with this axiom,[97] and he is in a position to codify much of the established view on this topic. Orne, however, is a veteran of MKULTRA, and furthermore seems to have lied - at least in his original communications - to author John Marks about his witting involvement in subproject 94.[98] While I respect much of Orne's ground-breaking work, his pronouncements do not hold, for this layman, an Olympian unassailability.

To be sure, many other hypnosis experts, untainted by Company connections, also discount the possibility that anti-social actions can be induced. But a number of highly-experienced professionals - including Milton Kline, William Kroger, George Estabrooks, John Watkins, and Herbert Spiegel - have argued that such actions can, at least to some degree, be elicited by an outside manipulator.

Occasionally, claims of hypnotically-induced anti-social behavior find their way into the courtroom; one such case, which led to the incarceration of the hypnotist, was the Palle Hardrup affair. This incident occurred in Denmark in 1951.[99] Palle Hardrup robbed a bank, killing a guard in the process, and later claimed that he had been instructed to do so by the hypnotist Bjorn Nielsen. Nielsen eventually confessed to having engineered the crime as a test of his hypnotic abilities.

FIRE FROM THE SKY

The most significant aspect of this incident concerns the "pose" Nielsen adopted to work his malicious designs. During the hypnosis sessions, Nielsen hypnotically suggested that he was Hardrup's "guardian angel," represented by the letter X. Hardrup testified that "There is another room next door where Nielsen and I go and talk on our own. It is there that my guardian spirit usually comes and talks to me. Nielsen says that X has a task for me."

One of these tasks was arranging for Hardrup's girlfriend to have sex with the hypnotist. The other tasks, he mentioned, included robbery and murder. Nielsen convinced his victim that "X" wanted the robbery funds to be used for worthwhile political goals. The end, Hardrup was told, justified the means.

Compare this scenario to that encountered in the typical contactee case, in which alien "guardians" convince their victims/subjects that the encounter will eventually serve some unspecified "higher purpose." Indeed, in my interviews with abductees who have established a "long-term" relationship with their visitors, I have found that some of them originally believed themselves in contact with Hardrup-like angelic guardians. Only in recent years was the "angel" pose discarded and the true "alien" form revealed.

Thus we have one possible means of overcoming the proposition that hypnosis cannot induce anti-social behavior. If a hypnotist lacks scruples, and has access to a particularly susceptible subject, he can induce a misperceived reality. Actions which we would abhor in an everyday context become acceptable in specialized circumstances: A citizen who could never commit murder on a surburban street might, if drafted into an army, kill on the field of battle. In hypnosis, the mind becomes that battlefield. In the words of Dr. John Watkins,

We behave on the basis of our perceptions. If our perceptions of a situation can be altered so as to cause us to misconstrue it, or to develop a false belief, then our behavior in relation to it will be drastically altered. It is precisely in the area of changing perceptions that the hypnotic modality demonstrates its most powerful effects. Hallucinations both under hypnosis, and posthypnotic, can easily be induced in the suggestible subject. He can be made to ignore painful stimuli, be apparently unable to hear loud sounds, and "see" individuals who are not present [my italics]. Moreover, attitudes and beliefs can be initiated in him which are quite abnormal and often contrary to those which he previously held.[100]

If traditional hypnosis, unaided, can achieve such changes in perception, one can only imagine the possibilities inherent in the combination of hypnotic techniques with the psychoelectronic research previously described.

Scientists such as Orne and Milton Erickson[101] have taken issue with Watkins' assertions. But the Hardrup case would appear to bear Watkins out. If someone can be convinced that he, like Jeanne D'Arc, acts under the influence of a supernatural higher power, then previously unthinkable capabilitites may be evinced and "impossible" actions carried forth. Indeed, when we consider the extreme personality changes - and occasionally, the heinous actions, elicited by leaders of certain cults, and occult groups,[102] we understand the desirability of installing a hypnotic "cover story" within a supernatural matrix. People will do for God - or the Devil, or the Space Brothers - what they would not do otherwise.

FIRE FROM THE SKY

The date of the Hardrup affair corresponds to the institution of BLUEBIRD/ARTICHOKE; it doesn't require much imagination to see how this case could have served as a model to the scientists researching those and subsequent projects.

Screen Memory

According to declassified documents in the Marks files, a major difficulty faced by the MKULTRA researchers concerned the "disposal problem." What to do with the victims of CIA-sponsored electroshock, hypnosis, and drug experimentation? The Company resorted to distressing, but characteristic, tactics: They disposed of their human guinea pigs by incarcerating them in insane asylums, by performing icepick lobotomies, and by ordering "executive actions."[103]

A more sophisticated solution had to be found. One of the goals of the CIA's mind control efforts was the erasure of memory via hypnosis (and drugs, electronics, lobotomies, etc.); not only would this hide what occurred during the experimental indoctrination/programming sessions, it would prove useful in the field. "Amnesia was a big goal," confirms Victor Marchetti, who points out its usefulness in dealing with contract agents: "After you've done it, the agent doesn't even know what he's done... you send him in, he does the job. When he comes out, you clean his head out."[104]

The big problem: Despite hypnotically-induced amnesia, there would be memory leaks - snippets of the repressed material would arise spontaneously, in dreams, as flashbacks, etc. A proposed solution: Give the subject a "screen memory," a false story; thus, even if he starts to recall the material, he will recall it incorrectly.

Even the conservative Dr. Orne notes that:

A S [subject] who is able to develop good posthypnotic amnesia will also respond to suggestions to remember events which did not actually occur. On awakening, he will fail to recall the real events of the trance and will instead recall the suggested events. If anything, this phenomenon is easier to produce than total amnesia, perhaps because it eliminates the subjective feeling of an empty space in memory.[105]

Not only would the screen memories fill in the uncomfortable blanks in the subjects' recollection, they would protect against revelation. One fear of the MKULTRA scientists was that a hypno-programmed individual used as, say, a courier, could be un-programmed by another hypnotist, perhaps working for the enemy. Thus, the MKULTRA scientists decided to instill multiple personalities - multiple cover stories, if you will - to confuse any "unauthorized" hypnotist.[106]

One case using this technique centered on an assassin named Luis Castillo, who, after his capture in the Philippines, was extensively de-briefed and studied by experts in the employ of the National Bureau of Investigation, that country's equivalent to our FBI. Castillo was discovered to have had at least four separate personalities hypnotically instilled; each personality could be triggered by a specific cue. In one state, he claimed to be Sgt. Manuel Angel Ramirez, of the Strategic Air Tactical Command in South Vietnam; supposedly, "Ramirez" was the illegitimate son of a certain pipe-smoking, highly-placed CIA official whose initials were A.D.[107] Another personality claimed to be one of John F. Kennedy's assassins.

The main hypnotist involved with this case labelled these hypnotic alter-egos "Zombie states." The report on the case stated that "The Zombie phenomenon referred to here is a somnambulistic behavior displayed by the subject in a conditioned response

FIRE FROM THE SKY

to a series of words, phrases, and statements, apparently unknown to the subject during his normal waking state."

Upon Castillo's repatriation to the United States, the FBI claimed that he had fabricated the story. In his book OPERATION MIND CONTROL, Walter Bowart makes a convincing case against the FBI's claims. Certainly, many aspects of the Castillo affair argue for his sincerity - including his hypnotically-induced insensitivity to pain,108 his maintenance of the story (or stories) even when severly inebriated, and his apparently programmed suicide attempts.

If Castillo told the truth, as I believe he did, then he manifested both hypnotically-induced multiple personality and pseudomemory. The former remains controversial; the latter has been repeatedly replicated in experimental situations.109

This point is vitally important for students of the abduction phenomenon. We CANNOT assume the accuracy of abduction descriptions given during subsequent hypnotic regression. Moreover, we cannot even assume the accuracy of spontaneously-arising recollections (i.e., abduction memories not elicited through hypnotic regression). Indeed, responsible skeptics have argued that hypnotic regression may prove inadvertently harmful, in that it may lock in place a false remembrance. (Note, however, that other psychiatric professionals consider hypnotic regression the best technique, however flawed, in unlocking amnesia.110 For my part, I maintain an ambivalent and cautious attitude toward the use of hypnosis in abductee work.)

Granted, it is all too easy for the debunkers to cry "confabulation" to dismiss hypnotic testimony which does not conform to our preconceptions about the possible; I do not intend to make this same error. Whenever skeptics offer the phenomenon of pseudomemory to rationalize abduction claims, they cite experimental situations in which pseudomemory was originally created by a hypnotist 111 These experiments can not be cited as proof that an individual abductee spontaneously conjured up a fantasy (which just happens to correspond to the details of hundreds of similar "fantasies"). Rather, laboratory studies of pseudomemory creation prove my point: Pseudomemory can be induced by previous hypnosis.112

In other words, an abductee may talk of aliens - when the reality was something else entirely.

In correspondence with me, a noted abduction researcher wrote of an instance in which an abductee recounted seeing a helicopter during his experience; as the abductee testimony progressed, the helicopter turned into a UFO. During one of the (quite few) regression sessions I attended, I heard an exactly similar narrative. Hopkins would argue that the helicopter was a "screen memory" hiding the awful reality of the UFO encounter. But does Occam's razor really cut that way? Shouldn't we also consider the possibility that the object in question really WAS a helicopter - which the abductee was instructed to recall as a UFO?

The Super Spy
Among the released BLUEBIRD/ARTICHOKE/MKULTRA papers was the following handwritten memorandum, unsigned and undated:

I have developed a technic which is safe and secure (free from international censorship). It has to do with the conditioning of our own people. I can accomplish this as a one-man job.

FIRE FROM THE SKY

The method is the production of hypnosis by means of simple oral medication. Then (with NO further medication) the hypnosis is re-enforced daily during the following three or four days.

Each individual is conditioned against revealing any information to an enemy, even though subjected to hypnosis or drugging. If preferable, he may be conditioned to give FALSE information rather than NO information.

In the margin of this document, one of Marks' assistants wrote, "Is this Wendt?" The reference here is to G. Richard Wendt, a professor employed by Project CHATTER who, in 1951, led both his Naval employers and the CIA on a mind control merry goose chase, when an experiment similar to that described above failed to produce results.113 Even if the above memorandum does describe an operational failure (and the tactics described in this memo do not seem very feasible to me), we should not rest complacent. We now know that, in at least ONE case, more sophisticated techniques made the above scenario a reality.

I refer to the case of Candy Jones.

Her story has filled at least one book 114 and ought, one day, to give rise to another. Obviously, I cannot here give all the details of this fascinating and frightening narrative. But a precis is mandatory.

Ms. Jones (born Jessica Wilcox) achieved star status as a model during World War II, and later established her own modelling agency. An FBI man requested her to allow her place of business to be used as a "mail drop" for the Bureau and "another government agency" (presumably, the CIA); Candy, deeply patriotic, accepted the proposition gladly. Toiling on the fringes of the clandestine world, Candy eventually came into contact with a "Dr. Gilbert Jensen," who worked, in turn, with a "Dr. Marshall Burger." (Both names are pseudonyms.) Unknown to her, these doctors had been employed as "spy-chiatrists" by the CIA. Using a job interview as a cover, Jensen induced hypnosis, found Candy to be a particularly responsive subject - and proceeded to use her as other scientists would use a rhesus monkey. She became a test subject for the CIA's mind control program.

Her job - insofar as it is known - was to provide a clandestine courier service.115 Estabrooks had outlined the basic idea years earlier: Induce hypnosis via a disguised technique, give the messenger information to memorize, hypnotically "erase" the message from conscious memory, and install a post-hypnotic suggestion that the message (now buried within the sub-conscious) will be brought forth only upon a specific cue. If the hypnotist can create such a courier, ultra-security can be guaranteed; even torture won't cause the messenger to tell what he knows - because he doesn't know that he knows it.116 According to the highly respected Dr. Milton Kline, "Evidence really does exist that has not been published" proving that Estabrooks' perfect secret agent could be successfully evoked.117

Candy was one such success story. Success, in this context, means that she could be - and was - brutally tortured and abused while running assignments for the CIA. All the MKULTRA toys were brought into play: hypnosis, drugs, conditioning - and electronics. Using these devices, Jensen and Burger managed to:

install a "duplicate personality,"

create amnesia of both the programming sessions and the field assignments,

FIRE FROM THE SKY

turn Candy into a vicious, hate-mongering bigot, the better to isolate her from the rest of humanity (previously, her associates considered her noteworthy for her racial tolerance; her modelling agency was one of the first to break the color barrier), and

program her to commit suicide at the end of her usefulness to the Agency.

The programming techniques used on her were flawed. She breached security when she married famed New York radio personality John Nebel,[118] who, using hypnotic regression, elicited the long-repressed truth. Eventually, the "Other Candy" was bade farewell, and the programming broken.

Skeptics might find Candy's story as incredible as the abduction accounts - after all, an amateur had conducted her hypnotic regression, and the possibility of confabulation always lurks. Nevertheless, I feel that the veracity of her narrative has been established beyond reasonable doubt. In her hypnotic regression sessions, she recalled being programmed at a government-connected institute in northern California - which, as John Marks' investigators later proved, was indeed heavily involved with government-funded brainwashing research.[119] Marks himself believes Candy's story - not least, because the details of the programming methods used on her were substantiated by documents released AFTER her book was published.[120] Interviews with Milton Kline, Dr. Frances Jakes, John Watkins and others provided the testimony that the programming of Candy Jones was feasible - and Deep Trance substantiated the story.[121]

Recently, the case has received important "indirect" confirmation: Investigators interested in follow-up research have filed FOIA requests with the CIA for all papers relating to Candy Jones. The agency admits that it has a substantial file on her, but refuses to release any part of it. If her tale is false, then why would the CIA be so reluctant to deliver the information? Indeed, why would they have a file in the first place?[122]

The final confirmation of Candy's tale requires a revelation - one which I make with some trepidation, even though the individual named is dead.

"Marshall Burger" was really Dr. William Kroger.[123]

Kroger, long associated with the espionage establishment, had written the following in 1963:

...a good subject can be hypnotized to deliver secret information. The memory of this message could be covered by an artificially induced amnesia. In the event that he should be captured, he naturally could not remember that he had ever been given the message... however, since he had been given a post-hypnotic suggestion, the message would be subject to recall through a specific cue.[124]

If Candy confabulated her story, why did she name this particualr scientist, who, writing theoretically in 1963, predicted the subsequent events in her life?[125]

After l'affair Jones, Kroger transferred his base of operations to UCLA - specifically, to the Neuropsychiatric Institute run by Dr. Louis Jolyon West, an MKULTRA veteran. There he wrote HYPNOSIS AND BEHAVIOR MODIFICATION,[126] with a preface by Martin Orne (another MKULTRA veteran) and H.J. Eysenck (still another MKULTRA veteran). The finale of this opus contains chilling hints of the possibilites inherent in combining hypnosis with ESB, implants, and conditioning - though Kroger is careful to point out that "we are not concerned that man might be conditioned by rewards and punishments through electronic brain stimulation to be controlled like robots."127 HE may not be concerned - but perhaps WE ought to be.

The control of Candy Jones gives us much information useful to our "alien abduction" hypothesis.

1. Her torture sessions - inflicted during her programming by her CIA masters, and on missions by as-yet mysterious persons - seem strikingly like the otherwise senselessly painful "examinations" allegedly conducted aboard alien spacecraft.

2. Her personality shifts roughly parallel those experienced by certain UFO abductees.

3. Despite her brutalization, she remained "loyal" to Drs. Jensen and Burger. This bewildering behavior reminds me of my first abductee interviews, during which I heard ghastly descriptions of UFO torture sessions - followed by protestations of limitless love for the alien pain-mongers.

4. Like many abductees, Candy had to attend regular "conditioning" sessions. Repeated exposure to the programming is necessary to effect continuous control.

5. To maintain their hammerlock on her mind, Candy's handlers programmed her to remain isolated. Specifically, they instilled a deep paranoia toward other human beings; "outsiders" were probable enemies, out to use or abuse her. I have seen this pattern consistently in my own work with abductees.128 Skeptics would argue that unreasonable abductee fears probably indicate paranoid schizophrenia - one symptom of which can, indeed, be hallucinatory experiences. But most abductees are easily hypnotized, while paranoid schizophrenics are extremely difficult to "put under," according to Dr. Edward Simpson-Kallas, a psychiatrist with wide experience in the area of forensic hypnosis.129 If, however, those unreasonable fears had been hypnotically induced, the contradiction is resolved.

6. Candy was the product of an unhappy childhood, hence her propensity toward multiple personality.130 Many of the "repeater" abductees I have interviewed had similarly depressing family histories.131

7. The story of Candy Jones also has what we might call a "negative relevance" to the abduction accounts. Because the Controllers did not establish a hypnotic cover story, or pseudomemory, the true facts of the case managed to percolate into her conscious mind. No matter how thorough the posthypnotic amnesia, leaks will occur - hence the need for a false memory, to fill the gap of recollection. The CIA learns from its mistakes. Candy's hypno-programming broke down in early 1973 - the year the "alien disguise" became (if my hypothesis proves correct) standard operating procedure.132 (Milton Kline accepted the Candy Jones story, but considered the job amateurish and inconsistent with the best work done at that time.133 Perhaps the major fault was the lack of a pseudomemory cover story?)

Bases of Suspicion

"Underground base" rumors are as hot as jalapenos in the UFO field right now, and several of these stories involve abductions.

For example, a sideshow of the famous Bentwaters UFO case involves the abduction of an airman named Larry Warren to an underground cavity beneath the military base. There, while in what he later described as "a bit of a drugged state," he saw aliens and human beings - military figures - working side-by-side.134

FIRE FROM THE SKY

I have spoken to another abductee, Nancy Wright, who was allegedly taken to an underground chamber ten miles north of Edwards AFB, California. As this was a multiple-witness event, and Ms. Wright has not attempted to capitalize on the story for financial gain, I tend to credit her story.135

According to abduction researcher Miranda Parks, an elderly couple living in the vicinity was also abducted in an exactly similar fashion.136

In 1979, Paul Bennewitz and Leo Sprinkle researched a particularly controversial abduction involving a young woman (name unrevealed) who was apparently taken to a facility where aliens processed fluids and body parts from a cattle mutilation. This investigation seems to have led to the government harassment of Bennewitz, in which some form of mind control (or, as I have previously referred to it, "electronic GASLIGHT") may have played a part.137

How do we account for these tales of alleged alien skullduggery carried out in conjunction with the military? I, for one, cannot credit the generally unsubstantiated tales of "cosmic conspiracy" now promulgated by ex-intelligence agents such as John Lear and William Cooper. While I cannot assert insincerity on the part of these men, I often wonder if they have been used as conduits - witting or unwitting - in a sophisticated disinformation scheme.

A simpler, though no less chilling, explanation for the "base" abductions may be found in the story of Dr. Louis Jolyon West, now notorious for his participation in MKULTRA experiments with LSD.138 Inspired by VIOLENCE AND THE BRAIN (a book by Drs. Frank Ervin and Vernon H. Mark which ascribed inner city turmoil to a "genetic defect" within rebellious blacks), West proposed, in 1973, a Center for the Study and Reduction of Violence, where potentially violent individuals could be dealt with prophylactically.

And who were these individuals? According to West's proposal, the noteworthy factors indicating a violent predisposition were "sex (male), age (youthful), ethnicity (black) and urbanicity." How to deal with them? "...by implanting tiny electrodes deep within the brain, electrical activity can be followed in areas that cannot be measured from the surface of the scalp... it is even possible to record bioelectrical changes in the brains of freely-moving subjects, through the use of remote monitoring techniques..." By monitoring the subjects' EEGs remotely, potentially violent episodes could be identified.

For our purposes, the most significant aspect of this proposal had to do with location. In a secret communication to Dr. J.M. Stubblebine, director of the California State Department of Health (fortunately, this missive was "leaked" to the public), West disclosed that he intended to house his Center in an abandoned Nike missile base, whose location was accessible yet relatively remote. "The site is securely fenced," West wrote. "Comparative studies could be carried out there, in an isolated but convenient location, of experimental model programs, for the alteration of undesirable behavior."139

Public outcry stopped these plans. But was this scheme truly eliminated? Or was it merely modified, stripped (temporarily) of its overtly racial overtones and relocated to some less-accessible spot?

One thing is certain: A CIA "spy-chiatrist" favored secret behavior control experimentation in a remote military installation. Perhaps someone within the espionage establishment's mind-modification divisions still thinks highly of the idea. If so, the disposal problem would once again rear its ugly head, should "visitors" to these installations ever reappear in outside society. Again, a hypno-programmed cover story - the less believable, the better - would prove invaluable.

The Scandinavian Connection

Many books have been written about abductees, yet few exist about the victims of mind control. I cannot understand this situation; the reality of UFOs is still controversial, yet the existence of mind control was verified in two (heavily compromised) congressional investigations and in thousands of FOIA documents. Nevertheless, the abductees find many a sympathetic ear, while those few who dare to proclaim themselves the victims of known government programs rarely find anyone to hear them out. Our prejudices on this score are regrettable, for if we listened to the "controllees" we would hear many details strikingly similar to those mentioned by UFO abductees.

Two cases in point: Martti Koski and Robert Naeslund.

Koski, a Finnish citizen, claims to have been a victim of mind control experimentation while visiting Canada. Shortly after his experience began, he attempted to broadcast his situation to the world and draw attention to his plight. Few listened. Many of his details were bizarre, and not being a native speaker of English, he could not express himself convincingly to those he approached for help. Yet many aspects of his story correspond closely to known details of MKULTRA and related programs.

Naeslund, a Swedish citizen, tells a similar story. Moreover, his claims were backed by special evidence: X-rays revealed an implant in his brain. Naeslund actually went to the extreme of having his implant tested by electronic technicians employed by Hewlett-Packard. A Greek surgeon performed the necessary trepanation to remove the device.

Many aspects of the Koski and Naeslund stories correspond to my hypothesis. Koski, for example, was at one point told that the doctors afflicting him were actually "aliens from Sirius." At another point, he was led to believe that he was under direction of "the Lord." (As I previously indicated, manipulation of religious imagery could help induce anti-social behavior; the subject's super-ego can be nullified if he believes that he follows commands from on high. Such manipulation may explain the more bizarre aspects of Betty Andreasson Luca's abduction.140)

Naeslund's implant was originally placed through his nasal cavity. He first realized that something terrible had happened to him after an experience of missing time, followed by an inexplicable nosebleed.

This detail will be instantly familiar to anyone who has studied abductions; I have encountered it in my own conversations with abductees. For an excellent example in the UFO literature, I refer the reader to the case of Susan Ransted, as detailed in Kevin D. Randle's THE UFO CASEBOOK;141 the background of alleged contactee Diane Tessman is also noteworthy in this regard.142 Intriguingly, I have located a reference in the open literature to the use, in animal study, of nasally-implanted electrodes for the measurement of electro-magnetic radiation effects.143

There are other claimed mind control victims bearing evidence of implants; note, especially, the fascinating case of James Petit, a CIA-connected pilot and alleged brainwashing alumnus; X-rays of his cranium have revealed abductee-style implants - fitting, perhaps, since his body bears abductee-style scars.144 Conversely, certain abductees will, if allowed a thorough and sympathetic hearing, deliver testimony strongly agreeing with Koski's narrative.

FIRE FROM THE SKY

Helicopters and Disks

The bizarre story of Rex Niles and his sister (not named in news accounts) may shed interesting light on a variety of abductee cases, particularly that of Betty and Barney Hill.145 Niles, the high-rolling owner of a Woodland Hills defense subcontracting firm (Rex Rep) was fingered by authorities investigating defense industry kickbacks. He became an extraordinarily cooperative witness in the investigation - until he was targeted by his enemies, who allegedly used psychoelectronics as harassment.

The following excerpt from the LOS ANGELES TIMES article on Niles is particularly compelling:

He [Niles] produced testimony from his sister, a Simi Valley woman who swears that helicopters have repeatedly circled her home. An engineer measured 250 watts of microwaves in the atmosphere outside Niles' house and found a radioactive disk underneath the dash of his car. [my italics]

A former high school friend, Lyn Silverman, claimed that her home computer went haywire when Niles stepped close to it.

No aliens in this story - yet how similar it is to tales of alien abduction! The low-flying helicopters, of course, are frequently reported by abduction victims - the Betty Andreasson Luca case provides the best known example.146 The haywire electronics equipment is also frequently encountered in putative abduction cases; I have spoken (independently) to three women who claimed to have been able to disturb or shut off televisions and stereos simply by walking past the devices; one woman even claimed she had switched off her TV simply by pointing at it.

But the radioactive disk is especially intriguing. As former FBI agent Ted Gunderson recently explained to my associate Alexander Constantine, magnetic radioactive disks have long been used by the clandestine services as cancer-inducing "silent killers" - i.e., as tools of assassination. Not only that. The disc calls to mind one little-remembered detail of the Hill case - the dozen-or-so circular "shiny spots," each the size of a silver dollar, found on the trunk of her car directly after the abduction. A compass needle reacted wildly when placed near these spots. Could they have marked the location where an electromagnetic or radioactive device, similar to that found by Niles, was placed on the car? (Such a device might have been held to the spot magnetically, hence the circular impressions.) If so, then the disorienting EMR could have helped induce the Hills' "UFO sighting."

The Military and Mind Control

Some time ago, I attended hypnotic regression sessions in which the subject - a claimed UFO abductee - recalled undergoing a mysterious "brain operation" at a veteran's hospital in California. The operation was performed by human beings, not aliens. Interestingly, this same hospital was mentioned in two other cases I encountered. These other claims were not made by abductees, but by people alleged to have been victims of mind control experimentation.

One of these claimants, a former Navy SEAL who undertook numerous dangerous missions in Vietnam, favorably impressed me with the wealth of detail in his story.147 This individual - I've taken to calling him "the trained SEAL"- had received specialized

141

FIRE FROM THE SKY

combat training at a military base in California; he claims that at one point during this training he was drugged, hypnotized, possibly placed under some form of electronic control, and subjected to the extremes of pain/pleasure operant conditioning. One peculiar detail of his story concerns the "reward" aspect of the conditioning: When properly acquiescent, he was given unlimited sexual access to a woman who, the SEAL avers, was herself the victim of brainwashing.

Unbelievable as this last claim may seem, I found it oddly resonant when I later interviewed a prominent abductee in the Southern California area, who bravely offered me details on a puzzling, albeit quite delicate, incident in her past. Still an attractive woman, she recalled for me - indeed, seemed strangely compelled to describe - an early love affair with a young soldier training at a military base near her home. She cannot recall the soldier's name. All she remembers is that one day he started living at her family's house; she has no memory of how the arrangement began, and her parents have never felt comfortable discussing the matter. Although unattracted to this soldier, she felt compelled to become intimate with him, adopting a pliant, obeisant attitude that was quite out of character for her. Later, the soldier went on to covert missions in Vietnam.

Of course, a young person's psycho-sexual development is never smooth, and the incident related above may merely have represented one peculiarly upsetting bump in that notoriously rough road. Still, some of the details of this story - particularly the parents' attitude, the woman's personality shift, and her subsequent memory lapses - are striking, and I treat with respect the abduc- tee's intuition that this minor enigma in her personal history could, if properly understood, shed light on her later "missing time" experiences.

Could the "trained SEAL" have been right? Was there, is there, a coterie of hypno-programmed soldiers conducting particularly hazardous missions? And do the programmers have at their disposal a "ladies' auxiliary," so to speak, of hypnotized camp followers?

If the SEAL's story stood alone, skeptics could easily dismiss it (provided they did not sit, as I did, face-to-face with the story's teller, listening to all the grisly and unsettling details). But other veterans have added their voices to this grim tale. Daniel Sheehan, of the Christic Institute, claims that his organization has spoken to half-a-dozen individuals with narratives similar to my SEAL informant. All had received "processing," so to speak, within the context of standard military training; after programming and specialized combat instruction by mercenaries, the recruits were placed "on hold," to be used as situations arose - and some of those situations occurred within the United States.[148]

Walter Bowart began his own researches into mind control by placing an ad in SOLDIER-OF-FORTUNE-style publications, asking for correspondence from veterans who experienced inexplicable lapses in memory or strange behavior modification techniques while serving in Vietnam; he received over 100 replies. Bowart devoted an entire chapter to one of these respondents - an Air Force veteran named David, who ended his four-year tour of duty recalling only that he had spent the time, "having fun, skin diving, laying on the beach, collecting shells.... It never dawned on me until later that I must have DONE something while I was in the service." (An obvious example of screen memory.) He was also "assigned" a girlfriend whose name he cannot now recall, despite the length and deep intimacy of the affair.[149] The parallels to the SEAL's story and the abductee's account should be obvious.

We even have a confession, of sorts, from a scientist who specialized in one aspect of this sort of training. Lt. Commander Thomas Narut, of the U.S. Naval Hospital at the NATO headquarters in Naples, Florida, [Ed: ???] admitted during a lecture in Oslo that recruits in Naples underwent CLOCKWORK ORANGE-style behavior modification sessions. Trainees would be strapped into chairs with their eyelids clamped open while watching films of industrial accidents and African circumcision ceremonies - films frequently used by psychologists as a means of inducing stress in experimental situations. Unlike the protagonist in A CLOCKWORK ORANGE, who learned revulsion at the sight of violence, Narut's soldiers were taught to accept and enjoy bloodshed, to view it with equanimity. Similar techniques were used to dehumanize potential enemies. Graduates of this program became, in Narut's words, "hit men and assassins," to be placed in American embassies throughout the world.

When questioned by reporters about these claims, the American government denied the story; Narut - after a long incommunicado period and apparent coercion - later explained to journalists that he had merely spoken theoretically. If so, why did he originally describe the behavior modification procedure as an ongoing program?150

And while it may seem frivolous to return to the subject of abductions after examining such grim data, I should remind the reader of the many abduction accounts in which abductees recall being forced to watch certain stress inducing motion pictures. The aliens, it seems, have learned a few lessons from Dr. Narut.

Narut, of course, concentrated on selective programming of individual American soldiers; on the other side of the mind control spectrum, Defense Department specialists have also concentrated on methods to render entire enemy battalions "combat ineffective." Electromagnetic weaponry, intended to wipe out the aggression of the enemy, is the province of DARPA, under the direction of Dr. Jack Verona. These projects remain fairly mysterious; we do know, however, that one operation, SLEEPING BEAUTY, employed the services of Dr. Michael Persinger, a scientist who has expressed interesting views regarding UFOs.

Persinger discovered a method of using ELF waves to induce the brain's MAST cells to release histamine; should a battlefield commander wish to subject his enemy to mass bouts of vomiting, Persinger's trick could do the job even faster than a Tobe Hooper movie. The method works on animals. "The question," writes mind control researcher Larry Collins, "is how to get from point A to point B without violating one of the most rigorous commandments of Government ethics - thou shalt not conduct experiments like that on human beings."151

If Collins had studied the record a little more carefully, he might realize that the government hasn't always regarded this commandment as something graven in stone. As Milton Kline put it:

*Ethical factors involved in most research would preclude having positive results. Those ethical factors don't always hold with government research. The research which has given really positive results has not been limited by ethical constraints.*152 [my italics]

The Ultimate Motive for Mind Control

FIRE FROM THE SKY

Hypnosis hard-liners of the Orne school would almost certainly dismiss the foregoing veterans' accounts of the use of hypnosis, drugs and behavioral conditioning on American fighting men. Why, the skeptics would ask, would anyone attempt to create a "Manchurian Candidate" when the military services, using entirely conventional means, can create a "Rambo"? There have always been recruits for even the most hazardous duties; what need of hypnosis?

The need, in fact, is absolute.

The modern battlefield has little place for the traditional soldier. Advanced weaponry requires an increasing level of technical sophistication, which in turn requires a cool-headed operator. But the all-too-human combatant - though capable of extraordinary acts of courage under the most stressful conditions imaginable - does not possess inexhaustible reserves of *sang-froid*. Eventually, breakdowns will occur. Per-capita psychiatric casualties have increased dramatically in each successive American conflict. As Richard Gabriel, the excellent historian of the role of psychiatry in warfare, writes:

Modern warfare has become so lethal and so intense that only the already insane can endure it.... Modern war requiring continuous combat will increase the degree of fatigue on the soldier to heretofore unknown levels. Physical fatigue - especially the lack of sleep - will increase the rate of psychiatric casualties enormously. Other factors - high rates of indirect fire, night fighting, lack of food, constant stress, large numbers of casualties - will ensure that the number of psychiatric casualties will reach disastrous proportions. And the number of casualties will overburden the medical structure to the point of collapse.

The ability to treat psychiatric casualties will all but disappear. There will be no safe forward areas in which to treat soldiers debilitated by mental collapse. The technology of modern war has made such locations functionally obsolete...[153]

According to Gabriel, the military intends to meet this challenge by creating "the chemical soldier," a designer-drugged zombie in fighting man's uniform:

On the battlefields of the future we will witness a true clash of ignorant armies, armies ignorant of their own emotions and even of the reasons for which they fight. Soldiers on all sides will be reduced to fearless chemical automatons who fight simply because they can do nothing else.... Once the chemical genie is out of the bottle, the full range of human mental and physical actions become targets for chemical control.... Today it is already possible by chemical or electrical stimulation to increase the aggression levels of the human being by stimulating the amygdala, a section of the brain known to control aggression and rage. Such "human potential engineering" is already a partial reality and the necessary technical knowledge increases every day.[154]

While this passage speaks of drugs and electronics, we can safely assume that the planners of battle would not refrain from using any other promising technique.

Gabriel writes primarily of large-scale battle scenarios, but based on his information, we can fairly deduce that the mind-controlled soldier will also play a role in the surgical strike, the covert operation, the infiltration behind enemy lines by units of the Special Forces. On such missions, United States personnel have increasingly relied on torture as a means of interrogation and intimidation,[155] and as such barbarism becomes standard procedure the American fighting man of the future will need to find within himself unprecedented reserves of brutality. Will the average recruit, culled from the nation's suburbs and reared on traditional ideals, possess such reserves?

Vietnam proved that the soldier, despite a barrage of propaganda intended to cloud his discernment, will sense the difference between fighting for legitimate defense interests and fighting to protect political hegemony. To forestall this realization, or to render it irrelevant, military planners must withdraw the human combatant and replace him with a new species of warrior. The soldier of the future will not discern; he will merely do. He will not be a butcher; he will be the butcher's knife - a tool among tools, thoughtless and effective.

And it is my contention that to create this soldier of the future, the controllers will need a continuing program, one designed to test each new method and combination of methods for conquering the human mind.

One primary goal of this program must include expanding the human capacity for stress and violence. Subjects enrolled in such experimental procedures will experience pain, and will learn to accept the pain. Eventually, they will learn to inflict it, without remorse or even remembrance. The nation who first creates this new soldier will possess a decisive advantage on the "conventional" battlefield - as will the nation which first develops a means of using mass mind control techniques to disable entire enemy platoons. This paramount military necessity is the reason why I will never believe any unconvincing reassurances that our nation's clandestine scientists have foregone or will forego research into behavior modification. This research will never be mere history. What's past is present, and today's covert experimentation will become tomorrow's basic training.

A prototype of the future warrior may already be with us. The Navy SEAL I interviewed spoke in horrifying detail of dismemberment without emotion, of rape as routine, of killing without affect. And then forgetting that he has killed. Even years later, he could not recall the stories behind many of the wounds on his own body. He claims that whenever he would need the services of the veteran's hospital, doctors would re-hypnotize him shortly after his admission, while a physician specifically cleared for such work would examine his medical history, which was highly classified and kept under lock and key.

According to the SEAL's testimony, his memory block cracked little by little, as a result of events too complex to recount here. Finally, years after Vietnam, he was able to remember what he did.

Amnesia was a blessing.

IV. Abductions

Press and public now regard abductees as tony curiosities, yet science, for the most part, still banishes their tales to the domain of the damned, as Charles Fort defined damnation. So too with claimed victims of mind control. The Voice of Authority tells us that MKULTRA belongs to history; like Hasdrubal and Hitler, it threatened once, but no more. Anyone insisting otherwise must be silenced by glib rationalization and selective inattention.

FIRE FROM THE SKY

Yet these two topics - UFO abductions and mind control - have more in common than their mutual ostracization. The data overlap. If we could chart these phenomena on a Venn diagram, we would see a surprisingly large intersection between the two circles of information. It is this overlap I seek to address.

Note, however, that I can NOT address all the other interesting and important issues raised by the UFO abduction experience. For example, I have written, admittedly rather vaguely, of nasal implants reported by abductees - the sort of detail which might place an account in the "high strangeness" category, and of course, a detail central to my thesis. But what percentage of the percipients speak of such implants? A truly scientific analysis would provide a figure. Unfortunately, I haven't the resources to compile a sufficiently large abductee sample from which one could draw statistics. Nor can I make an over-arching qualitative analysis, measuring the value of "high strangeness" reports against other abductee claims. All I can do is note the available literature, and leave the reader to wonder, as I do, whether the compilers of that literature concentrated on exceptional cases or were biased in favor of the less fantastic abductee accounts. I have supplemented readings of the abduction literature with my own interviews with percipients - which, since abductees tend to know other abductees, can give a surprisingly wide view of the phenomenon. This view has been broadened still further by my talks and correspondence with other members of the UFO community.

Of course, we must recognize the difference between testimony and proof. No one can state definitively that abduction reports have a basis in objective reality (however misperceived). Ultimately, all we have are stories. Some of these stories may be of questionable veracity; others may be contaminated by investigator bias; many are insufficiently detailed. No one research paper can resolve all abduction controversies, and many necessary battles must be fought on other fields.

Still, the testimony won't go away - and we certainly have enough to allow for comparisons. I maintain that an unprejudiced overview of abduction reports in the popular press and the less-familiar material on mind control will demonstrate a striking correlation. Once other abduction researchers have been educated in the ways of MKULTRA (and this paper is intended as an introductory text) they may note a similar pattern. If so, we can then begin to write a revisionist history of the phenomenon.

The abduction enigma contains within it sub-mysteries that slide into the mind control scenario with surprising ease, even elegance - mysteries which fit the E.T. hypothesis as uncomfortably as a size 10 foot fits into a size 8 shoe. As we have seen, the MKULTRA thesis explains the reports of abductee intracerebral implants (particularly reports involving nosebleeds), unusual scars, "telepathic" communication (i.e., externally induced intracerebral voices) concurrent with or following the abduction encounter, allegations that some abductees hear unusual sound effects (similar to those created by the hemisynch and cognate devices), haywire electronic devices in abductee homes, personality shifts, "training films," manipulation of religious imagery, and missing time. Needless to say, the thesis of clandestine government experimentation readily accounts for abductee claims of human beings "working" with the aliens, and for the government harassment that plays so prominent a role in certain abductee reports.

Let's look at some more correlations.

The Hill Case and the "Advanced" Aliens

Earlier, I asked, "Do the aliens also watch black-and-white television?" in reference to their alleged use of old-fashioned, Terra-style brain implantation devices. Abduction accounts abound in other examples of alien "retro-technology." The most striking example can be found in the Betty and Barney Hill incident, the details of which are too well-known to recount here.156 As we have already glimpsed during our discussion of the Rex Niles affair, the Hills' "interrupted journey" abounds in data which, taken together, permits the construction of an alternative explanation.

At one point during the alleged UFO abduction, the "examiners" inserted a needle in Betty Hill's navel, telling her that this practice constituted a test for pregnancy.157 Some ufologists158 rashly assume that Betty Hill's "pregnancy test" is evidence of advanced extraterrestrial technology, since her 1961 account pre-dates the official announcement of amniocentesis, which does indeed make use of a needle inserted into the navel. But we now have much less invasive means of testing for pregnancy than amniocentesis. True, amniocentesis is still sometimes used to gather information about the fetus, but the wielders of a highly evolved technology would certainly use other methods of determining the existence of pregnancy in the first place.

Betty Hill's testimony reminds us of certain other abduction accounts, which contain descriptions of "healings" surprisingly similar to the procedures associated with still-experimental electromagnetic therapy techniques, such as those described in Robert O. Becker's THE BODY ELECTRIC. For example, abductee Deanna Dube described for me an abduction-related "regeneration" of her long-damaged heart; had she been familiar with Becker's work,159 she might have been a bit less rapid to ascribe her healing to otherworldly influences.

Medical breakthroughs often undergo years of testing before their official "discovery." For some of these tests, finding volunteers present a major obstacle. If we accept the proposition that the Hill incident originated in an external and objective stimulus, we must then ask ourselves which scenario is more likely: Did Betty Hill encounter human beings using a technique ten years ahead of its time? Or did she encounter aliens (reputedly a "billion years ahead of us") using science from eons before their time?

One must also ask why Betty Hill's aliens seemed to have no grasp of basic human concepts (such as how we measure time) - yet they knew enough about us to speak English fluently and had even mastered our slang. Were these real aliens, or humans engaging in theatricals (and occasionally muffing their lines)? For that matter, why did Betty Hill originally recall her abductors as humanoid, only later describing them as aliens?

FIRE FROM THE SKY

The Hill case provided a particularly controversial piece of evidence - the celebrated "star map" recalled by Betty Hill under hypnosis. In later years, an Ohio schoolteacher named Marjorie Fish made an ingenious and laudable attempt to discover a match for this map by constructing an elaborate three-dimensional model of nearby star systems; whether she succeeded remains a matter for keen debate.160 For now, I prefer to avoid taking sides in this dispute and will confine myself to insisting that pro-ET ufologists answer (without resorting to glib ripostes) a point first raised by Jacques Vallee: the map makes no sense as a navigational aid. Vallee notes that, even if we grant the Fish interpretation, the stars are not drawn to scale - and at any rate, alien spaceships would surely be navigated the same way we guide our own spacecraft: via computers and telemetry161 The validity of the Fish interpretation is irrelevent; the point is that any such chart would have no value to an interstellar star-farer.

Fish's work raises other controversies: Allegedly, the map points to Zeta Reticuli as the aliens' home system and pictures Zeta Reticuli as a single star, a view consistent with scientific opinion of the 1960s. Yet in later years scientists discovered that Zeta Reticuli is binary.162 Moreover, how did our abductee manage to remember so accurately a complex chart glimpsed in passing? Even allowing for the possibility of increased accuracy of recollection under hypnotic regression, the memory feat here seems remarkable. Consider the circumstances of the abduction: Kafka on hallucinogens couldn't have conceived of the nightmare vision confronting Betty Hill that night - yet for some reason this particular arrangement of stars emerged as her most intensely-detailed recollection of the experience.

This memory (if not confabulated during regression, a possibility we should always weigh) is comprehensible only as an example of artificially-induced hypermensia. In other words, Betty Hill was directed to store that chart within her subconscious. The celebrated star map ought to be recognized for what it was: a prop, a seemingly confirmatory circumstantial detail meant to convince her - and perhaps us - of the reality of her abduction.

The question of motive arises. Why - if my thesis is correct - were these two fairly innocuous individuals chosen for this new variation on the old MKULTRA tricks?

The selection might, of course, have been arbitrary. Or perhaps circumstances now irretrievably lost to history rendered the couple a convenient target. Interestingly, Barney Hill had become acquainted (through church functions) with the head of Air Force intelligence at Pease Air Force Base; perhaps this relationship first brought the Hills to the attention of members of the intelligence community. Arguably, the Hills could have been fingered for a wide variety of reasons; as a general rule, the clandestine services prefer to satisfy a number of itches with one scratch.

In fact, the espionage establishment had one particularly compelling reason to focus on the Hills. Barney Hill (a black man) and his wife held important positions in several civil rights organizations, including the NAACP.163 The abduction took place during the 1960s, when the NAACP and allied groups fell victim to an increasingly paranoid series of attacks from the FBI and other governmental agencies (under operations COINTELPRO, CHAOS, GARDEN PLOT, etc.).164 At that time, infiltration of civil rights groups proved a difficult chore; while most left-leaning groups provided easy targets for FBI stooges, the average undercover operative would have had an exceptionally difficult time posing as

FIRE FROM THE SKY

a black activist. (In 1961, the only black people on the FBI's payroll were the servants in J. Edgar Hoover's home.)

In light of these facts, we should recall Victor Marchetti's anecdote about the cat that the CIA had "wired for sound." Perhaps an ambitious covert scientist proposed a similar experiment, in which a human being would play the role that had once been assigned to the unfortunate feline? As Estabrooks noted, the ultimate espionage agent would be the spy who doesn't KNOW he is a spy. Barney Hill, a well-regarded figure with a near-genius-level IQ, was a safe bet to obtain a leadership role in any group he joined; he would have been remarkably well-positioned, had any outsiders wished to use his ears to overhear prominent black organizers in confidential discussion.

Of course, many intelligence professionals would counter this suggestion by reminding us that eavesdroppers on the civil rights movement had plenty of less-flamboyant methods: Bugging, "black bag" jobs, paying for information, etc. The point is valid. But if the technology to create a "human bug" was developed circa 1961 - and there is documentation suggesting that such is indeed the case[165] - the intelligence agencies would surely have wanted to test the possibilities in the field. And considering the expense of such a test, why not conduct the experiment in such a way as to reap the maximum benefits? Why NOT choose a Barney Hill?

Arms and the Abductee

Budd Hopkins told the follwing story during his lecture at the Los Angeles "Whole Life Expo."[166] He considers the case "very good... lots of corroborating witnesses for parts of it." Though not, presumably, for this part.

Hopkins' informant, after the by-now familiar UFO abduction, was given a gun by the aliens. Not a Buck Rogers laser weapon - this was something Dirty Harry might have packed.

The abductee was also given someone to shoot. Not a little grey alien, another human being, tied to a chair. The "visitors" told their armed abductee that this captive had done "evil on earth, and he's a bad person. You have to kill him." If the abductee didn't do as asked, he would never leave the ship.

The captive proclaimed his innocence, and pleaded for his life. The abductee, caught in the middle of all this, became quite upset. (Worth noting: he seems to have at least considered the aliens' request to shoot someone he had never met.) Ultimately, the abductee turned the gun on the aliens and said, "Nobody's going to get shot here."

According to Hopkins, "The aliens said 'Fine. Very good.' They took the gun from him; the man [presumably, the captive] got up, walked away, disappeared, and they went on to the next thing." Obviously, this little drama had been staged - a test of some sort.

I submit that this surreal incident is incomprehensible as either an example of alien incursion or of "Klass-ical" confabulation. The scenario described here EXACTLY parallels numerous experiments in the hypnotic induction of anti-social action as revealed both in the standard hypnosis literature and in declassified ARTICHOKE/MKULTRA documents. For example, compare Hopkins' account to the following, in which Ludwig Mayer, a prominent German hypnosis researcher, describes a classic experiment in the hypnotic induction of criminal action:

FIRE FROM THE SKY

I gave a revolver to an elderly and readily suggestible man whom I had just hypnotized. The revolver had just been loaded by Mr. H. with a percussion cap. I explained to [the subject], while pointing to Mr. H., that Mr. H. was a very wicked man whom he should shoot to kill. With great determination he took the revolver and fired a shot directly at Mr. H. Mr. H. fell down pretending to be wounded. I then explained to my subject that the fellow was not yet quite dead, and that he should give him another bullet, which he did without further ado.167

Of course, if a conservative hypnosis specialist were asked to comment on the above account, he would quickly point out that hypnotic suggestions which work in an experimental situation would not easily succeed outside the laboratory; on some level, the subject will probably sense whether or not he's playing the game for real.168 Similarly, a conservative abduction researcher would, in reviewing Hopkins' material, emphasize the problems inherent in using testimony derived during regression, where the threat of confabulation lurks. I'll concede both arguments - for the moment - only to insist that they are beside the point. The matter of primary importance, the sticking point which neither Klass nor Hopkins can comfortably confront, is the convergence of detail between Mayer's hypnosis experiment and the testing event related by Hopkins' abductee. Why are these two stories so similar? Did the good Dr. Mayer take pupils from Sirius?169

Hopkins says he knows of other instances in which abductees found themselves in similar crucibles. So do I.

One person I spoke to can remember (sans hypnosis) being handed a gun inside a ziplock baggy and receiving instructions that she will have to use this weapon "on a job." Early in my interviews with her (and with no prompting from me) she recited an apparent cue drilled into her consciousness by the "entities" (as she calls them): "When you see the light, do it tonight," followed by the command, "Execute." (One can only speculate as to how such commands would be used in the field; we will discuss later the use of photovoltaic hypnotic induction.) Though her personal feelings toward firearms are decidedly negative, she vividly describes periods in her "everyday" life when she feels an uncharacteristic, yet overpowering urge to be near a gun - a quasi-sexual desire to pick one up and touch the metal.170

She is not alone. Another has been so affected by gun fever that he became a security guard, just to be near the things.171 The abductees I have spoken to connect this sudden surge of Ramboism to the UFO experience. But I suggest that the UFO experience may be merely a cover story for another type of training entirely.

One of the primary goals of BLUEBIRD, ARTICHOKE, and MKULTRA was to determine whether mind control could be used to faciliate "executive action" - i.e., assassination.172

It isn't difficult to imagine the media's reaction if a public figure were murdered by someone acting at the behest of the "space brothers." Who would dare to speak of conspiracy under such circumstances? The hidden controllers could choose a myth structure that conform's to the abductee's personality, then pose as higher beings, who would whisper violence into the ear of the percipient. Using this ruse, the trick that scientists such as Ludwig Mayer could perform in the lab might now be accomplished in the field. As Estabrooks' associate Jack Tracktir (professor of hypnotherapy at Baylor University) explained to John Marks, anti-social acts can be induced with "no conscience involved"

FIRE FROM THE SKY

once the proper pretext has been created.173

They Will Think It's Flying Saucers

Jenny Randles contributes an anecdote from Great Britain which dovetails nicely with this hypothesis.

In 1965, "Margary" (a pseudonym) lived in Birmingham with her husband, who one night told her to prepare for a "shock and a test." As Randles describes what she calls a "rogue case":

They got into his car and drove off, although her memory of the trip became hazy and confused and she does not know where they went. Then she was in a room that was dimly lit and there were people standing around a long table or flat bed. She was out on it and seemed "drugged" and unable to resist. The most memorable of the men was tall and thin with a long nose and white beard. He had thick eyebrows and supposedly said to Margary, "Remember the eyebrows, honey." A strange medical examination, using odd equipment, was performed on her.

Both the husband and the scientists, using (apparently) hypnotic techniques, flooded her mind with images that, she was told, would be understood only in the future. According to Randles, "At one point one of the 'examiners' in the room said to Margary in a tone that made it seem as if he were amused, "They will think it's flying saucers." The husband also revealed that he had a second identity. After the abduction, this husband (am I going too far to assume his employment with MI6 or some cognate agency?) left, never to be seen again.174 Margary did not recall the abduction until 1978.

This affair can only baffle a researcher who insists on fitting all abduction accounts into the ET hypothesis; once we free ourselves from that set of assumptions, explanations come easily. I interpret this incident as a case in which the controllers applied the flying saucer cover story sloppily, or to an insufficiently receptive subject. If my thesis is correct, the UFO "hypnotic hoax" technique would still have been fairly new in 1965, particularly outside the United States; perhaps the manipulators hadn't yet got the hang of it. The odd comment about the scientist's eyebrows may refer to an item of disguise donned for the occasion. The unscrupulous hypnotist, unsure about his ability to induce an impenetrable amnesia - and mindful of the price paid by his forerunners in mesmeric criminality175 - would understandably want to hedge his bets; by indulging in the British penchant for theatrics, he could further protect his anonymity.

A similar incident was brought to my attention by researcher Robert Durant.

The relevant excerpt of his letter follows:

Now I want to turn to a case that I have been investigating for several months. The subject is an abductee. Standard abduction scenario. Twice regressed under hypnosis, the first time by a well-known abduction researcher, the second time by a psychologist with parapsychology connections.

In the course of many hours of listening to the subject, I discovered that she has had close personal contact over a long period of time with several individuals who have federal intelligence connections. She was hypnotized many years ago as part of a TV program devoted to hypnosis. Her abductions began shortly after she attended several long sessions at a

FIRE FROM THE SKY

laboratory where, ostensibly, she was being tested for ESP abilities. Two other people who were "tested" at this same laboratory have also had abductions. All three were told by the lab to join a local UFO group. During her abductions, the principal alien spoke to the subject in the English language in a normal manner, not via telepathy. She recognized the voice, which was at one time that of her very close friend of yesteryear who was then and is now employed by the CIA. The other voice was that of an individual who works in Washington, has what I will call very strong federal connections as well as a finger in every ufological pie, and who just happened to bump into her at the aforementioned laboratory.

*He also anticipated, in the course of telephone conversations, her abductions. When the subject confronted him about this and the voice, he claimed to be psychic. (!)*176

The "ESP" connection is suggestive; the MKULTRA documents betray an astonishing interest on the part of the intelligence agencies in matters parapsychological.

Some researchers would object that examples such as this are rare; most abductions contain no such overt indications of intelligence involvement. But have investigators looked for them? As mentioned in the introduction, a false dichotomy limits much ufological thought; as long as the abduction argument swings between the ET hypothesis and purely psychological theories, researchers will not recognize the relevance of certain key items of background data.

Glimpses Of The Controllers

In an interview with me, a northern-California abducteee - call him "Peter" - reported an experience which was conducted NOT by a small grey alien, but by a human being. The percipient called this man a "doctor." He gave a description of this individual, and even provided a drawing.

Some time after I gathered this information, a southern-California abductee told me her story - which included a description of this very same "doctor." The physical details were so strikingly similar as to erase coincidence. This woman is a leading member of a Los Angeles-based UFO group; three other women in this group report abduction encounters with the same individual.177

Perhaps those three women were fantasists, attaching themselves to another's narrative. But my northern informant never met these people. Why did he describe the same "doctor"?

One of the abductees I have dealt with insisted, under hypnosis, that her abduction experience brought her to a certain house in the Los Angeles area. She was able to provide directions to the house, even though she had no conscious memory of ever being there. I later learned that this house is indeed occupied by a scientist who formerly (and perhaps currently) conducted clandestine research on mind control technology.

This same abductee described a clandestine brain operation of some sort she underwent in childhood. The neurosurgeon was a human being, not an alien. She even recalled the name. (Note: This is not the same individual referred to above.) When I heard the name, it meant nothing to me - but later I learned that there really was a scientist of that name who specialzed in electrode implant research.

Licia Davidson is a thoughtful and articulate abductee, whose fascinating story closely parallels many found in the abductee literature - except for one unusual detail. In an interview with me, described an unsettling recollection of a human being, dressed nor-

FIRE FROM THE SKY

mally, holding a black box with a protruding antenna. This odd snippet of memory did NOT coincide with the general thrust of her abduction narrative. Could this remembrance represent an all-too-brief segment of accurately-perceived reality interrupting her hypnotically-induced "screen memory"? Peter clearly recalls seeing a similar box during his abduction.

Interestingly, Licia resides in the Los Angeles suburb of Tujunga Canyon, a prominent spot on the abduction map; Many of the abductees I have spoken to first had unusual experiences while living in this area. Near Tujunga Canyon, in Mt. Pacifico, is a hidden former Nike missile base; more than one abductee has described odd, seemingly inexplicable military activity around this location.178 The reader will recall the connection of Nike missile bases to the disturbing story of Dr. L. Jolyon West, a veteran of MKULTRA.

Cults

Some abductees I have spoken to have been directed to join certain religious/philosophical sects. These cults often bear close examination.

The leaders of these groups tend to be "ex"-CIA operatives, or Special Forces veterans. They are often linked through personal relations, even though they espouse widely varying traditions. I have heard unsettling reports that the leaders of some of these groups have used hypnosis, drugs, or "mind machines" on their charges. Members of these cults have reported periods of missing time during ceremonies or "study periods."

I strongly urge abduction researchers to examine closely any small "occult" groups an abductee might join. For example, one familiar leader of the UFO fringe - a man well-known for his espousal of the doctrine of "love and light" - is Virgil Armstrong, a close personal friend of General John Singlaub, the notorious Iran-Contra player, who recently headed the neo-fascist World Anti-Communist League. Armstrong, who also happens to be an ex-Green Beret and former CIA operative, figured into my inquiry in an interesting fashion: An abductee of my acquaintance was told - by her "entities," naturally - to seek out this UFO spokesman and join his "sky-watch" activities, which, my source alleges, included a mass channelling session intended to send debilitating "negative" vibrations to Constantine Chernenko, then the leader of the Soviet Union. Of course, intracerebral voices may have a purely psychological origin, so Armstrong can hardly be held to task for the abductee's original "directive."179 Still, his past associations with military intelligence inevitably bring disturbing possibilities to mind.

Even more ominous than possible ties between UFO cults and the intelligence community are the cults' links with the shadowy I AM group, founded by Guy Ballard in the 1930s.180 According to researcher David Stupple, "If you look at the contactee groups today, you'll see that most of the stable, larger ones are actually neo-I AM groups, with some sort of tie to Ballard's organization."181 This cult, therefore, bears investigation.

Guy Ballard's "Mighty I AM Religious Activity," grew, in large part, out of William Dudley Pelly's Silver Shirts, an American Nazi organization.182 Although Ballard himself never openly proclaimed Nazi affiliation, his movement was tinged with an extremely right-wing political philosophy, and in secret meetings he "decreed" the death of President Franklin Roosevelt.183 The I AM philosophy derived from Theosophy, and in this author's estimation bears a more-than-cursory resemblance to the Theosophically-based teachings that informed the proto-Nazi German occult lodges.184

After the war, Pelley (who had been imprisoned for sedition during the hostilities)

FIRE FROM THE SKY

headed an occult-oriented organization call Soulcraft, based in Noblesville, Indiana. Another Soulcraft employee was the controversial contactee George Hunt Williamson (real name: Michel d'Obrenovic), who co-authored UFOs CONFIDENTIAL with John McCoy, a proponent of the theory that a Jewish banking conspiracy was preventing disclosure of the solution to the UFO mystery.185 Later, Williamson founded the I AM-oriented Brotherhood of the Seven Rays in Peru.186 Another famed contactee, George Van Tassel, was associated with Pelley and with the notoriously anti-Semitic Reverend Wesley Swift (founder of the group which metamorphosed into the Aryan Nations).187

The most visible offspring of I AM is Elizabeth Clare Prophet's Church Universal and Triumphant, a group best-known for its massive arms caches in underground bunkers. CUT was recently exposed in COVERT ACTION INFORMATION BULLETIN as a conduit of CIA funds,188 and according to researcher John Judge, has ties to organizations allied to the World Anti-Communist League.189 Prophet is becoming involved in abduction research and has sponsored presentations by Budd Hopkins and other prominent investigators. In his book THE ARMSTRONG REPORT: ETs AND UFOs: THEY NEED US, WE DON'T NEED THEM [sic],190 Virgil Armstrong directs troubled abductees toward Prophet's group. (Perhaps not insignificantly, he also suggests that abductees plagued by implants alleviate their problem by turning to "the I AM force" within.191)

Another UFO channeller, Frederick Von Mierers, has promulgated both a cult with a strong I AM orientation192 and an apparent con-game involving over-appraised gemstones. Mierers is an anti-Semite who contends that the Holocaust never happened and that the Jews control the world's wealth.

UFORUM is a flying saucer organization popular with Los Angeles-area abductees; its founder is Penny Harper, a member of a radical Scientology breakaway group which connects the teachings of L. Ron Hubbard with pronouncements against "The Illuminati" (a mythical secret society) and other betes noir familiar from right-wing conspiracy literature. Harper directs members of her group to read THE SPOTLIGHT, an extremist tabloid (published by Willis Carto's Liberty Lobby) which denies the reality of the Holocaust and posits a "Zionist" scheme to control the world.193

More than one unwary abductee has fallen in with groups such as those listed above. It isn't difficult to imagine how some of these questionable groups might mold an abductee's recollection of his experience - and perhaps help direct his future actions.

Some modern abductees, with otherwise-strong claims, claim encounters with blond, "Nordic" aliens reminiscent of the early contactee era. Surely, the "Nordic" appearance of these aliens sprang from the dubious spiritual tradition of Van Tassell, Ballard, Pelley, McCoy, etc. Why, then, are some modern abductees seeing these very same otherworldly Uebermenschen?

One abductee of my acquaintance claims to have had beneficial experiences with these "blond" aliens - who, he believes, came originally from the Pleiades. Interestingly, in the late 1960s, the psychopathically anti-Semitic Rev. Wesley Swift predicted this odd twist in the abduction tale. In a broadcast "sermon," he spoke at length about UFOs, claiming that there were "good" aliens and "bad" aliens. The good ones, he insisted, were tall, blond Aryans - who hailed from the Pleiades. He made this pronouncement long before the current trends in abduction lore.

Could some of the abductions be conducted by an extreme right-wing element within

FIRE FROM THE SKY

the national security establishment? Disagreeable as the possibility seems, we should note that the "lunatic right" is represented in all other walks of life; certainly hard-rightists have taken positions within the military-intelligence complex as well.

Grounds For Further Research

John Keel's ground-breaking OPERATION TROJAN HORSE, written in an era when abductees still came under the category of "contactees," includes the following intriguing data, gleaned from Keel's extensive field work:

Contactees often find themselves suddenly miles from home without knowing how they got there. They either have induced amnesia, wiping out all memory of the trip, or they were taken over by some means and made the trip in a blacked-out state. Should they encounter a friend on the way, the friend would probably note that their eyes seemed glassy and their behavior seemed peculiar. But if the friend spoke to them, he might receive a curt reply.

In the language of the contactees this process is called being used...I have known silent contactees to disappear from their homes for long periods, and when they returned, they had little or no recollection of where they had been. One girl sent me a postcard from the Bahama Islands - which surprised me because I knew she was very poor. When she returned, she told me that she had only one memory of the trip. She said she remembered getting off a jet at an airport - she couldn't recall getting on the jet or making the trip - and there "Indians" met her and took her baggage.... The next thing she knew she was back home again.[194]

Puzzling indeed - unless one has read THE CONTROL OF CANDY JONES, which speaks of Candy's "blacked out" periods, during which she travelled to Taiwan as a CIA courier, adopting her second personality. The mind control explanation perfectly solves all the mysteries in the above excerpt - save, perhaps, the odd remark about "Indians."

Hickson and Mendez' UFO CONTACT AT PASCAGOULA contains the interesting information that Charles Hickson awakes at night feeling that he is on the verge of re-awakening some terribly important memory connected with his encounter - yet ostensibly he can account for every moment of his adventure.

Hickson also received a letter from an apparent abductee who claims that the grey aliens are actually automatons of some sort - perhaps an unconscious recognition of the unreality of the hypnotically-induced "cover story."[195] In this light, the film version of COMMUNION - whose screenplay was written by Whitley Strieber - takes on a new interest: The abduction sequences contain inexplicable images indicating that the "greys" are really props, or masks.

COMMUNION and TRANSFORMATION contain passages detailing what seems to be a hazily-recalled Candy-Jones-style espionage adventure, in which Strieber was shanghaied by a "coach" and a "nurse" (both human beings) who apparently drugged him.[196] Recall the example of Keel's informants. Moreover, TRANSFORMATION contains lengthy descriptions of alien beings working in apparent collusion with human beings.

Abductee Christa Tilton also recalls both human beings and aliens playing a part in her experience. Ever since her abduction, she claims, she has been "shadowed" by a mysterious federal agent she calls John Wallis.[197] Christa's husband, Tom Adams, has confirmed Wallis' existence.[198]

FIRE FROM THE SKY

In his REPORT ON COMMUNION, Ed Conroy - who seems to have become a participant in, and not merely an observer of, the phenomenon - describes harassment by helicopters, which as we have already noted, seems to be quite a common occurrence in abductee situations.199 Researchers blithely assume that these incidents represent governmental attempts to spy on UFO percipients. But this assertion is ridiculous. Helicopters are extremely expensive to operate, and the engines of espionage have perfected numerous alternative methods to gather information. After all, we now have a fairly extensive bibliography of FBI, CIA, and military efforts to spy on numerous movements favoring domestic social change. Why have no veterans of CHAOS or COINTELPRO (either victim or victimizer) spoken of helicopters? Obviously the choppers serve some other purpose beyond mere surveillance. One possibility might be the propagation of electromagnetic waves which might affect the perceptions/behaviors of an implanted individual. (Indeed, I have heard rumors of helicopters being used in electronic "crowd control" operations in Vietnam and elsewhere; alas, the information is far from hard.)

Contactee Eldon Kerfoot has written of his suspicions that human manipulators, not aliens, may be the ultimate puppeteers engineering his experiences. He describes a sudden compulsion to kill a fellow veteran of the Korean conflict - a man Kerfoot had no logical reason to distrust or dislike, yet whom he "sensed" to have been a traitor to his country. Fortunately, the assassination never materialized.200 But the situation exactly parallels incidents described in released ARTICHOKE documents concerning the remote hypnotic induction of anti-social behavior.

One last speculation

Renato Vesco's INTERCEPT BUT DON'T SHOOT201 outlines a fascinating scenario for the "secret weapon" hypothesis of UFOs. Vesco points out that if these devices are one day to be used in a superpower conflict, the attacking power would be well-served by the myth of the UFO as an extraterrestrial craft, for the besieged nation would not know the true nature of its opponent. Perhaps, then, one purpose of the UFO abductions is to engender and maintain the legend of the little grey aliens. For the hidden manipulators, the abductions could be, in and of themselves, a propaganda coup.

Final Thoughts

I do not insist dogmatically on the scenario that I have outlined. I do not wish to dissuade abduction researchers from exploring other avenues - indeed, I strongly encourage such work to continue. Nor can I easily account for some aspects of the abduction narratives - for example, any suggestions I could offer concerning the reports of genetic experimentation would be extremely speculative.

But I do insist on a fair hearing of this hypothesis. Criticism is encouraged; that which does not destroy my thesis will make it stronger. I ask only that my critics refrain from intellectual laziness; mere differences in world-view do not constitute a valid attack. God is found in the details.

I recognize the dangers inherent in making this thesis public. New and distressing abductee confabulations may result. I would prefer that the audience for this paper be restricted to abduction researchers, not victims, who might be unduly influenced. However, in a society that prides itself on ostensibly free press, such restrictions are unthinkable. Therefore, I can only beg any abduction victims who might read this paper to attempt a superhuman objectivity. The thesis I have outlined is promising, and (should

FIRE FROM THE SKY

trepanation ever provide us with an example of an actual abductee implant) susceptible of proof. But mine is not the only hypothesis. The abductee's unrewarding task is to report what he or she has experienced as truthfully as possible, untainted by outside speculation.

Whether or not future investigation proves UFO abductions to be a product of mind control experimentation, I feel that this paper has, at least, provided evidence of a serious danger facing those who hold fast to the ideals of individual freedom. We cannot long ignore this menace.

A spectre haunts the democratic nations - the spectre of technofascism. All the powers of the espionage empire and the scientific establishment have entered into an unholy alliance to evoke this spectre: Psychiatrist and spy, Dulles and Delgado, microwave specialists and clandestine operators.

A mind is a terrible thing to waste - and a worse thing to commandeer.

Endnotes

1. Budd Hopkins, MISSING TIME (New York: Richard Marek Publishers, 1981) and INTRUDERS (New York: Random House, 1987).
2. Whitley Strieber, COMMUNION (New York: Beech Tree Books, 1987).
3. Cannon, "Psychiatric Abuse of UFO Witness," UFO magazine, vol. 3, no. 5 (December, 1988)
4. Philip Klass, UFO ABDUCTIONS: A DANGEROUS GAME (Buffalo: Prometheus Books, 1988). Klass makes some sharp observations, which are undercut by his refusal to interview abductees directly. The work has no footnotes and depends heavily on the work of Dr. Martin Orne - of whom more anon.
5. See bibliography.
6. New York: Bantam Books, 1979.
7. See generally PROJECT MKULTRA, THE CIA'S PROGRAM OF RESEARCH IN BEHAVIOR MODIFICATION, joint hearing before the Select Committee on Health and Scientific Research of the Committee on Human Resources, Unites States Senate (Washington: Government Printing Office, 1977).
8. Robert Eringer, "Secret Agent Man," ROLLING STONE, 1985.
9. John Marks interview with Victor Marchetti (Marks files, available at the National Security Archives, Washington, D.C.).
10. In an interview with John Marks, hypnosis expert Milton Kline, a veteran of clandestine experimentation in this field, averred that his work for the government continued. Since the interview took place in 1977, years after the CIA allegedly halted mind control research, we must conclude either that the CIA lied, or that another agency continued the work. In another interview with Marks, former Air Force-CIA liaison L. Fletcher Prouty confirmed that the Department of Defense ran studies either in conjunction with or parallel to those operated by the CIA. (Marks files.)
11. Estabrooks, HYPNOSIS (New York: E.P. Dutton & Co., Inc., 1957 [revised edition]), 13-14.
12. A copy of this letter can be found in the Marks files.
13. Estabrooks attracted an eclectic group of friends, including J. Edgar Hoover and

FIRE FROM THE SKY

Alan Watts.

14. Interview with daughter Doreen Estabrooks, Marks files, Washington, D.C.

15. Martin A. Lee and Bruce Shlain, ACID DREAMS (New York: Grove Press, 1985) 3-4; Marks, THE SEARCH FOR "THE MANCHURIAN CANDIDATE", 6-8

16. Marks, ibid. 4-6.

17. Edward Hunter, BRAINWASHING IN RED CHINA (New York: Vanguard Press, 1951.). Hunter invented the term "brainwashing" in a September 24, 1950 Miami NEWS article.

18. "Japan's Germ Warfare Experiments," THE GLOBE AND MAIL (Toronto), May 19, 1982.

19. Walter Bowart, OPERATION MIND CONTROL (New York: Dell, 1978), 191-2, quoting Warren Commission documents. We cannot fairly derive from this statement a sanguine attitude about PRESENT Soviet capabilities; in this field, even outdated technology suffices for mischief.

20. Marks, THE SEARCH FOR "THE MANCHURIAN CANDIDATE", 60-61. A folk entymology has it that the "MK" of MKULTRA stands for "Mind Kontrol." According to Marks, TSS prefixed the cryptonyms of all its projects with these initials. Note, though, that MKULTRA was preceded by a still-mysterious TSS program called QKHILLTOP.

21. Ibid., 224-229. Seven MKULTRA subprojects were continued, under TSS supervision, as MKSEARCH. This project ended in 1972. CIA apologists often proclaim that "brainwashing" research ceased in either 1962 or 1972; these blandishments refer to the TSS projects, not to the ORD work, which remains TERRA INCOGNITA for independent researchers. Marks discovered that the ORD research was so voluminous that retrieving documents via FOIA would have proven unthinkably expensive.

22. For a description of the research into parapsychology, see Ronald M. McRae's MIND WARS (New York: St. Martin's Press, 1984). The best book available on a subject which awaits a truly authoritative text.

23. Abduction researcher and hypnotherapist Miranda Park, of Lancaster, California, reports that she has viewed such anomalies in abductee MRI scans. See also Whitley Strieber, TRANSFORMATION (New York: Beech Tree Books, 1988) 246-247. At this writing, both Strieber and Hopkins report initially promising results in their efforts to document the presence of these "extras" in abductees.

24. Allegedly, the experiment took place in 1964. However, in WERE WE CONTROLLED? (New Hyde Park, NY: University Books, 1967), the pseudonymous "Lincoln Lawrence" makes an interesting argument (on page 36) that the demonstration took place some years earlier.

25. New York: Harper and Row, 1969. Much of Delgado's work was funded by the Office of Naval Intelligence, a common conduit for CIA funds during the 1950s and '60s. (Gordon Thomas' JOURNEY INTO MADNESS (New York: Bantam, 1989) misleadingly implies that CIA interest in Delgado's work began in 1972.)

26. J.M.R. Delgado. "Intracerebral Radio Stimulation and Recording in Completely Free Patients," PSYCHOTECHNOLOGY (Robert L. Schwitzgebel and Ralph K. Schwitzgebel, editors; New York: Holt, Rinehart and Winston, 1973): 195.

27. David Krech, "Controlling the Mind Controllers," THINK 32 (July-August), 1966.

28. Delgado, PHYSICAL CONTROL OF THE MIND

29. Delgado, "Intracerebral Radio Stimulation and Recording in Completely Free Pa-

tients," 195.

30. Note, for example, Charles Hickson's account of the Pascagoula Incident. Charles Hickson and William Mendez, UFO CONTACT AT PASCOGOULA (Tuscon: Wendelle C. Stevens, 1983).

31. John Ranleigh, THE AGENCY (New York: Simon and Shuster, 1986): 208. Marchetti casts this story in the form of an amusing anecdote: After much time and expense, a cat was suitably trained and prepared - only, on its first assignment, to be run over by a taxi. Marchetti neglects to point out that nothing stopped the Agency from getting another cat. Or from using a human being.

32. Of course, this suggestion raises the knotty question of whether the abductees suffer from a form of schizophrenia, which may also be characterized by "voices." I refer the reader to the work of Hopkins, Strieber, Thomas Bullard, and others who have described the difficulties of ascribing all abductions to psychotic states.

33. Alan W. Scheflin and Edward M. Opton, Jr., THE MIND MANIPULATORS (London: Paddington Press, 1978), 347.

34. Thomas, JOURNEY INTO MADNESS, 276.

35. James Olds, "Hypothalamic Substrates of Reward," PHYSIOLOGICAL REVIEWS, 1962, 42:554; "Emotional Centers in the Brain," SCIENCE JOURNAL, 1967, 3 (5).

36. Vernon Mark and Frank Ervin, VIOLENCE AND THE BRAIN (New York: Harper and Row, 1970), chapter 12, excerpted in INDIVIDUAL RIGHTS AND THE FEDERAL ROLE IN BEHAVIOR MODIFICATION, prepared by the Staff of the Subcommittee on Constitutional Rights of the Committee of the Judiciary, United States Senate (Washington: Government Printing Office, 1974).

37. John Lilly, THE SCIENTIST (Berkeley, Ronin Publishing, 1988 [revised edition]), 90. Monkeys allowed to stimulate themselves continually via ESB brought themselves to orgasm once every three minutes, sixteen hours a day. Scientific gatherings throughout the world saw motion pictures of these experiments, which surely made spectacular cinema.

38. Scheflin and Opton, THE MIND MANIPULATORS, 336-337. Heath even monitored his patient's brain responses during the subject's first heterosexual encounter. Such is the nature of the brave new world before us.

39. Robert L. Schwitzgebel and Richard M. Bird, "Sociotechnical Design Factors in Remote Instrumentation with Humans in Natural Environments,"

40. Thomas, JOURNEY INTO MADNESS, 277. In the BEHAVIOR RESEARCH METHODS AND INSTRUMENTATION article referenced above, Schwitzgebel details how the radio signals may be fed into a telephone via a modem and thus analyzed by a computer anywhere in the world.

41. Scheflin and Opton, THE MIND MANIPULATORS, 347-349.

42. Louis Tackwood and the Citizen's Research and Investigation Committee, THE GLASS HOUSE TAPES (New York: Avon, 1973), 226.

43. Perry London, BEHAVIOR CONTROL (New York: Harper and Row, 1969), 145

44. Scheflin and Opton, THE MIND MANIPULATORS, 351-353; Tackwood, THE GLASS HOUSE TAPES, 228.

45. "Beepers in kids' heads could stop abductors," Las Vegas SUN, Oct. 27, 1987.

46. Lilly, THE SCIENTIST, 91.

47. Marks, THE SEARCH FOR "THE MANCHURIAN CANDIDATE", 151-154.

48. Interestingly, Lilly has come out of the closet as a sort of proto-Strieber; THE SCIENTIST recounts his close interaction with alien (though not necessarily extraterrestrial) forces which he labels "solid state entities."

49. The story of Deep Trance, an MKULTRA "insider" who provided invaluable information, is somewhat involved. I do not know who Trance is/was and Marks may not know either. He contacted Trance via the writer of an article published shortly before research on THE SEARCH FOR "THE MANCHURIAN CANDIDATE" began, addressing his informant "Dear Source whose anonymity I respect." I respect it too - hence my reticence to name the aforementioned article, which may mark a trail to Trance. The fact that I have not followed this trail would not prevent others from doing so.

50. London, BEHAVIOR CONTROL, 139.

51. See generally, UFO magazine, Vol. 4, No. 2; especially the interesting contribution by Whitley Strieber.

52. Lawrence, WERE WE CONTROLLED?, 36-37; Anita Gregory, "Introduction to Leonid L. Vasilev's EXPERIMENTS IN DISTANT INFLUENCE," PSYCHIC WARFARE: FACT OR FICTION (editor: John White) (Nottinghamshire: Aquarian, 1988) 34-57.

53. Lawrence, WERE WE CONTROLLED?, 38.

54. Bowart, OPERATION MIND CONTROL, 261-264.

55. Ibid., 263.

56. Lawrence, WERE WE CONTROLLED?, 52.

57. HUMAN DRUG TESTING BY THE CIA, 202.

58. Note especially the Supreme Court's decision in CENTRAL INTELLIGENCE AGENCY ET Al. V. SIMS, ET AL. (No. 83-1075; decided April 16, 1986). The egregious and dangerous majority opinion in this case held that disclosure of the names of scientists and institutions involved in MKULTRA posed an "unacceptable risk of revealing 'intelligence sources.' The decisions of the [CIA] Director, who must of course be familiar with 'the whole picture,' as judges are not, are worthy of great deference...it is conceivable that the mere explanation of why information must be withheld can convey valuable information to a foreign intelligence agency." How do we square this continuing need for secrecy with the CIA's protestations that MKULTRA achieved little success, that the studies were conducted within the Nueremberg statues governing medical experiments, and that the research was made available in the open literature?

59. Letter, P.A. Lindstrom to Robert Naeslund, July 27, 1983; copy available from Martti Koski, Kiilinpellontie 2, 21290 Rusko, Finland. Lindstrom writes that he fully agrees with Lincoln Lawrence, author of WERE WE CONTROLLED?

60. Bowart, OPERATION MIND CONTROL, 265. I have attempted without success to contact Dr. Lindstrom.

61. Ibid., 233-249. This interview was repinted without attribution in a bizarre compendium of UFO rumors called THE MATRIX, compiled by "Valdamar Valerian" (actually John Grace, allegedly a Captain working for Air Force intelligence).

62. Robert Anton Wilson, "Adventures with Head Hardware," MAGICAL BLEND, 23 [of course], July 1989.

63. Michael Hutchison, MEGA BRAIN (New York: Ballantine, 1986); Gerald Oster, "Auditory Beats in the Brain," SCIENTIFIC AMERICAN, September, 1973.

64. Marilyn Ferguson, THE BRAIN REVOLUTION (New York: Taplinger, 1973), 90.

65. Ibid., 91-92. The presence of delta in a waking subject can indicate pathology.

66. Bio-Pacer promotional and price sheet, available from Lindemann Laboratories, 3463 State Street, #264, Santa Barbara, CA 93105.

67. Hutchison, MEGA BRAIN, 117-118. Compare Light's observations about "the grant game" to Sid Gottlieb's protestations that nearly all "mind control" research was openly published.

68. Thomas Martinez and John Gunther, THE BROTHERHOOD OF MURDER (New York: McGraw-Hill, 1988), 230.

69. Interview, Sandy Monroe of the Los Angeles office of the Christic Institute.

70. See generally Paul Brodeur, THE ZAPPING OF AMERICA (Toronto, George J. MacLeod, 1977).

71. Until recently, the American Embassy was on a street named after the composer.

72. It was finally determined that the microwaves were used to receive transmissions from bugs planted within the embassy. DARPA director George H. Heimeier went on record stating that PANDORA was never designed to study "microwaves as a surveillance tool." See Anne Keeler, "Remote Mind Control Technology," FULL DISCLOSURE #15. I would note that the Soviet embassy was "bugged and waved" in Canada during the 1950s, and according to the Los Angeles TIMES (June 5, 1989), the Soviet embassy in Britain had been similarly affected.

73. Ronald I. Adams R.A. Williams, BIOLOGICAL EFFECTS OF ELECTROMAGNETIC RADIATION (RADIOWAVES AND MICROWAVES) EURASIAN COMMUNIST COUNTRIES, (Defense Intelligence Agency, March 1976.) Brodeur notes that much of the work ascribed to the Soviets in this report was actually first accomplished by scientists in the United States. Keeler argues that this report constitutes an example of "mirror imaging" - i.e., parading domestic advances as a foreign threat, the better to pry funding from a suitably-fearful Congress.

74. Keeler, "Remote Mind Control Technology."

75. R.J. MacGregor, "A Brief Survey of Literature Relating to Influence of Low Intensity Microwaves on Nervous Function" (Santa Monica: RAND Corporation, 1970).

76. Keeler, "Remote Mind Control Technology."

77. Larry Collins, "Mind Control," PLAYBOY, January 1990.

78. Allan H. Frey, "Behavioral Effects of Electromagnetic Energy," SYMPOSIUM ON BIOLOGICAL EFFECTS AND MEASUREMENTS OF RADIO FREQUENCIES/MICROWAVES, DeWitt G. Hazzard, editor (U.S. Department of Health, Education and Welfare, 1977).

79. Quoted in THE APPLICATION OF TESLA'S TECHNOLOGY IN TODAY'S WORLD (Montreal: Lafferty, Hardwood & Partners, Ltd., 1978).

80. Keeler, "Remote Mind Control Technology."

81. L. George Lawrence, "Electronics and Brain Control," POPULAR ELECTRONICS, July 1973.

82. Susan Schiefelbein, "The Invisible Threat," SATURDAY REVIEW, September 15, 1979.

83. E. Preston, "Studies on the Nervous System, Cardiovascular Function and Thermoregulation," BIOLOGICAL EFFECTS OF RADIO FREQUENCY AND MICROWAVE RA-

DIATION, edited by H.M. Assenheim (Ottawa, Canada: National Research Council of Canada, 1979), 138-141.

84. Robert O. Becker, THE BODY ELECTRIC (New York: William Morrow, 1985) 318-319.

85. Ibid.

86. Ibid., 321.

87. See Bowart's OPERATION MIND CONTROL, page 218, for an interesting example of this "rationalization" process at work in the case of Sirhan Sirhan, who was convicted for the assassination of Robert F. Kennedy. In prison, Sirhan was hypnotized by Dr. Bernard Diamond, who instructed Sirhan to climb the bars of his cage like a monkey. He did so. After the trance was removed, Sirhan was shown tapes of his actions; he insisted that he "acted like a monkey" of his own free will - he claimed he wanted the exercise.

88. Keeler suggests that the proposal was revealed only because Schapitz' sensationalistic implications may have worked to his discredit - and therefore hide - the REAL research. Personally, I don't accept this argument, but I respect Keeler's instincts enough to repeat her caveat here.

89. Margaret Cheney's TESLA: A MAN OUT OF TIME (New York: Dell, 1981), the most reliable book in the sea of wild speculation surrounding this extraordinary scientist, confirms Tesla's early work with the psychological effects of electromagnetic radiation. See especially pages 101-104; note also the afterword, in which we learn that certain government agencies have kept important research by Tesla hidden from the general public.

90. Noted in Lawrence, WERE WE CONTROLLED?, 29.

91. Particularly one Thomas Bearden of Huntsville, Alabama; I have in my possession a document written by Bearden associate Andrew Michrowski which identifies Bearden as an intelligence agent for an undisclosed agency.

92. Kathleen McAuliffe, "The Mind Fields," OMNI magazine, February 1985.

93. May 5, 1985.

94. I refer to an individual who later wrote a very clear-headed and thoughtful letter to Dr. Paul Lowinger, who has graciously made his files available to me. For now, I feel compelled to withhold this person's name.

95. Cameron became president of the American Psychiatric Association, the Canadian Psychiatric Association, and the World Association of Psychiatrists, He previously sat on the Nueremberg panel, helping to draw up the statutes governing ethical medical behavior!

96. In particular, Opton and Scheflin's overview, though excellent in scope and detail, continually seeks reassurring interpretations of evidence which points toward more distressing conclusions.

97. Martin T. Orne, "Can a hypnotized subject be compelled to carry out otherwise unacceptable behavior?" INTERNATIONAL JOURNAL OF CLINICAL AND EXPERIMENTAL HYPNOSIS, 1972, Vol. 20, 101-117.

98. Marks mentions, in a letter to Orne, the latter's claim to have been an unwitting participant in subproject 84. Yet the papers released concerning subproject 84 clearly establish the Agency's willingness to put Orne in the know; Orne later admitted to Marks that he was made aware of his CIA sponsorship (Marks, THE SEARCH FOR "THE MANCHURIAN CANDIDATE", 172-173). In an interview with Marks, Orne discounted the story

of Candy Jones (which we shall recount later) by insisting that if such an experiment had occurred "someone in some agency would have come to me." Why would they come to him about a super-secret project, unless Orne had a high security clearance and worked extensively with intelligence agencies? Note also that Orne conducted extensive studies for the Office of Naval Research from June 1, 1968 to May 31, 1971. He has also been funded by DARPA. Moreover, I consider noteworthy the fact that Orne somehow became president of the Society for Clinical and Experimental Hypnosis despite the fact that the organization had decided not to have a president. (This fact was related to Marks by a prominent hypnosis specialist in an off-the-record interview that I probably wasn't supposed to see.)

99. The story has been told many times. See Turner and Christian's THE KILLING OF ROBERT F. KENNEDY, 207-208; also Peter J. Reiter, ANTISOCIAL OR CRIMINAL ACTS AND HYPNOSIS (Springfield, Illinois: Charles C. Thomas, 1958).

100. John G. Watkins, "Antisocial behavior under hypnosis: Possible or impossible?" INTERNATIONAL JOURNAL FOR CLINICAL AND EXPERIMENTAL HYPNOSIS, 1972, Vol. 20, 95-100.

101. Milton H. Erickson, "An experimental investigation of the possible anti-social use of hypnosis," PSYCHIATRY, 1939, vol. 2. Erickson argues that if a hypnotist has convinced his subject to misperceive reality, then resulting actions cannot be considered "anti-social," for the actions would be acceptable within the subject's internal reality construct. This argument strikes me as semantic quibbling.

102. See generally Flo Conway and Jim Seigelman, SNAPPING (New York: Lippincott, 1978).

103. Lee and Schlain, ACID DREAMS, 8-9.

104. John Marks interview with Victor Marchetti, December 19, 1977 (Marks files).

105. Martin T. Orne, "On the Mechanisms of Posthypnotic Amnesia," THE INTERNATIONAL JOURNAL OF CLINICAL AND EXPERIMENTAL HYPNOSIS, 1966, vol. 14, 121-134. Orne's work with post-hypnotic amnesia was funded by NIMH, the Air Force Office of Scientific Research, and the Office of Naval Research. I should like to hear what innocent explanation, if any, the Air Force has to offer to explain their interest in post-hypnotic amnesia.

106. Bowart, OPERATION MIND CONTROL, 242-243.

107. Obviously Allan Dulles. This may have been a hypnotically-induced delusion; on the other hand, Dulles' legendary sexual rapacity makes this claim rather less unlikely than one might first assume.

108. Always the best indicator of whether or not hypnosis is genuine; I can't understand why Orne didn't use this test in the Blanchi case.

109. Herbert Spiegel, "Hypnosis and evidence: Help or hindrance," ANN. N.Y. ACAD. SCI.; 1980, 347, 73-85.

110. See, for example, Kroger, HYPNOSIS AND BEHAVIOR MODIFICATION, 21-22

111. See especially Klass, UFO ABDUCTIONS: A DANGEROUS GAME, 60-61. Orne, interviewed here, makes reference to the work summarized in his article "The use and misuse of hypnosis in court" (INTERNATIONAL JOURNAL OF CLINICAL HYPNOSIS, 1979, vol. 27, 311-341.)

112. Klass argues that ufologists, in conducting hypnotic regression sessions, inad-

FIRE FROM THE SKY

vertently cue their subjects. A close reading of his text reveals that he never proves or claims that such "cues" have taken place in any individual instance; he simply believes that cueing MIGHT have occurred. Had Klass been more willing to deal with abductees directly, he might have found evidence of cause and effect; as it stands, his argument really amounts to no more than a suggestion. For all that, I find his ideas regarding therunning of "clean" hypnotic regression sessions potentially valuable.

113. Marks, THE SEARCH FOR "THE MANCHURIAN CANDIDATE", 34-37.

114. Donald Bain, THE CONTROL OF CANDY JONES (Chicago, Playboy Press, 1976).

115. The use of hypnotized couriers in warfare goes back to the 19th century.

116. Estabrooks, HYPNOTISM, 193-214.

117. John Marks interview with Milton Kline, December 22, 1977 (Marks files). In another interview, Professor Clare Young (a colleague of Estabrooks' at Colgate University) confirmed that Estabrooks' hypnosis work for the government has never been published.

118. Or could her marriage have been part of the program? "Long John," as he was popularly known, was famous in UFO circles, and had provided a forum for such early-day contactees as Howard Menger. He also knew Jackie Gleason, a prominent (if unlikely) name in the "crashed disc" rumor vaults. Could Candy have been assigned to discover what Nebel knew?

119. Marks files. John Marks did excellent work on the Candy Jones story; he erred - almost unforgivably - on the side of conservatism when he refused to include information about this incident in his book. I know the name of the institute involved; however, since Candy saw fit to keep this aspect of her story secret (probably for sound legal reasons), I shall follow her lead.

120. Scheflin and Opton, THE MIND MANIPULATORS, 446-447.

121. Interviews, Marks files. One of Marks' informants offered the interesting speculation that Candy's torture sessions were not conducted in the field, but in the lab - her entire mission might have been a hypno-programmed fantasy.

122. The information about Candy's CIA files stems from a telephone interview with Candy Jones. A problem looms here: CIA cover stories unravel like the skin of an onion; once you remove the outer layer, the next lie is revealed. In the case of Candy Jones, the substrata of buncombe involves allegations that she WILLINGLY complied with the CIA, and used Jensen's hypnosis experiments as a rationalization for her compliance. Such is the explanation offered by certain of Marks' informants; alas, Opton and Scheflin seem to have bought this line. Anyone familiar with the vile acts of self-degradation to which Candy's programmers subjected her will laugh this story out of court. No one, short of a severely psychotic masochist, would willingly undergo what she went through.

123. Marks files.

124. William Kroger, CLINICAL AND EXPERIMENTAL HYPNOSIS (Philadelphia: Lippincott, 1963), 299.

125. Recently, ufologist Jim Moseley, an acquaintance of Candy's, has claimed that an unidentified source on Nebel's "inner circle" once, off-the-record, pronounced Candy's story "a crock." This assertion deserves careful and respectful consideration. Still, Moseley won't identify his source, and we have no way of telling if this insider spoke from instinct or certain knowledge, or indeed, what he really meant. Did he feel Candy

was fantasizing or fibbing? If the former, why did her hallucinations match details of MKULTRA released only after publication of her book? If the latter, how are we to explain the many hypnotic regression tapes, at least some of which were made available to outside investigators? (Fairly elaborate, for a hoax.) In any case, how could Candy have known the fact (confirmed by Marks' associates) that Kroger taught "Jensen" at a certain West-coast institute? Why, if the story was "a crock," would Candy risk libel suits by naming - to associates and investigators, if not to the general public - real-life hypnotherapists? All in all, I would suggest that Moseley's "insider" was speaking glibly, and did not know the true facts.

126. Philadelphia, Lippincott, 1976.

127. Ibid., 415.

128. Similar paranoid outbreaks led to the dissolution of Dr. Richard Neal's UFO abductee group in Los Angeles, according to a phone interview I had with Dr. Neal.

129. Affidavit of Dr. Simpson-Kallas in the case of Sirhan-Sirhan, 1973; see Bowart, OPERATION MIND CONTROL, 225.

130. All true MPs have experienced some form of abuse or trauma, psychological or physical, during childhood.

131. One was ritually abused in an occult setting. If I were a "spy-chiatrist" scouting potential fodder for mind control experiments, I would seek out abused children from military families. (A military background would ensure that the "right" doctor gets access to the child.) Abduction researchers should look for such a pattern.

132. I refer here to the vast upsurge in alien abductions which took place that year; see generally Kevin Randle, THE OCTOBER SCENARIO (Middle Coast, 1988). Of course, abductions (or, according to my hypothesis, disguised mind control operations) occurred previous to this year.

133. John Marks interview with Milton Kline, December 22, 1977 (Marks files).

134. Brenda Butler ET AL., SKY CRASH, expanded edition (London: Grafton Books, 1986), 305-321, 354-355.

135. Telephone interview with Nancy Wright.

136. Telephone interview with Miranda Parks.

137. William Moore, "UFOs and the U.S. Government," FOCUS, vol. 4, June 30, 1989. Moore's role in the affair strikes me as highly questionable, even scandalous - although at least here we have one instance of direct and irrefutable "insider" testimony of government harassment.

138. Some have also raised questions about his psychiatric treatment of Oswald assassin Jack Ruby. I find it odd that a CIA mind control veteran - who did NOT reside or practice in Dallas - should have been assigned to the Ruby case.

139. Samiel Chavkin, THE MIND STEALERS (New York: Houghton Mifflin, 1978), 96-107.

140. Raymond Fowler, THE ANDREASSON AFFAIR (New York: Prentice Hall, 1979).

141. New York: Warner Books, 1989; 198-202.

142. Ruth Montgomery, ALIENS AMONG US (Ballantine, 1985), 49. My article "Psychiatric Abuse of UFO Witness," referred to earlier, also documents this phenomenon.

143. Chung-Kwang Chou and Arthur W. Guy, "Quantization of Microwave Biological Effects," SYMPOSIUM OF BIOLOGICAL EFFECTS AND MEASUREMENT OF RADIO FRE-

FIRE FROM THE SKY

QUENCY/MICROWAVES, edited by Dewitt G. Hazzard (U.S. Department of Health, Education and Welfare, 1977).

144. MIAMI HERALD, May 28, 1984 and June 6, 1984; NATIONAL EXAMINER, vol. 22, no. 18, April 30, 1985. Although the EXAMINER is a supermarket tabloid, and therefore a questionable source, this periodical has rendered researchers the service of printing the X-ray of Petit's brain, showing the implant.

145. Los Angeles TIMES, March 28, 1988.

146. Raymond Fowler, THE ANDREASSON AFFAIR, PHASE TWO (Reward, 1982). This book includes rare photographs of the unmarked helicopters which have plagued this abduction victim and her family.

147. A mutual friend described for me an incident in which the former SEAL, mistakenly perceiving a threat, almost instantly felled, and nearly killed, a man twice his size. Whatever the truth of my informant's other statements, he certainly has received advanced combat training.

148. Fenton Bresler, WHO KILLED JOHN LENNON? (New York: St. Martin's Press, 1989), 45-46.

149. Bowart, OPERATION MIND CONTROL, 27-42.

150. Denise Winn, THE MANIPULATED MIND (London, Octagon Press, 1983), 72-73; Bresler, WHO KILLED JOHN LENNON?, 41; see generally: Peter Watson, WAR ON THE MIND (London: Hutchison, 1978) (Watson broke the story on Narut for the London TIMES).

151. Larry Collins, "Mind Control," PLAYBOY, January 1990.

152. John Marks interview with Milton Kline, December 22, 1977 (Marks files).

153. Richard A. Gabriel, NO MORE HEROES (New York: Hill and Wang, 1987), 124.

154. Ibid., 150-151.

155. See generally: Mark Lane, CONVERSATIONS WITH AMERICANS (Simon and Shuster, 1970); A.J. Langguth, HIDDEN TERRORS (New York: Pantheon, 1978).

156. John G. Fuller, THE INTERRUPTED JOURNEY (New York: Dell, 1966).

157. This detail plays a part in other abductions - for example, it crops up in the Betty Andreasson Luca case. See Raymond Fowler, THE ANDREASSON AFFAIR (New York: Bantam, 1980), 50-51.

158. Stanton Friedman, for example; the reader is referred to his 1988 Whole Life Expo lecture, "UFOs: A Cosmic Watergate."

159. THE BODY ELECTRIC, 196-202.

160. The Fish map has received wide discussion; for a representative sampling, the reader is directed to the aforementioned Friedman lecture (note 158); Terence Dickenson, "The Zeti Reticuli Incident," ASTRONOMY, December, 1974; Klass, UFO ABDUCTIONS: A DANGEROUS GAME, 20-23; and John Rimmer, THE EVIDENCE FOR ALIEN ABDUCTIONS (Weillingborough: Aquarian, 1984), 88-92. Incidentally, Klass has proposed to Friedman a test regarding the ability to recall such material accurately under hypnotic regression; Friedman, for reasons best known to himself, declined the offer to participate.

161. Jacques Vallee, DIMENSIONS (Chicago: Contemporary, 1988), 266.

162. See Rimmer, THE EVIDENCE FOR ALIEN ABDUCTIONS, 91-92. None of this is meant to denigrate Marjorie Fish, whose work has received universal praise.

163. Fuller, THE INTERRUPTED JOURNEY, 18-19.

164. Athan G. Theoharis and John Stuart Cox, THE BOSS: J. EDGAR HOOVER AND THE

FIRE FROM THE SKY

GREAT AMERICAN INQUISITION (Philadelphia: Temple University Press, 1978), 325; Chip Berlet, "The Hunt for the Red Menace," COVERT ACTION INFORMATION BULLETIN, no. 31 (winter, 1989); J. Edgar Hoover, COINTELPRO (memo), March 4, 1968.

165. For example, Delgado's work pre-dates the Hill incident. Moreover, one of the few pages released on MKULTRA subproject 119 concerns "a critical review of the literature and scientific developments related to the recording, analysis and interpretation of bioelectric signals from the human organism, and activation of human behavior by remote means." The review took place in 1960-61. Presumably, the CIA wanted to DO something with the information so derived.

166. "UFO Abductions Workshop," Whole Life Expo, March, 1988.

167. Ludwig Mayer, DIE TECHNIC DER HYPNOSE (Munich: J.H. Lehmanns Verlag, 1953), 225; quoted in: Heinz E. Hammerschlag (translation: John Cohen) HYPNOTISM AND CRIME (Hollywood: Wilshire Book Company, 1957), 24-25.

168. Numerous articles discuss this possibility; see, for example, William C. Coe ET AL. "An Approach Toward Isolating Factors that Influence Antisocial Conduct in Hypnosis," THE INTERNATIONAL JOURNAL OF CLINICAL AND EXPERIMENTAL HYPNOSIS, 1972, vol XX, no. 2, 118-131, as well as other reports in that issue. The difference between the laboratory and the "field" settings may account for the success of Mayer's experiment and the apparent failure of the "aliens."

169. For a description of a quite similar experiment conducted under CIA auspices in 1954, see "CIA able to control minds by hypnosis, data shows," THE WASHINGTON POST, February 19, 1978.

170. Abductee interview, "Veronica." The reader will, I hope, forgive my use of a pseudonym here. For the most part, I hope to deal in this work with published cases. Suffice it to say, Veronica's testimony proved fascinating, troubling, convoluted, problematical; in spite of all the questions raised by this case, I still believe it to have substantial bearing on my thesis. The reader will forgive me for severing relations with this abductee before completing an investigation; she keeps a mini-armory next to her bed.

171. Abductee interview, "Veronica," At one point, she ran an informal abductee/contactee group; as a result, she was able to describe many other cases to me.

172. One ARTICHOKE document explicitly details a failed attempt to use hypnosis to induce the assassination of a foreign leader. The document is undated; the experiment took place January 8-January 15, 1954. Document reproduced in CIA PAPERS, vol. 1 (Ann Arbor, MI: Capitol Information Associates, 1986),39-41.

173. John Marks interview of Prof. Jack Tracktir (Marks files).

174. Jenny Randles, ABDUCTIONS (London: Robert Hale, 1988), 52-53.

175. As in, for example, the Palle Hardrup affair.

176. Private correspondence, Robert Durant to the author.

177. Abductee interview, "Polly." I won't give the facial details here; suffice it to say that this abductor, like Margary's (noted earlier), has something of the smell of greasepaint about him.

178. The base is mantioned in Ann Druffel's and D. Scott Rogo's THE TUJUNGA CANYON CONTACTS (New York: Signet, 1989) [expanded edition], 157.

179. On the other hand, Armstrong asks us to accept his own channelled material, so he would have an awkward time should he choose to challenge the "psychic impres-

sions" of others.

180. Jacques Vallee, MESSENGERS OF DECEPTION (Berkeley: And/Or Press, 1979), 192-193.

181. Curtis G. Fuller (editor), PROCEEDINGS OF THE FIRST INTERNATIONAL UFO CONGRESS (New York: Warner Books, 1980), 307.

182. For information of Pelley, see John Roy Carlson, UNDER COVER (New York: Dutton, 1943).

183. Gerald B. Bryan, PSYCHIC DICTATORSHIP IN AMERICA (Los Angeles: Truth Research, 1940). An essential book-length expose of Ballardism. One of Bryan's sources alleges that Ballard, before founding the I AM group, may have practiced some variety of black magic.

184. The student should carefully compare the I AM dogma with the available information on pre-Third Reich occultism; the best sources are James Webb's masterful analyses, THE OCCULT ESTABLISHMENT and THE OCCULT UNDERGROUND (La Salle, Illinois: Open Court Publishing, 1976).

185. Vallee, MESSENGERS OF DECEPTION, 192-194.

186. Even a cursory examination of Williamson's SECRET OF THE ANDES (London: Neville Superman, 1961), written under the pseudonym Brother Philip, will reveal the I AM connections.

187. Personal sources. Van Tassell's "Integration," a domed structure allegedly built under extra-terrestrial guidance (located near Twentynine Palms, California) prominently displays, to this day, key I AM artifacts

such as the portraits of Jesus and Saint Germain (commissioned by Ballard).

188. "The Afghan Arms Pipeline," COVERT ACTION INFORMATION BULLETIN, no. 30 (summer, 1988).

189. Telephone interview with John Judge.

190. Village of Oak Creek, Arizona: Entheos, 1989, 119. I can't recall ever encountering another book title which contained so many grammatical errors. Armstrong's accomplishment is genuinely impressive.

191. For further information on I AM, Prophet's organization, saucer cults, and other groups, see the appropriate sections of J. Gordon Melton's ENCYCLOPEDIA OF AMERICAN RELIGION.

192. Ruth Montgomery, ALIENS AMONG US (New York: Ballantine, 1985), 128-188.

193. Penny Harper, "Are Aliens Taking Over the Earth?" WHOLE LIFE TIMES, January 1990.

194. John Keel, WHY UFOS: OPERATION TROJAN HORSE (New York: Manor Books, 1970) [paperback edition], 228.

195. Hickson and Mendez, UFO CONTACT AT PASCAGOULA, 242.

196. Strieber, COMMUNION, 134; TRANSFORMATION, 109.

197. "Contactee: Firsthand," UFO magazine, vol. 4, no. 2, 1989.

198. Telephone conversation, Tom Adams.

199. Ed Conroy, REPORT ON COMMUNION (New York: William Morrow, 1989), 365-385.

200. "Contactee: Firsthand," UFO magazine, vol. 3, no. 3.

201. New York: Zebra, 1971. See especially note 2, Chap. 9.

FIRE FROM THE SKY

Selected Bibliography On Mind Control

ACID DREAMS, by Martin A. Lee and Bruce Shlain (Grove, 1985). Outstanding work on MKULTRA and drugs.

THE BODY ELECTRIC, by Robert Becker (Morrow, 1985). Important.

THE BRAIN CHANGERS, by Maya Pines (Signet, 1973). Outdated, but an excellent chapter on the stimoceiver and related technologies.

BRAIN CONTROL, by Elliot Valenstein (John Wiley and Sons, 1973). Highly conservative; outdated; still worth reading.

CIA PAPERS, compiled by Capitol Information Associates (POB 8275, Ann Arbor, Michigan, 48107). Interesting selection of MKULTRA documents.

THE CONTROL OF CANDY JONES, by Donald Bain (Playboy Press, 1976). Mandatory reading.

HUMAN DRUG TESTING BY THE CIA, hearings before the Subcommittee on Health and Scientific Research on the Committee on Human Resources, United States Senate (Government Printing Office, 1977).

HYPNOTISM, by George Estabrooks (Dutton, 1957). See especially the chapters on hypnosis in warfare and crime. Some modern experts in clinical hypnosis decry Estabrooks' work. These "experts" tend to have a history of funding by CIA cut-outs and military intelligence. I suspect they denounce Estabrooks not because his work was shoddy, but because he let the cat out of the bag.

INDIVIDUAL RIGHTS AND THE FEDERAL ROLE IN BEHAVIOR MODIFICATION, by the Staff of the Subcommittee on Constitutional Rights of the Committee of the Judiciary, United States Senate (Government Printing Office, 1974).

MEGABRAIN, by Michael Hutchison (Ballantine, 1986). The only popular book on modern mind machines.

MESSENGERS OF DECEPTION, by Jacques Vallee (And/Or, 1979). Vallee has been criticized, correctly, for including in this book invented "conversations" with a composite character he calls Major Murphy. But the section on cults in this book bears a haunting resemblance to stories I have heard in my own investigations.

THE MIND MANIPULATORS, by Opton and Scheflin (Paddington Press, 1978). Conservative, but extremely useful as a reference work.

MIND WARS, by Ronald McCrae (St. Martin's Press, 1984).

OPERATION MIND CONTROL, by Walter Bowart (Dell, 1978). The best single volume on the subject. Difficult to find; indeed, this book's rapid disappearance from bookstores and libraries has aroused the suspicions of some researchers. (Tom David Books, POB 1107, Aptos, CA 95001, carries this work.)

PHYSICAL CONTROL OF THE MIND, by Jose Delgado (Harper and Row, 1969). Outdated but still essential.

PROJECT MKULTRA, joint hearing before the Select Committee on Health and Scientific Research of the Committee on Human Resources, United States Senate (Government Printing Office, 1977).

PSYCHIC WARFARE: FACT OR FICTION? edited by John White (Aquarian, 1988). See especially Michael Rossman's contribution.

FIRE FROM THE SKY

PSYCHOTECHNOLOGY, Robert L. Schwitzgebel and Ralph K. Schwitzgebel (Holt, Rhinehart and Winston, 1973).

THE SCIENTIST, by John Lilly (expanded edition: Ronin, 1988). Bizarre - Lilly is an ex-"brainwashing" specialist who claims to be in contact with aliens. Is he controlled or controlling?

THE SEARCH FOR "THE MANCHURIAN CANDIDATE", by John Marks (Bantam, 1978). An invaluable book. However, many people have made the mistake of assuming it tells the full story. It does not.

WERE WE CONTROLLED? by Lincoln Lawrence (University Books, 1967). Explores possible connections to the JFK assassination. Dr. Petter Lindstrom's endorsement of this work makes it mandatory reading.

WHO KILLED JOHN LENNON? by Fenton Bresler (St. Martin's Press, 1989). Interesting thesis concerning the possible use of mind control on Mark David Chapman. Better in its analysis of Chapman than in its history of mind control. In my own work, I have encountered data which may help confirm Bresler's theory.

THE ZAPPING OF AMERICA, by Paul Brodeur (MacLeod [Canadian edition], 1976). Contains a good chapter on microwave mind control technology.

ORDER THE WORLD'S GREATEST CONSPIRACY BOOK AND RECEIVE THE WORLD'S GREATEST CONSPIRACY VIDEO AS A BONUS!

Learn How And Why You Became A Slave And Why You And Your Children Are Property Of The State!

HERE IS INFORMATION YOU THOUGHT YOU KNEW ABOUT! NOW YOU'LL LEARN THAT EVERYTHING YOU WERE TAUGHT IN THAT MILITARY CONTROLLED SCHOOL WAS NOTHING BUT...

SUPPRESSED INTELLIGENCE REPORTS VOLUME TWO

Now Is The Time To Open Your Eyes To The Truth! Here Is A Guide For The "Know It All" Patriot, Conspiracy Buff and Unconventional Thinker. Open Your Mind And Read About:

SECTION ONE: ✓ The Law of the Land ✓ Complete Overthrow of the Public Liberties ✓ The Greatest Lie Never Told ✓ Founding Fathers Were NOT Christians ✓ The Word Game ✓ The Lexicon of Doublespeak ✓ We Are Property of the State! ✓ The Constitution Unmasked ✓ Influence of Freemasonry On Cultural Beliefs ✓ The U.S. Remains A Colony of Great Britain ✓ The Inmates Are In Charge of the Asylum ✓ The Arrival of Orwellian America ✓ Slaves of the Fascist State ✓ Schools and Churches Under Military Tribunal.

SECTION TWO: ✓ Lost Civilizations ✓ The Lost World Re-Discovered ✓ Dogon – The People From Sirius ✓ The Reptilian Aliens ✓ Sightings and More ✓ A Selected Chronology of Historical "Sightings."

SECTION THREE: ✓ School of American Assassins ✓ Textbook Repression ✓ Torture 101 ✓ 4 Mexico Practices What America Teaches ✓ Reagan's Links To Guatemalan Terrorists ✓ The CIA Out of Control ✓ The Corruption of Covert Actions ✓ Death Squads in Columbia ✓ Cocaine and Culpability in South America.

SUPPRESSED INTELLIGENCE REPORTS VOLUME TWO is a hefty book that will enthrall you for hours, and one you will reference repeatedly. And if you order now we will include an absolutely fantastic companion 115 minute DVD that expands on some of the same topics, but also exposes the Jesus "myth," 9/11 lies, a thorough condemnation of the international banking cartel and the scam artists at the Federal Reserve who are now about to take over America by controlling the flow of money.

Send $29.95 + $5.00 S/H for these MUST HAVE items!

P.S. Did you miss *Volume One* of the *SUPPRESSED INTELLIGENCE REPORTS* series? It normally sells separately for $39.95, but just add an additional $25 and get over 15 complete reports on banned and covered up topics that the world is thirsting to know about. (**$54.95 total + $5 S/H**) Includes *"The Car That Runs On Water,* and underground alien bases.

Global Communications • Box 753 • New Brunswick, NJ 08903 • PayPal: MrUFO8@hotmail.com

REEXAMINATION OF AN HISTORICAL UFO CASE!

Behind The Flying Saucers And The Truth About The Aztec UFO Crash!

Were sixteen alien bodies recovered from a dome-shaped device that crashed near the town of Aztec, NM circa 1948? Why does the FBI continue to withhold 200 pages of classified material on the case for alleged "national security reasons?" Was the incident covered up with a camouflaged "front story" presided over by con men and scam artists, who were perhaps in the government's pay? Did President Eisenhower make contact with aliens around the same time, thus adding weight to this and other UFO crash cases?

When Variety columnist Frank Scully's *BEHIND THE FLYING SAUCERS* burst upon the literary scene in 1950, it was an immediate bestseller, but also shrouded in a controversy that has lasted for over half a century.

It was the first hardback, nonfiction book on what were then the relatively new subjects of UFOs, crashed saucers and a conspiracy to cover up the truth that the government was clearly engaged in at the highest levels, especially in regard to crash retrievals. Scully was a respected journalist, the kind of trustworthy reporter that people could feel confident in revealing their secrets to, and was thus able to provide a lot of insider information on the apparent alien invasion that had people everywhere watching the skies.

The Conspiracy Journal is very proud to offer this expanded version of perhaps the most seminal book in the history of the unexplained... a case that now stands right beside the UFO crash at Roswell, NM for its credibility and veracity. For years the Aztec case was spurned by serious researchers who did not have access to all the information now available on the crash. In addition to reprinting the entire, unabridged, text to the rare 50's Scully book (reset in an easy to read style), journalist Sean Casteel has dug deep to provide the reader with an updated account of what really transpired outside this isolated desert town near the Four Corners. His up to date research on the Aztec case is presented through interviews with top investigators like Nick Redfern, Scott and Suzanne Ramsey, Stanton Friedman and others.

FREE AUDIO CD TO OUR CUSTOMERS ONLY!

Be among the first to get all the facts in the shocking, 200+ page *BEHIND THE FLYING SAUCERS – THE TRUTH ABOUT THE AZTEC UFO CRASH* for the special price of **$20.00 + $5.00 S/H** to our readers (suggested retail $25.00). Order now and receive an exclusive audio interview with a university professor who claims inside information on UFO crashes.

❏ **AZTEC 1948 UFO CRASH** — Additional Evidence *NOW ON DVD!* – In total, 16 alien bodies were recovered and immediately transported to Wright Patterson Air Force Base where all traces of this event disappeared into a web of secrecy. This 60 minute program documents the shocking facts that surround this disturbing mystery and includes a walking tour of the UFO crash site as well as the secret U.S. radar station that tracked the craft. - **$22.00 + $5.00 S/H**

SPECIAL: Behind The Flying Saucers and Aztec UFO DVD just $39.95 + $5 S/H
Global Communications • Box 753 • New Brunswick, NJ 08903
Credit Card Hotline-732-602-3407 • PayPal at MrUFO8@hotmail.com

www.ingramcontent.com/pod-product-compliance
Lightning Source LLC
Chambersburg PA
CBHW080506110426
42742CB00017B/3015